AFRICADIAN ATLANTIC:
Essays on
George Elliott Clarke

ESSENTIAL WRITERS SERIES 35

Guernica Editions Inc. acknowledges the support of the Canada Council for the Arts and the Ontario Arts Council. The Ontario Arts Council is an agency of the Government of Ontario

AFRICADIAN ATLANTIC:
Essays on
George Elliott Clarke

Edited by
Joseph Pivato

GUERNICA
TORONTO—BUFFALO—BERKELEY—LANCASTER (U.K.) 2012

Michael Mirolla, general editor
Joseph Pivato, series editor
Guernica Editions Inc.
P.O. Box 117, Station P, Toronto (ON), Canada M5S 2S6
2250 Military Road, Tonawanda, N.Y. 14150-6000 U.S.A.

Interior Design by Sun Editing & Book Design

Distributors:
University of Toronto Press Distribution,
5201 Dufferin Street, Toronto (ON), Canada M3H 5T8
Gazelle Book Services, White Cross Mills, High Town, Lancaster
LA1 4XS U.K.
Small Press Distribution, 1341 Seventh St., Berkeley, CA
94710-1409 U.S.A.

First edition.
Printed in Canada.

Legal Deposit – First Quarter
Library of Congress Catalog Card Number: 2012938357

Library and Archives Canada Cataloguing in Publication

Africadian Atlantic : essays on George Elliott Clarke / Joseph Pivato, editor.

(Writers series ; 35)
Issued also in electronic format.
ISBN 978-1-55071-627-6

1. Clarke, George Elliott, 1960- --Criticism and interpretation. 2. Black Canadians in literature. I. Pivato, Joseph II. Series: Writers series (Toronto, Ont.) ; 35

PS8555.L3748Z56 2012 C811'.54 C2012-902903-3

Contents

Introduction in Two Parts

JOSEPH PIVATO

This essay collection is the first devoted entirely to the work of George Elliott Clarke, a writer whose critical and literary *intervention* in Canadian and post-colonial, English-speaking cultures merits examination. Clarke is an imaginative and authoritative scholar who has contributed mightily to efforts to democratize how we read Canada's history, languages, and diverse cultures. His production has raised questions about race, ethnic identity, and the position of minority women. In my own work on Italian-Canadian writers working in English, French and Italian, I have found Clarke's creative work and academic essays invaluable for their insight into the racialization of ethnic minority people in North America and Europe. Likewise, he has graciously cited my scholarship as an inspiration and incitement to his own. I have organized this introduction into two parts: part one, my personal experience of George Elliott Clarke and his work, and, part two, my commentary on the essays in this collection.

Part One: Personal Journeys

I have known George for two decades—primarily through my work on ethnic minority writers and the academics who write about post-colonial literature. We share a positive view about Canadian multiculturalism as actually working when we see different communities acknowledge each other and discuss similar experiences. We do not ignore the problems that cultural diversity can produce, since these are often what we write about in our studies. We both believe that ethnic minority writers must also review critically works by other minority writers in order to establish the critical recognition of different literatures. For this reason, for example, Clarke was invited as the keynote speaker at the biannual conference of the Association of Italian-Canadian Writers in 2002. He spoke about the importance of creating anthologies for groups of ethnic minority writers by comparing the first *national* Black-Canadian anthology, *Canada In Us Now* edited by Harold Head (1976) and the first Italian-Canadian anthology, *Roman Candles* edited by Pier Giorgio Di Cicco (1978). Clarke holds that these are positive examples that other groups of minority writers should follow.

George Elliott Clarke has received considerable critical recognition for his original poetry, plays, novels and libretti and also for his studious essays and books on post-colonial literature. His literary achievements alone are significant, but to me, a fellow minority intellectual, the social contribution he has made to the fostering of Black literature in Canada is also vital. He has done this through his own work, through his anthologies and studies of other Black writers, by lecturing on these writers overseas, and by considering the historical experience of other ethnic minority groups in Canada.

He began this enterprise in 1991 by editing the two-volume *Fire on the Water: An Anthology of Black Nova Scotian Writing* and, later, *Eyeing the North Star: Directions in African-Canadian Literature* (1997). He has urged on further academic recognition of this writing by publishing pioneering essays in many literary journals. This project culminated in his seminal book, *Odysseys Home: Mapping African-Canadian Literature* (2002), a 490-page outline of the history and particular challenges of Black writing—and critique thereof—in Canada. In this work, Clarke confronts several of the ideological issues in post-colonial theory, identifies the major texts and focuses on some of the most published authors such as Austin Clarke, Dionne Brand, Marlene NourbeSe Philip, and Claire Harris. His follow-up tome is *Directions Home: Approaches to African-Canadian Literature* (2012), which builds on the earlier volume and expands Clarke's analysis of little-known texts, post-colonial theory, as well as significant contemporary writers.

My views on Clarke as the post-colonial scholar changed when I saw his opera, *Beatrice Chancy*, performed in Edmonton in 2001. This new Canadian opera had such an impact on me that it inspired me to compile this book of studies devoted to Clarke's creative writing. Clarke has published several provocative essays such as, "Treason of the Black Intellectuals?" and "Must All Blackness Be American?" and his academic book, *Odysseys Home*, but his lasting legacy to literature may primarily be his lettered art.

When *Beatrice Chancy* was staged in Edmonton in 2001 at the Citadel Theatre, the performances were sold-out and critically lauded. The Citadel Theatre, the most important venue for live theatre in Alberta, made this new Canadian opera the highlight of the season. Fascinatingly, this Canadian opera also has Italian connections. Clarke's verse play, *Beatrice Chancy*, was inspired by the tragic story of the Cenci family, Roman nobles of the late 1500s, and by Percy Bysshe Shelley's verse play, *The Cenci* (1819). Clarke completed this work in 1998 during his sojourn in Bellagio, Italy, while on a Rockefeller Foundation Fellowship. Between 1999 and 2001, *Beatrice Chancy* was performed as a chamber opera in Halifax, Edmonton, and Toronto. It was also aired by CBC television in February 2001, thus becoming the first Canadian opera to receive a television broadcast in roughly three decades. The music was composed by James Rolfe. The lead, Beatrice, was sung by the young soprano, Measha Bruggergosman, who is now an international opera star. Clarke has since written libretti for two other operas, thus continuing to experiment with this medium and its conventions.

I attended two performances of *Beatrice Chancy*. Rolfe's use of a variety of contemporary musical genres—in response to Clarke's richly multicultural libretto—contrasted dramatically with the stylized conventions of European opera in every element: music, lyrics, themes, plots, characterization, setting, and even the movements of the singers. It made me appreciate how creative and courageous Clarke was in his new opera since, as the librettist, he had very little control over the final performance—the sound and the visual spectacle on the stage. And I also wondered how much the genre of opera and the medium of the stage affected the final product. Clarke himself realized the limitations of the genre while he was drafting the original libretto. For this reason he also wrote the longer five-act verse drama *Beatrice*

Chancy, which was published separately and has received dramatic readings in Toronto and Winnipeg.

Another work by Clarke to reach the stage is *Whylah Falls*, which began as a verse-novel in 1990, but became a verse play in 1999. The play, *Whylah Falls*, was translated into Italian for a 2002 production in Venice. Called *Le Cascate di Whylah*, the Italian chorus sang jazz, blues, and spirituals in an ornate Venetian theatre named after author Carlo Goldoni. This Venetian wrote many plays, not in standard Italian but rather in Veneto, a dialect similar to Italian and for centuries the official language of the Venetian Republic. In Goldoni's work, we hear the voices of Venetian men and women. In parallel fashion, George Elliott Clarke is a master of the Black dialect of Nova Scotia. We need only read aloud his poems in *Whylah Falls* (1990), in *Execution Poems* (2001), and dialogues in his novel *George and Rue* (2005), to hear the transfiguring voices of his Black Nova Scotian (he says, "Africadian") men and women, themselves a strong combo of West Indian, African-American, and First Nations peoples.

To me, it is ironic that this play about Black Nova Scotians should be staged in Venice. The Venetian Republic lasted over one thousand years, but this important naval power and vast, Mediterranean trading empire utilized slavery. In the 1400s, for instance, over 10,000 slaves from Eastern Europe were sold in Venice. Genoese merchants organized the modern slave trade from the Crimea and Egypt. The Portuguese explorers began the slave trade in Black Africa in 1452. The first modern European explorer to set foot on the territory of Nova Scotia was a Venetian citizen, Giovanni Caboto, in 1497.

The production of Clarke's verse play, *Whylah Falls*, in Italy is just one indication of the international recognition that his work has received. In addition to Italian, *Whylah Falls* has been translated into Mandarin (2006), and a collection of his poems appeared in Romanian (2006). Individual poems have been published in Finnish, French, Catalan, Spanish, Czech, Hungarian, and Italian. (As this book goes to press, a volume of Clarke's poetry will soon be published, in Italian, in Italy.) Clarke has received the Rockefeller Foundation Fellowship, the Dr. Martin Luther King Jr. Achievement Award (2004), the Premiul Poesis (Romania, 2005), the Pierre Elliott Trudeau Fellowship Prize (2005–08), the Dartmouth Book Award for Fiction (2006), the Eric Hoffer Book Award for Poetry (2009), and many other awards, including a Canadian Governor General's Award for his *Execution Poems* in 2001.

I share with Clarke a mission to promote Canadian ethnic minority writing—both in North America and beyond. I have been an invited speaker in the UK, Holland, Italy, Greece, Taiwan, and Australia. Clarke has done extensive travel for his mission as well. In 2008, I met Clarke by chance at Charles De Gaulle International Airport at Roissy, near Paris. We shared breakfast before he went off to Nantes and I took my flight to Venice. In 2011, we were both invited to speak at the University of Udine, Italy, to celebrate the 10th Anniversary of their Centro di Cultura Canadese.

For many years Clarke has been returning to Italy by invitation from the Università Ca'Foscari di Venezia and other institutions. So it seems appropriate that this first volume of studies on his work should be edited by an ethnic writer born near the historic city of Venice, but who grew up a Canadian in Toronto and Edmonton. When I arrived in Canada, I came ashore at Pier 21 in Halifax, the receiving port for millions of other immigrants to Canada.

Part Two: The Essays

The major contributor to the critical study of African-Canadian writing is Clarke himself. The number and variety of his books and media works are impressive. The essays in this volume have been selected to represent the diversity of Clarke's writing, both in subjects and in genres.

Wayde Compton looks at the recreation of history in Clarke's debut poetry collection, *Saltwater Spirituals and Deeper Blues* (1983). In his close readings, Compton explores the patterns of repetition as Clarke reconstructs the history and geography of his people—"Coloured Christians" and "African Baptists" (but not yet "Africadians"), contesting white-authored, colonial history.

The blues in the poetry of *Whylah Falls*—the 1990 verse-novel—is the subject of H. Nigel Thomas' essay. Thomas uses the term African-American to include African-Canadians too. It strikes me as a controversial assumption, one that Clarke and many of this book's contributors might contest. Thomas discusses the various genres which make up this narrative in dramatic poetry, while also exploring the personal dialogue of blues.

Jennifer Andrews looks at the representation of Fredericton in *Execution Poems* (2000). Against the troubled historical context of Acadia and Loyalist New Brunswick, Andrews examines how Clarke's poems explore the racism around the 1949 trials and executions of two mixed-race brothers, George and Rufus (Rue) Hamilton (Clarke's own cousins), whose upbringings in rural Nova Scotia were violent and impoverished.

In "The Mask of Aaron," Susan Knutson draws comparisons between the brutality in *Execution Poems* and Shakespeare's *Titus Andronicus*, a play so violent that it is rarely staged. She explains that: "The rhetorical excess and the violent action place *Execution Poems* in the tradition of revenge tragedy."

Cultural memory is the focus of Maureen Moynagh's study of *Beatrice Chancy* (libretto 1998; verse-play 1999). She explores the history of racial and sexual violence in the context of colonialism and slavery. She distinguishes *Beatrice Chancy*, the verse drama which is to be read as poetry, from the opera, which is based on the libretto. Moynagh argues convincingly that both works are provocative performance texts. She borrows the term "indigenizing" from Len Findlay's influential 1999 article on "decolonizing" English literature in the Canadian academy.

In a comparative essay Amanda Montague examines the intertexts of *Beatrice Chancy*, in the context of the tragic legend and Shelley's *The Cenci* and Clarke's methods of creating an original adaptation. With Moynagh's and Larson's essays, Montague argues that *Beatrice Chancy*, as verse drama and opera, is one of Clarke's major texts.

From Venice, Italy, Giulio Marra gives us a close reading of Clarke's *Black* (2006) in the context of *Blue* (2001) and *Execution Poems*. Marra examines the poetic language and the references to the history of slavery and the influences of African-American writers.

Clarke's jazz opera is *Québécité: A Jazz Fantasia in Three Cantos* (2003), featuring the lush, scintillating music composed by D.D. Jackson. Here again harmony and dissonance are used to explore the different ethnic identities of the four characters. In her essay, "*Oui,* let's scat," Katherine McLeod examines how sound can be used to deconstruct cultural differences and otherness. In the contexts of debates about performing multiculturalism, she argues "that *Québécité* exemplifies the ways in which sound offers a medium through which to redefine understandings of multicultural and multivocal improvisations."

Clarke continued his collaboration with D.D. Jackson in his third opera, *Trudeau: Long March/Shining Path* (2007), which uses world-music traditions to trace Pierre Elliott Trudeau on his cosmopolitan travels. Chinese string instruments, Cuban dance music, and Montreal jazz piano position Trudeau as a Ulysses figure who fostered multicultural values in Canada and elsewhere. In "Creating a Canadian Odyssey," Lydia Wilkinson gives us a critical reading of these global perspectives in Clarke's *Trudeau: Long March/ Shining Path.* In her essay, she treats both the printed text and the opera workshop performance.

The notion of Africadian writing in the cultural landscape of Atlantic-Canadian literature is explored in critical detail by Alexander MacLeod. In his essay he argues that Clarke's work on identifying an Africadian literary canon "transgresses the normal boundaries between real and imagined social space and, in the process, extends regionalist discourse into new areas of political and social action."

From Brazil, South America, Maristela Campos compares Négritude in Clarke's poetry with that of Brazilian poet Solano Trindade. She situates Clarke in a resolutely pan-African tradition.

In "Resistance from the Margin," Katherine Larson examines the intertexts of *Beatrice Chancy*, the verse-drama, and argues that it is framed and infused by the paratexts and peritexts that Clarke has deliberately constructed around his work.

Collectively, these essays frame the poetry, plays, libretti, and fiction of George Elliott Clarke as exemplary of the whole enterprise of African-Canadian literature, a body of significant authors and texts that has achieved a sudden clamour of national and international recognition. It is telling that Clarke has helped teach us how to read these works, not only through his own criticism, but through his own practice.

Reference

Clarke, George Elliott. "Correspondences and Divergences Between Italian-Canadian and African-Canadian Writers." *Canadian Multicultural Dreams, Realities, Expectations.* Eds. Matthew Zachariah, Allan Sheppard, Leona Barratt. Edmonton: Canadian Multicultural Education Foundation, 2004.

"Even the stars are temporal": The Historical Motion of George Elliott Clarke's *Saltwater Spirituals and Deeper Blues*[1]

WAYDE COMPTON

George Elliott Clarke's collection of poems, *Saltwater Spirituals and Deeper Blues*, is a poetic chronicle of the black population of Nova Scotia. The black Nova Scotian (Africadian) community traces its roots back to the first wave of Loyalist immigrants who arrived in 1782 after the British loss in the American Revolution. In 1792 many of the black Loyalists of Nova Scotia "repatriated" to Sierra Leone, this "decolonization" being similar in spirit to the later American establishment of Liberia by abolitionists and free blacks. These "repatriations" served equivocally voiced purposes: on one hand to free blacks from colonialism; on the other hand to empty North America of its "race problem." A second wave of black immigration to Nova Scotia came after the War of 1812, known as the Black Refugees. Clarke is a descendant of these migrants who put down roots in Nova Scotia, and *Saltwater Spirituals and Deeper Blues* sings their genealogy.

Clarke's poetics derives from a distinct engagement of history (time) and geography (space). *Saltwater Spirituals and Deeper Blues* was written in 1983 and self-consciously walks in a tradition of black Nova Scotian music, literature, orature, arts, and preaching—all modes of indigenous black expression. Clarke's self-conscious placement produces a definitive text that spiritually "maps" his community-subject. The Nova Scotian geography is touched and held and turned over in Clarke's hands, tilled, and used to divine ancestral moods, aspirations, and senses. As part of the larger black tradition, the Africadian knows the arbitrariness of geography for the diasporic black; tensions between migration, settlement, flight, and foundation permeate *Saltwater Spirituals and Deeper Blues*. Similarly, history and time take particular places for the diasporic black who lives out a fragmented and displaced lineage nationally, racially, within the kinship patterns of former slave societies, within oral culture, and within a culture destabilized by racism. Historical discourse is at once self-reflection and self-creation for such a community. The sense of time itself is expressed in a distinct style that originates in the diasporic circumstance. Clarke surfaces from his community as the conduit of invocation, as both historian and seer, looking back in both directions. *Saltwater Spirituals and Deeper Blues* is comfortably both documentation (like footprints) and art (like dance).

In his essay "Repetition as a figure of black culture," James A. Snead assesses the particular value placed on perpetual immanence in black expression. Defined against the Western interpretation of repetition as valuable only if it is innovative (what is known as "progress," or as Snead calls it, the "not yet there" model), Snead suggests a black cultural paradigm he calls the "always already there" model, or simply a model that embraces repetition (63–64). He notes that black culture's emphasis on repetition stems partly from the logic of an oral culture and partly from a culture which does not view the subjugation of nature as a desirable goal, but a culture which listens to nature for its understanding of temporality, rhythm, cycle.

Snead identifies what he calls the repetitive "cut"—that is the moment at which a cycle returns to its beginning and repeats, "an abrupt, seemingly unmotivated break (an accidental *da capo*) with a series already in progress and a willed return to a prior series" (67). Snead examines the philosophical production of a culture that centres the "cut" contrasted with Western notions of history being "played out" or reaching some sort of perceived goal. Black culture traditionally conflates history with the present, and is socially inclusive in that any event or change is easily integrated into the narrative at the next "cut." Whereas Western culture's "progress" weeds out the accidental and the tributary, black culture's repetition integrates the accidental and the new into the repeating patterns. Snead contrasts European classical music with black musical forms such as African drumming, jazz, and blues. Classical European music distinctly starts towards a goal and finishes while black music subsumes its own creation into its form; Snead points to jazz improvisation and James Brown's music in which Brown's instructions to the band as to how many bars to play or where to insert the next bridge are themselves musical (68–69).[2]

Clarke's *Saltwater Spirituals and Deeper Blues* presents history in the pattern of repetition identified by Snead. The first section of Clarke's collection is "Soul Songs," which consists of twelve—with apostolic significance—shorter lyrics ("songs") ranging between eleven and twenty-two lines. Each song is titled after a church in Nova Scotia, mostly members of the African United Baptist Association, which was founded in 1854 and still serves as a focal point for the Africadian community. Clarke's "Soul Songs" have titles such as "The Sermon on the Atlantic: Africville Seaview African Baptist Church," "Amherst African Methodist Episcopal Church," "Musquodoboit Road Church," and "Cherrybrook African Baptist Church." The repetition of the word "church" in each title is similarly reflected in the ordering of the songs; each song (each church) could be read in any order because each is a closed lyric, or cycle in Snead's model of repetition. Keeping in mind Snead's notion of the "cut," reading the "Soul Songs" feels as if, once finished a song, we "return" to another version of the same; after finishing "Horton Church" we "cut" back to "Fall River Church"—the next cycle.

Repetition also exists in both form and theme in the "Soul Songs." In "Guysborough Road Church" the phrase, "we are the" repeats like an invocation, successively singing an identity:

> we are the black loyalists:
> we think of the bleak fundamentalism
> of a ragged scarf of light
> twined and twisted and torn
> in a briar patch of pines.
> and then, of steel-wool water,
> scouring the dull rocks of bonny
> bonny nova scotia –

the chaste, hard granite
coastline inviolate; the dark,
dreary mountains where sad Glooscap broods
over waters void [...]
we are the world-poor.
we are the fatherless.
we are the coloured Christians
of the african united baptist association. (14)

The effect is indeed song-like. Repetition as a theme appears in the "Souls Songs" read in the natural imagery of "Hammonds Plains African Baptist Church":

i dream of a dauntless dory
battling the blue, cruel combers
of a feral, runaway ocean –
a trotskyite ocean in permanent revolution
turning fluid ideas over and over
in its leviathan mind,
turning driftwood, drums, and conundrums

over and over ... (24)

Here change and repetition are forced together; the very euphemism of progress—revolution—is itself "battled" by the human motion towards repetition. As Snead describes the black cultural urge to subsume the accidental, counter to the progressive "weeding out" of the arbitrary, Clarke's "trotskyite ocean in permanent revolution" is grafted to the natural, the "conundrums" of doubt, and the "driftwood" of emotion, uncertainty, and the openness of nature. The poem is integrative but not dialectical; rather, it presents a unified moment, "fluid" in its waves of thought and reconsideration.

Clarke not only exposes the self-defeating linearity of progress, but also the rigidity of tradition. In "Fall River Church" Clarke again uses the ocean as a metaphor for change:

> a steamer-tractor parts
> a shifting sea, churning the thick,
> dry earth near weary horses
> that flounder in the dust,
> gasp for grass,
> drown.
> soon, some saint will find them,
> floating in the sargasso drought,
> jettisoned from care like sick or
> dead slaves,
> and he will cast out a net,
> like one who founds a church,
> to rescue those flailing,
> to bury deeper those sunken. (18)

Though it is again alienating and "battled," the chaotic earth-ocean of this song has a solution: the establishment of the church (community, tradition). However, Clarke reveals the limits of such tradition, and the limits of the repetition model, for the individual who cannot or will not be subsumed, like the "sinner" in "Fall River Church," but just as easily the non-conformist of any tendency. The poem's metaphorical "net" which inclusively swallows targets accidental and intended can be seen at once as a tool of unifying power and a trap. Here Clarke shows a rare hint of malevolence in the communitarian approach he overall appears to advocate.

The tilling of unfamiliar, alienating soil in "Fall River Church" reflects the geographical and spatial burden of diasporic blackness. Similar again to Snead's "cut" of temporal repetition, the migrations of black people to Nova Scotia are part of the larger condition which Kamau Brathwaite, with some irony, describes as:

> 'the seemingly
> endless
> purgatorial
> experience
> of black
> people' (132).[3]

For the diasporic black, where history has given settlement it has also given unsettlement, migration, root-laying, uprooting, more migration, and so forth. The Africadian community, as a refugee population, contends with the landscape in a particular, disjunctive manner. In her essay "An Unimpoverished Style: the Poetry of George Elliott Clarke," M. Travis Lane suggests that Clarke engages a familiar "Canadian" style which attempts to make sense of a perceived barrenness of the Canadian landscape and how to compose a culture from this barrenness. Lane writes:

> Like [A.G. Bailey and Ralph Gustafson] Clarke possesses a sense of history as continuous and present in his own context. But, and here again he reminds me of A.G. Bailey, Clarke also possesses a rich sense of what the Canadian found in Canada—of Indian history, of nature—as well as what the Canadian brought. Not even the arctic tundra was barren. (47)

Lane tries to understand Clarke in a Canadian historical context of colonization and settlement, which inadequately describes the larger context of black diasporic migration and, specifically, the fact of the disempowered and racially objectified refugee. For Clarke's Africadian community, Nova Scotia has never been part of a colonialist project to be written and claimed with confidence. Clarke's description of the Canadian landscape is terrifying not because it is an untamable or chaotic expanse, but because it is yet another station removed from Africa, yet another level of alienation, yet another arbitrary repositioning that may or may not prove to be *home*. The material conditions of a slave-turned-cheap-labour community punctuate the Africadian—not Canadian—relationship to the land:

> ah, national sea products limited
> shackles the deeps to our eyes,
> clamps the storm-winds to our ears,
> fetters us to death by water (20)

In "North Atlantic" the ocean itself echoes slavery and the middle passage but also announces itself as unclaimable to the speaker:

> white, bleached tombstones, mute,
> overlook brackish, brawling, breaking
> water that loudly lashes the lamenting land—
> water, ivory with ice and violence,
> striking implacable igneous rocks,
> and insatiable sedimentary rocks,
> and rolling up into thunderous,
> mad, crashing, incomprehensible fury (45)

Apart from the fugitive disrepair as itself problematizing, the geography is marked with the signs of white power, the Canadian claim:

> the classical wind blows at cross-purposes,
> tactile in backwoods forest,
> intangible on sun-fired tors,
> becomes invisible bagpipe
> to a ragged tartan of blue sky and green tree tops (17)

Perhaps the above imagery of Scottish signifiers appearing in the very landscape is what Lane refers to when she suggests that "[t]he sensuous vitality and multiculturalness of this verse is as Canadian as those sharply fragrant beach roses" (48) in "Musquodoboit Road Church":

> micmac windpoems sing
> Spring's resurrection,
> foretold by the sharp, fused fragrances
> of jubilee roses [...]
> ....
> knowing this sensual verse
> we ensure fertility.
> we prepare a path through the wilderness. (21)

Whereas Lane reads the imagery of classical wind, bagpipes, and tartan resident in the Canadian landscape as "multicultural," a black diasporic reading suggests that what is signified is Scottish-Canadian ownership over the land, segregation, political relationships of race/power. Clarke does not celebrate these relationships; the above-quoted lines from "Musquodoboit Road Church" are Clarke's celebration. Just as the geography has been used as a weapon against blacks, Clarke "prepare[s] a path through the wilderness" by *knowing* the disruption of migration, exile, geographical dissociation, and building from that foundation a black national consciousness. The "jubilee roses," like the last section of *Saltwater Spirituals and*

Deeper Blues, "The Book of Jubilee," mark a beginning of a specifically cultural emancipation.

While I reject the term "multiculturalism" as a euphemism for white containment of rival cultures, Clarke's poetry *is* syncretic. Another image of bagpipes appears in "East Coasting," a poem from the collection's middle section "Blues Notes":

> bagpipe jazz hymns sermonize
> sunday air; oh amazing
> grace of sounds, maritime
> music; ocean voices
> ....
> saxophone sea spirituals,
> moaning blacks in clapboard churches,
> bagpipe jazz hymns
> testifying their atlantic geneology. (49)

Here Clarke truly "prepare[s] a path through the wilderness" of the diasporic black condition: if the land is white-owned and suffused with the signifiers of a dominant culture, those very tools of repression can be re-mythologized. In "Can't Seem to Settle Down" Clarke composes the poetry of rootlessness:

> motion is religion: a fast, non-stop,
> irresistable faith.
> i, its disciple, do not want roots, not yet
> ....
> i long to marry atlases
> and sire cosmopolitan, postcard children,
> and never be chained
> to clocks and calendars, but go on forever
> and never
> come to a conclusion. (43)

The word "roots" is used here with the individualistic meaning of the traveller or bachelor without a permanent home; the word is also a black signifier of unity, black nationalism, Africa. Clarke playfully subverts both meanings of "roots" in a traditional blues gambit. In order to deal with the rejection of the dominant society (*you have no roots*), the blues lyricist uses the mask of individuality (*I can't seem to settle down*) to signify the national situation (*they won't let us have roots*). Another black signifier which is turned on its head, encoded in the blues form, is the phrase "never be chained." The obvious allusion is slavery but the metaphorical shackling is to the time of long-term plans, goals, and even history—again things which have been forcibly kept from black people. To embrace literally the land ("marry atlases"), Clarke must be transient. "Can't Seem to Settle Down" works ironically against the "Souls Songs" section in which the churches of Africadia are very carefully mapped out in verse. In direct opposition to the line "motion is religion," the whole first section carefully describes the setting down of a black national foundation, church by church and brick by brick. With its humour and irony, "Can't Seem to Settle Down" is an example of the traditional method of cultural survival for black people in the diaspora. When the culture is extremely compromised by oppression, defining oneself with whatever means are left open, whether through new mythologies or even the knowing hyperbolization of stereotype, is the necessary act of making culture.

Clarke's usages of time and space, history and geography, era and nation are foundational. In the sense that *Saltwater Spirituals and Deeper Blues* is historical in its appearance and somewhat documentary, it is aware of this potential impediment to the aesthetic. Beyond the invocation of traditional black artistic forms—blues, spirituals, preaching—Clarke suggests a "reading" of black history and migration itself. The roads of Africadia, the churches, and their people are carefully versified; the verse is then returned to them as *Saltwater Spirituals and Deeper Blues*. The pattern is a familiar one, Clarke's text being merely another cycle of the rhythm, but only if one can understand the churches, the old photographs interspersed throughout the text, the roads, fields, Atlantic, all as textual. In this way, the people are sung.

Endnotes

1. "[E]ven the stars are temporal" is a quotation from M. Travis Lane's explication of "The Emissaries" (54).
2. Snead also notes that post-structuralism and post-modernism are part of a Western re-evaluation of the progress model, and something of a "return" to the cyclical, repetition model.
3. Brathwaite borrows this description from an unnamed critic who was writing about his work.

Works Cited

Brathwaite, Kamau. "Dream Haiti." *Hambone* 12 (1995): 123–185.

Clarke, George Elliott. *Saltwater Spirituals and Deeper Blues*. Porters Lake, NS: Pottersfield Press, 1983.

Lane, M. Travis. "An Unimpoverished Style: the Poetry of George Elliott Clarke." *Canadian Poetry Studies* 16 (1985): 47–54.

Snead, James A. "Repetition as a figure of black culture." *Black Literature and Literary Theory*. Ed. Henry Louis Gates, Jr. New York: Routledge, 1990. 59–79.

Re-Visioning Fredericton: Reading George Elliott Clarke's Execution Poems

JENNIFER ANDREWS

> *O snow-washed city of cold, white Christians,*
> *So white you will not cut a black man's hair.*
> – Fred Cogswell, "Ode to Fredericton"

If Northrop Frye's "Where is here?" remains a critical touchstone for literary scholars in the twenty-first century[1], then the city of Fredericton, New Brunswick, as a birthplace of English Canadian poetry, offers a particularly fascinating subject for discussion (see, e.g., Bailey; Brown; and Smith). It first gained prominence in the late nineteenth century as the hometown of the so-called Confederation poets, a group that included Sir Charles G.D. Roberts, Bliss Carman, and Francis Sherman. Their interest in Maritime topography and eagerness to create romantically charged visions of Canada's birth were often extrapolated from the scenic vistas and refined living offered in the relatively tiny city of Fredericton and its surrounding areas.[2] And in 1947, the federal government declared the city to be "The Poets' Corner of Canada," in honour of the contributions of Roberts, Carman, and Sherman to a national tradition of poetry.[3] Yet over time, representations of Fredericton in Canadian poetry have changed; over the past five decades, poets such as Alden Nowlan, Fred Cogswell, and George Elliott Clarke have begun to explore the issue of racism in the provincial capital. In Clarke's 2001 award-winning poetry collection, *Execution Poems*, Fredericton is the setting for the downfall of George and Rufus Hamilton, two African Canadian relatives of Clarke who murdered a taxi driver with a hammer and were subsequently executed by hanging. In these powerfully evocative poems, Clarke explores the impact of the city's Loyalist history and privileged population on the brothers. Conversely, he examines the brothers' brutal murder of a taxi driver, a crime that remains discursively imprinted on the local community; the area of Fredericton where the murder took place, Barker's Point, is still nicknamed Hammertown.

Born and raised in Windsor Plains, Nova Scotia, Clarke sees himself as intimately connected to the Maritimes and, as an African Canadian writer and scholar, he feels a "responsibility, too, to contest the erasure and silencing of black culture and history in Canada" (*Odysseys* 6).[4] Given the representation of Fredericton in Clarke's *Execution Poems*, how might one reread the city's status in the annals of Canadian literary history? How does Clarke's depiction of Fredericton through the voices of George and Rufus shape his efforts to consciously construct an "imagined community" or nation for African Canadians, an "Africadia" in his rural Nova Scotia birthplace? In this article, by attending to the dominant whiteness of the city—so aptly depicted in the last lines of Cogswell's "Ode to Fredericton"—in conjunction with Clarke's poems, the literary locale of Fredericton becomes a critical site for examining not only questions of Canadian literary identities and the historical absence of black voices, but also the changing psychological and cultural landscape of this provincial capital. *Execution Poems* gives voice to otherwise disenfranchised African Canadians in the Maritimes and thus counters the predominantly Loyalist tone of Maritime literature in the twentieth century and beyond.

(Re)Presenting Fredericton

In a millennial special issue of *Essays on Canadian Writing*, called *Where Is Here Now?*, a plethora of Canadian critics took the opportunity to revisit Frye's famous query, including Diana Brydon, who persuasively argues that "our actions are constrained but not predetermined by location" (14). Given Fredericton as a locale with a long and illustrious literary pedigree, how might Clarke reconfigure the "Where is here?" of this white Loyalist town to enable the voices of Rue and George to be heard? Brydon helpfully poses two alternative questions that are particularly applicable to Clarke's *Execution Poems*: "What are we doing here?" and "What is here doing to us?" (14). These self-conscious formulations move beyond location by focusing on the positioning of both place and individual within a specific community context. The interactive dimensions of self-identification and differentiation are not only central to understanding the individual and tragic stories of Rue and George in *Execution Poems* but also clarify Clarke's larger aims as an African Canadian and Maritime-born poet writing about racism both in Fredericton specifically and in the region as a whole.

The arrival of the Loyalists in the Maritimes at the end of the American Revolution forever changed the area. With the combined population of the provinces totalling fewer than twenty thousand, the influx of over thirty thousand Loyalists had a dramatic impact (see Reid 64). New Brunswick was the most affected; the province went from 4,000 to 18,500 residents as a result of the American War of Independence, giving the Loyalists a strong majority (see Reid 70). While blacks were a significant part of this fleeing population, once settled in the Maritimes they quickly discovered that "their supposedly equal rights and privileges would not be tolerated by fellow migrants" (Reid 74).[5] Fredericton was shaped by this vision, with the white Loyalist elite establishing the capital intent on making it a model colony. As Janice Kulyk Keefer explains, the Loyalists aimed "to create a well-appointed, graded society of landed gentry whose eminence [would be] based on the ownership of land, supported by a disciplined yeomanry" (124). In choosing a site for the capital, they displaced long-established Maliseet and Acadian residents (see Reid 78–80) and, as in the other Maritime provinces, blacks in Fredericton were typically either slaves or relegated to menial labour and forced to reside on the outskirts of the city, in areas such as Barker's Point.[6] Moreover, during the eighteenth and nineteenth centuries, the Fredericton Loyalists and their descendants placed a special emphasis on the education of the white upper and middle classes, in a bid to make the city, as Desmond Pacey puts it, "the most gentlemanly on earth" (177). Not surprisingly, then, A.J.M. Smith observes that the poetry of Roberts and Carman, among others, reflected a society that was "calm, settled, and certain; conservative and ... rather narrow; a beautiful flowering of many traditions—the Loyalist, the Anglican, and the classical" (71).

The most famous of the Fredericton Confederation poets, Sir Charles G.D. Roberts, pays tribute to the provincial capital in his 1881 poem "To Fredericton in May-Time." Roberts employs the traditional Petrarchan sonnet form, written from the viewpoint of an adoring male lover (see Abrams 197), to describe the natural beauty of an early summer morning in Fredericton. The octave focuses on how the local elm trees create their own majestic vision, one that mirrors the elegance of one of the most visible buildings on the skyline, Christ Church Cathedral, with its 198-foot-high spire and location on prime riverfront real estate: "thy close elms assume / Round earth and spire the semblance of green billows." (l. 6) In the sestet that follows, Roberts shifts focus to the image of the city as a female temptress who tantalizes the speaker with her soft spring air but ultimately leaves him unsatisfied. Notably, this image of Fredericton as siren is echoed and refigured in the manuscript of a 1942 public lecture, delivered at the provincial capital, in which Roberts explicitly personifies the natural beauty and insularity of the city: "But because she has sat long aloof, Narcissus-like admiring her own image in her splendid threshold water, and too loftily indifferent to proclaim her merits to the world, travel has gone blindly past her gates" ("City" 2). His selection of the Narcissus myth is especially significant because in Ovid's *Metamorphoses* the young man is cursed—as punishment for mocking Echo—to forever be enamoured of his reflection, an image without substance that eventually kills him (see Ovid 149–61). Such blindness is literally echoed in Roberts' later characterization of Fredericton, a portrait that may be read as reflecting the poet's ambivalence about his hometown and the dangers of a city that does not look beyond its own riverbanks.

Subsequent writers—including Nowlan, Cogswell, and Clarke—have written poems about Fredericton that depict the city in far less glowing terms. They also highlight, by implication, what Roberts hints at but does not probe in his representation of the capital, namely a place whose history has been written to suit the desires of its most powerful occupants. Nowlan, who spent much of his life in New Brunswick, penned "Ancestral Memories Evoked by Attending the Opening of the Playhouse in Fredericton, New Brunswick" (1967), a poem that recalls the 1861 visit to Fredericton of Prince Arthur, Duke of Connaught and Victoria's seventh child, an event that was much celebrated at the time by the city's Loyalist descendants. In the poem, Nowlan explores the racial and class hierarchies that exist within the city of Fredericton that relegated "the lower orders, / ... the Frenchies / and ... the sly and treacherous Indians," to the riverbanks while privileged whites dine at nearby Government House.

Cogswell is even more overt and specific in his critique of the city's prejudices in "Ode to Fredericton," first published in his 1959 collection, aptly titled *Descent from Eden*. The poem was inspired by several incidents that took place in Fredericton in late November and early December of 1947, when Cogswell was a student at the University of New Brunswick. Three black students, two of whom were Second World War veterans, attempted to get haircuts at local barbershops and were turned away because of their skin colour. In protest, over five hundred UNB students signed a petition boycotting downtown barbers and pledged to open a shop of their own, open to anyone, to be located on campus.[7]

For Cogswell, a young white New Brunswicker with Acadian and Loyalist roots, the injustice of these events clearly resonated for years to come. In "Ode to Fredericton," he takes aim at Fredericton's local elite, whose Christian charity and goodness, as the poem reveals, is tinged with hypocrisy. He employs winter weather to convey the prejudicial "whiteness" of those who control the city, as epitomized by the epigraph of this article. The exclusionary politics of the capital city are masked by the apparent purity and virtuousness of the snow, the cathedral so gloriously depicted by Roberts, and those who occupy the large houses of wealthy—primarily Loyalist—descendants that populate the downtown core:

> White are your housetops, white too your vaunted elms
> That make your stately streets long aisles of prayer,
> And white your thirteen spires that point to your God
> Who reigns afar in pure and whiter air,
> And white the dome of your democracy—
> The snow has pitied you and made you fair. (23)

Cogswell turns the elm-lined streets of downtown Fredericton into mock church aisles that lead to the cathedral spires and, by implication, God. But the "democracy" of the community appears to extend only as far as those whose complexions match the snow that blankets downtown. And as the poetic "I" suggests, the weather conditions reflect the natural world's feelings of pity for the capital city and its prejudices; the luminescence of snow—its whiteness—does not necessarily breed justice for all citizens. In the final lines of the ode, Cogswell specifically recalls the 1947 barbershop incidents, overtly linking the coldness of snow and its ability to conceal the racial biases of good Christians whose attempts to preserve their community include the clearly un-Christian act of refusing to "cut a black man's hair." Cogswell suggests that a Fredericton barbershop—much like the separate drinking fountains and designated seats at the back of the bus that dominated the American South throughout the 1960s (and beyond)—can also be read as a site of explicit racism. And by labelling the poem an ode, he reverses expectations: his poem may seem, at least initially, to praise Fredericton, with its elevated language and rich expressiveness, but the message delivered is highly critical, pointing to the longstanding marginalization of African Canadians in this provincial capital.

Fredericton's Blackness

George Elliott Clarke's acclaimed collection *Execution Poems*, published by Gaspereau, a small press in Nova Scotia, renders in poetic terms the stories of two mixed-race men hanged for murder in Fredericton, displacing the fixed physical location of the city with the public and private positioning of Rufus and George Hamilton, whose race, poverty, and poor planning doom them to certain death. The collection has a striking cover design that visually conveys the exclusion that Cogswell describes in "Ode to Fredericton." *Execution Poems* has a thick, textured black cover with the title and author's name embossed on it, as if to obscure it from vision, implicitly reversing the "whiteness" of the cold, Christian Frederictonians. And the poems themselves sustain this tension, with titles in blood-like red ink and the texts of the poems in black ink on creamy white paper.

The story that Clarke tells in the voices of Geo and Rue, shortened versions of their given names, is of African Canadian brothers whose anger, frustration, hunger, and feelings of "otherness" lead them to commit several crimes, including the heinous murder of a white cab driver. The gruesome details of the event, the punishments that follow, and the locale of Fredericton within this narrative are meticulously woven together in a series of first-hand poetic accounts of the murder itself and of life both before and after the crimes, including Clarke's own summary of their lives from the perspective of a living relative in "George and Rue: Pure, Virtuous Killers." In that poem, Clarke describes them as "rough dreamers, raw believers," whose "clear Negro and semi-Micmac" roots did not help their cause: "They were dangled from the gallows in the third hour of July 27, 1949 A.D. / They were my cousins, dead a decade before I was born. / My bastard phantoms, my dastard fictions" (12). Himself visibly African Canadian and born in the same rural community as his cousins, Clarke wrestles with the fate of these men and their self-negation, explaining in the first poem of the collection: "*Le nègre* negated, meagre, *c'est moi* / … My black face must preface murder for you" (11).

Fredericton does figure prominently in *Execution Poems* as the location where Geo and Rue commit their deeds, but it is certainly not the only cause of their violent behaviour. Clarke's poems outline a family and community legacy of abuse and neglect in Windsor Plains, with their father beating their mother because she is mulatto. Moreover, as children, Geo and Rue witness neighbours being horrifically murdered and lament their inability to describe what they have seen. As Rue puts it in "Child Hood II": "A poor-quality poet crafting hoodlum testimony, / my watery storytelling's cut with the dark rum of curses. / / This is how history darkens against its medium" (17). Through the voices of his cousins' memories, Clarke articulates how race—this heritage of darkness and accompanying self-hatred that can be traced back to the days of slavery in Nova Scotia and New Brunswick—has shaped the lives and actions of these men.

While such a representation of rural Nova Scotia is not entirely new to Clarke—violence, poverty, and racism are endemic to the area, Rue and George's stories of Windsor Plains lack the Edenic plenitude of natural vegetation, human hope, and passionate love that characterizes Clarke's previous depictions of the more positively inflected imagined community of Africadia in *Whylah Falls* and *Beatrice Chancy* (see, e.g., Banks 66, 68–69). One notable exception is two poems in the middle of *Execution Poems*, titled "Duet" and "Rue's Blues," in which Rufus recalls a youthful love affair in Windsor Plains with an exotic and beautiful black woman who picks apples from the local orchards. In "Duet," the woman, aptly named India, speaks for herself, lamenting Rue's physical absence in terms of the natural world:

> I miss the cool ceramic smoothness of your shoulder.
> I miss the scent of apple blossoms in the field
> and the scent of apple blossoms in our hair—
> especially me confusing the two. (29)

But the overwhelming bliss of this intense attraction within an idyllic setting is undercut in the poem that follows, an expression of "blues" that suggests there has been a literal and figurative fall, much like Eve's tasting of the forbidden apple in the Garden of Eden, an act that has altered the future forever. Rue turns to "black liquor" and a life of crime, knowing that "all the Latin in a church / Can't union ex-lovers again" (30). If, as Clarke has suggested, his representation of Africadia is intended to rewrite the map of Nova Scotia and more broadly the Maritime provinces, including New Brunswick,[8] to create "a green space where the free [black] self can live," then the lives of Rufus and George provide an explicit contrast to such idealism ("Mapping" 77). Positive memories of the abundance and nourishment that such a landscape might provide are displaced by the brutality and violence of childhood and the brothers' sense of being thrown out of whatever Eden may have existed. Instead, Rufus and George move to Halifax and eventually to Fredericton, a city where they are outcasts because of their skin colour and, in time, because of their crimes.

Fredericton takes on a life of its own in these poems by virtue of its impact on the Hamilton brothers and Clarke himself. Such interaction is exemplified by "Public Enemy," a text that consists of nine couplets narrated with great élan by Rue, who begins with the lines "Fredericton—fucking—New Brunswick. / A decade of Depression, then the Hitler War" (32). Plagued by the poverty around them, the two brothers, as Rue explains,

> drift into Fredtown like so much black sky—
> squinting at the frigid, ivory, strait-laced streets
>
> speckled by dung of Orange politicians' grins.
> (Spy ingots of shit oranging the snow). (32)

Rue's vivid description turns the Orange Party, whose slogan was "Keep Canada British and Protestant," into the equivalent of dog excrement, dotting the pure white snow not with darkness but with the evidence of political domination. The anger of the brothers, their desire to shake up "their white little paradise here" (32), becomes especially evident when Rue juxtaposes the city's often unacknowledged roots with its publicly celebrated heroes:

> Fredtown was put up by Cadians, Coloureds,
> and hammers. Law and lumber get made here.
> Bliss Carman got made here. Why should I put up with
> this hard-drinking, hard-whoring, hardscrabble town? …
> I want to give them all headaches and nausea:
> I'll play fortissimo Ellington, blacken icy whiteness. (32)

Here the physical building of the capital city by otherwise silenced populations is countered with the creation of poets such as Carman, word-makers who are little more than constructed entities, at least to Rue and George. In response, Rue turns to the musical rhythms of Duke Ellington, the famous African American pianist who in 1933 composed a tongue-in-cheek piece aptly titled "Rude Interlude" (see Holmes for more information). Similarly, Clarke, with his own "Ru(d)e Interlude," challenges the quiet iciness of Fredericton with the brash innovation of Ellington's music and Rue's own rage, both designed to shatter the city's veneer. The poem concludes with Rue's punning promise that he'll "draw blood the way Picasso draws nudes—voluptuously" (32), an image that, given the grotesque distortion of Picasso's portraits, anticipates the horror of the murder to come but frames it with a cultural sophistication intended to speak to Fredericton high society.

The aftermath of the taxi driver's murder is shaped by the conservative city's shock and the brothers' differing attempts to escape death. George claims innocence and insists that Rue committed the murder, fingering his brother in an effort to save himself. In "Ballad of a Hanged Man," George claims that the hunger of his child has motivated robbery but not murder:

> I had the intention to ruck some money.
> In my own heart, I had that, to rape money …
> Have you ever gone in your life, going
> two days without eating, and whenever
> you get money, you're gonna eat and eat
> regardless of all the bastards in Fredericton. (13)

Notably, George also differentiates himself from his sartorially resplendent brother, who apparently purchased, among other items, new clothes with the driver's stolen money the morning after the murder. George aligns Rue with the zoot-suit riots of the era, distinguished by the exaggerated shoulder pads and sharply tapered legs of dark suits worn by young African Americans and Mexican Americans in an expression of anger over their marginalization during the Second World War (see Daniels, et al.; and White and White). George, however, is a family man who cannot afford to make such a fashion statement. He appears at the trial in work overalls: "I know Fredericton reporters can prove / zoot-suit vines style not my viciousness" (13).

In contrast, Rue, newly released from the Dorchester Penitentiary in southeastern New Brunswick, having served time for a previous assault in Fredericton, is a self-styled ladies' man who responds to his brother's snitching with a combination of bravado and recognition that his destiny "was always murder and to be murdered" (21).[9] Rue has been accused of wielding the hammer that killed the taxi driver as well as plotting the dumping of the body and the car. His arrogance and anger at the racism that has shaped his life sustain him to the end:

> Here's how I justify my error:
> The blow that slew silver came from two centuries back.
> It took that much time and agony to turn a white man's whip
> into a black man's hammer. (35)

Rue remains unrepentant and well aware that the hanging of himself and his brother is inevitable because "blood must expunge, sponge up blood" (37), especially when blacks kill innocent whites.

In *Execution Poems*, Clarke's narrator repeatedly suggests that the brothers are roundly condemned to death by the local community for being almost but not quite the Maritimers they are supposed to be. They are destined to die partly because of the location of their crimes. More importantly, their race, their class status, and their geographic positioning at the edge of Fredericton ensure that they will be treated as "other" when put on the stand at the downtown courthouse. However, Clarke complicates this in explicitly linguistic terms by having the two brothers use different forms of "blackened English" to plead their case and tell their story. In "Malignant English," for instance, the Crown praises Rue for speaking "our English well," to which he replies, "But your alabaster, marble English isn't mine," and explains, "My duty is to make narrative more telling, / Yours is to make malice more malicious" (38). The cancerous elements of the conventional English language are pointedly mocked by Rue, whose poetic turns of phrase and highly imagistic vocabulary exceed the plodding conformity of the legalese that he must respond to in court. His language mirrors his dress, as a man whose meticulously styled zoot-suit ensembles and elegantly violent discourse separate him from his working-class roots, yet also suggests that he has no wish to become part of the white mainstream. In contrast, George's inelegant discourse is the subject of a monologue in a poem titled "Trial I," in which George vividly characterizes his speech in relation to location:

> My English is like fractured china—broken.
> I really speak *Coloured*, but with a Three Mile Plains accent.
> See, I can't speak Lucasville and my New Road's kinda weak.
> Ma English be a desert that don't bloom less watered by rum. (36)

Rue may choose to mock the static statue of marbled English that he associates with the courtroom and the discourse of white privilege more generally, but George actually describes the roots of his language use, making distinctions between geographic locations within rural Nova Scotia and taking pride in both the general inflection of blackness in his speech and the particularity of his accent, one grounded in place. As Clarke himself has argued in *Odysseys Home: Mapping African-Canadian Literature*: "Since standard English was thrust upon African diasporic peoples against their wills, it is marvelous justice that, in every exilic African culture, from New Brunswick to New Orleans … that tongue now meets a different standard" (276). Both brothers suggest that their resistance to and fragmentation of a standard English are important acts of self-definition and resistance against a city and a legal system that do not want to hear voices—each distinctive in its own right—that deviate from the dominant white Loyalist heritage of Fredericton, of New Brunswick, and of the Maritimes more generally.

The inevitability of the hanging becomes, for Rue and Geo, an opportunity to reflect on their sacrificial status in the place where they will be hanged, not like the "Hanging Gardens of Babylon," one of the seven wonders of the world, but, in the words of the men, "like Christ hanged" (41). As "*disjecta membra*" of Loyalist New Brunswick, Rue and George in the poem "Famous Last" narrate their own demise in the city of stately elms in decidedly ironic terms:

> *Geo*: The laws preach Christ but teach crucifixion.
> Folks glance through us like we're albino ghosts.
>
> *Rue*: Hanging's a lot like drowning:
> The condemned pedal in air,
> while constriction inundates the throat …
>
> *Rue*: We will fall into our sentence: silence. (41)

Fredericton, by implication, is not only the physical site of their death sentences but also the place of their final doing-in, yet another fall from grace. Virtually invisible to the local population except when considered a threat, the Hamilton brothers must negotiate their status in the capital city by virtue of their marginalization. Clarke's choice of title, "Famous Last," and the absence of the expected final, "Words," suggest that even in death the brothers resist deliverance through Christian grace. Rather than relegating them to silence or illiteracy once condemned, Clarke grants them the power of speech to the bitter end. The brothers may not escape the death penalty, but their eloquence, as he renders it, serves as a lasting rebuke of the capital city.

In a final satiric stab at Fredericton and those who inhabit the city, Clarke concludes his volume with three items: first, a letter addressed to the Governor General of Canada in 1949, Viscount Alexander of Tunis, a British war general, written by a citizen of Fredericton whose English pales in comparison with that of Rue and George; second, a newspaper item on the hanging from a paper aptly named the *Casket*,[10] prefaced by several fabricated entries outlining the paper's criminal and literary reporting inaccuracies; and third, two photos, placed side by side, of a black man being hanged (though notably the photo is of a man who died in 1932 and is taken from the National Defence Collection of the National Archives of Canada). The anonymous letter writer denounces both brothers, insisting in an impoverished English dialect that they are obviously guilty: "wee the peepul of Fredericton feel they must hang fore the bluddy homaside they did" (43). In the corrections on the following page, both from the imaginary local paper, the *Casket*, the royal "we" of the paper's staff are forced to acknowledge their inaccurate recounting of a 1948 murder (44). Clarke's poetic "I" employs a series of fairly overt puns here to make his point; the killer, aptly named Spears Flowers, explains that he actually committed the crime in 1947, strangling Nicey Pew not because he was intoxicated but because, as he puts it, "she had begun to write poetry, though he prefers true crime" (44). Likewise, the paper admits to having wrongly attributed the novel *Cane* to W.B. Yeats and not its actual author, African American Jean Toomer. Located adjacent to these pointedly subversive alterations of the literary and historical record is the account of the brothers' hanging, an event that brought out a huge number of spectators even though the execution was done within a constructed shed. The event is still etched in the memories of some older Fredericton residents.

Clarke's collection is a sprawling and politically invested representation of Fredericton and its surrounding areas, one that must inevitably narrow, ending with the executions in the old jailhouse courtyard—located two blocks from the cathedral—where the two young black men are confined to a shed for their hangings. To commit their crime, Geo and Rue take a long journey. The two men move on separate occasions from Nova Scotia to Barker's Point, an area of Fredericton's north side, and settle in. And the crime itself takes place in Barker's Point, but over the next twenty-four hours Rue and Geo travel between multiple places with the driver's body in the trunk in an effort to dump the evidence. Geo, following his brother's instructions, takes Rue on the highway east to Minto, a small town outside Fredericton, where he plays cards all night in an effort to secure a solid alibi. Geo then proceeds to drive roughly a hundred kilometres down to the port city of Saint John, where he spends the night at a brothel and returns to Fredericton the next morning. Rue has suggested that Geo should abandon the car in Saint John, which has a larger black population, and take a bus home. But Geo ignores this advice. His fateful road trip, during which he returns the car to the area of the crime, is represented in Clarke's text by the "Silver coiled—… void noose—in the trunk" (12), an image that also appears on the title page of the collection, coupled with a hammer. That noose, though initially unfilled, becomes symbolic of the increasingly tight geographic circle that draws the two brothers in from the suburbs of the capital, taking them to Minto, Saint John, the south side of the river in Fredericton (where they finally abandon the car), and Barker's Point before returning them to the downtown core, turning relegation to the periphery into visibility at the centre with the double hanging of the two men.

Roberts characterizes Fredericton as beautifully narcissistic, too consumed by its own reflection to pay much attention to what passes by the river's edge; Nowlan and Cogswell explore the lengthy history of racism in the provincial capital, whether aimed at Natives or African Canadians. Yet Rue and Geo, themselves of mixed blood, change that, intruding with violence and hatred on the rarefied atmosphere of the city in an effort to make their mark. In doing so, they blacken the centre of the city both literally and figuratively, revealing the Fredericton community's fascination with their lives and especially their public deaths. Clarke deconstructs this objectification by giving voice to the two men as they live through the crime and its aftermath. He also playfully notes at the end of the text under the "Author's Disclaimer" that those who have helped to produce the book "bear no responsibility for its harms. Only the author deserves hanging" (46). With this, Clarke stresses the need to examine what has led to the resolute condemnation of his two cousins. Furthermore, Clarke's interest in "rewriting the map of Nova Scotia" and of the presence of blacks in the Maritimes takes a considerably different turn in this text by focusing on a city that is outside of—and outcast from—the geographic and imaginary space of Africadia ("Mapping" 75). The collection implicitly delineates the boundaries of Africadia and the potential loss for those, like George and Rufus, who, once in Fredericton, can no longer remember the beauty of their birthplace and are reduced to describing it in predominantly ugly and violent terms.

Clarke, as a poet and scholar who has spent considerable energy pioneering the field of African Canadian literature, has much at stake in *Execution Poems*. As *Odysseys Home* attests, there is a rich and lengthy history of Africadian literature in particular that has been sorely neglected in the study and teaching of Maritime cultures, an area that has been dominated primarily by white Loyalist traditions.[11] To provide better access to these works, Clarke has already published two volumes of *Fire on the Water: An Anthology of Black Nova Scotian Writing*, which survey the writings of blacks in that Maritime province from 1785 onward. *Execution Poems* adds yet another dimension to his fictional depictions of Africadia and reflects his broader desire to make the complex and diverse voices of Maritime blacks available. In his collection, Clarke reclaims an otherwise unknown branch of his family and offers a personalized account of the ghosts whose positioning in relation to Fredericton society has shaped his own understanding of the city and the region. And the language that Clarke uses to tell their story, and his own, is not surprisingly a blackened or broken English, a deliberate choice that accords with his assertion in *Odysseys Home* that such speech is a means of maintaining a distinctive racial consciousness and sense of black solidarity (*Odysseys Home* 86). Writing in this tongue within the setting of 1940s Fredericton takes Cogswell's ironically charged ode a step further by giving voice to Africadians living in the city and paying tribute to their varied linguistic expertise.

Clarke's poems assert a presence in Fredericton and New Brunswick that is black and proudly so—exposing the legacy of racism that has shaped the birthplace of Canadian poetry and conversely ensuring the inclusion of what Clarke calls "Africadian" stories and voices while introducing another set of paradoxes. In November 2003, Clarke was named the inaugural E.J. Pratt Professor in

Canadian Literature at the University of Toronto, a position co-funded by Victoria College, where Frye spent his career. The choice of Clarke was justified by the English department chair with the explanation that, "Like Pratt, much of Professor Clarke's identity is shaped by his Maritime roots. And like Pratt, Professor Clarke is one of the country's most respected poets. So the choice was natural" ("Award-Winning Poet"). "Nature," it appears, has come full circle. Africadia may be a site of Edenic abundance, "an ideal place" with an imaginary geography that powerfully counters the historical erasure of the presence of blacks throughout the Maritimes (Clarke, "Mapping" 77); Fredericton, in contrast, becomes a space for those who have been cast out, a site of dastardly deeds that reveal the narrow geographic and imaginative potential of the city and the impact of that narcissism.

With *Execution Poems*, Clarke asks his readers to again examine Fredericton as an undeniably significant—but extremely vexed—site of poetic inspiration. Rather than seeing the city of spires as a bucolic, pastoral setting, Clarke's collection demonstrates that New Brunswick is also a place of racial conflict and execution with a heritage that tinges the capital city's whiteness and reframes its place in Maritime and Canadian literary history. As the voices of Rufus and George so powerfully suggest, there needs to be a wider reconsideration of the history—and legacy—of racism in the Maritimes and New Brunswick in particular. George Elliott Clarke's *Execution Poems* demands that we begin to undertake such a process by looking, at least in the case of Fredericton, not to the cathedral and the river but to the jail and those it has housed.

Author's Note

Many thanks to the staff of Science East and to Linda Baier and Mary Flagg at the Archives and Special Collections in the Harriet Irving Library for their help in making sense of Fredericton's past and present; Mary Rimmer also provided useful secondary sources. I am particularly grateful to Tanya Butler for giving me a tour of Windsor Plains and for her many thoughtful interventions throughout the writing of this article. As always, John Ball deserves credit for his careful reading of a draft of this article; thanks also to the editors of this special issue for their apt suggestions.

Endnotes

1. See *Essays on Canadian Writing* 71 (Flynn) for an extensive discussion of this question. See also Blodgett 122, 211; and Kertzer 42, 120.
2. Barry Davies notes that the population of Fredericton would have been approximately six thousand in the late eithteenth century (117).
3. A plaque erected on the University of New Brunswick campus by the Historic Sites and Monuments Board of Canada recognizes the lives and careers of Carman, Roberts, and Sherman under the heading "POETS' CORNER / LE BERCEAU DES POÈTES," with the following inscription: "Born in or near Fredericton, these three poets were educated in this University and are buried in the cemetery of Forest Hill. Their gifts of verse enriched Canadian literature and gained for their common birthplace the designation 'The Poets' Corner of Canada'." It can be viewed online at the following URL: <http://www.brokenjaw.com/GovCanada-PoetsCorner.htm> .

4. See, for example, Clarke's interview with Anne Compton in which he describes himself as "the scribe of a marginalized and colonized community" (Clarke, "Standing" 143). Similarly, in an interview with Maureen Moynagh, Clarke contends that "the need to commemorate has fuelled my writing since my youth … There's a whole side of Maritime/Canadian life that has been repressed, and it's the duty of all of us who are creating right now to address that fact" (Clarke, "Mapping" 73).
5. See also Walker 97–99, who details the relegation of black Loyalists to the bottom of land claim lists and outlines their lack of rights in the Maritimes at the end of the eighteenth century: blacks were not allowed to vote, serve on a jury, ask for a jury trial, or hold a public office throughout the region. The result was an exodus of black Loyalists to Sierra Leone in 1792. The British government promised those who went grants of land and full political rights as members of that newly formed colony. As Walker notes, Confederation didn't improve the status of blacks in the Maritimes, nor did the end of the First World War and the coming of the Depression: "[T]he elite among the [black] men became railway waiters and porters … Waiting jobs and other personal contact positions passed increasingly to whites" (100), leaving African Canadians throughout the region heavily dependent on their local communities for survival.
6. See Reid 72–75; also see William Spray's extremely useful *The Blacks in New Brunswick.*
7. See the UNB student newspaper, the *Brunswickan* 5 Dec. 1947: 1–3, for detailed commentary on these events and student reactions to the racism of local businesses. Coverage of the incidents continued in the *Brunswickan* 13 Jan. 1948: 1–2.

8. See also Compton's interview with Clarke, where he states that "there is, at least in the Maritimes, specifically in parts of Nova Scotia—the Annapolis Valley—but also in Prince Edward Island and New Brunswick, the possibility for gardens, as opposed to wilderness, where one is, more or less, at peace and where one can find beauty" ("Standing" 143).
9. See Clarke, *George & Rue*, 217 for photographs of the two men; George is indeed in work clothes, while Rue wears a shirt and tie, a stylish topcoat, and an elegantly patterned scarf.
10. The *Casket* is, in fact, the name of the weekly Antigonish newspaper, and Clarke with his close ties to the province would presumably know this.
11. See *Odysseys Home* 118–23. See also Gwendolyn Davies; Mannette; and Walker.

Works Cited

Abrams, M.H. *A Glossary of Literary Terms*. 6th ed. Fort Worth: Harcourt, 1993.

"Award-Winning Poet Named First Professor in Canadian Literature." *University of Toronto: News @UofT*. Ed. Anjali Baichwal. 2003. Dept. of Public Affairs, U of Toronto. 2 Oct. 2004 <http://www.news.utoronto.ca/bin5/031126a.asp>.

Bailey, Alfred G. "Creative Moments in the Culture of the Maritime Provinces." *Dalhousie Review* 29 (1949–50): 231–44.

Banks, Michelle. "Myth-Making and Exile: The Desire for a Homeplace in George Elliott Clarke's *Whylah Falls*." *Canadian Poetry* 51 (2002): 58–85.

Blodgett, E.D. *Five Part Invention: A History of Literary History in Canada*. Toronto: U of Toronto P, 2003.

Brown, E.K. *On Canadian Poetry*. Toronto: Ryerson, 1943.

Brydon, Diana. "It's Time for a New Set of Questions." Flynn 14–25.

Buckner, Philip, ed. *Teaching Maritime Studies*. Fredericton: Acadiensis, 1986.

Clarke, George Elliott. *Beatrice Chancy*. Vancouver: Polestar, 1999.

—. *Execution Poems: The Black Acadian Tragedy of "George and Rue."* Wolfville: Gaspereau, 2001.

—, ed. *Fire on the Water: An Anthology of Black Nova Scotian Writing*. 2 vols. Halifax: Pottersfield, 1991–92.

—. *George & Rue*. Toronto: HarperCollins, 2005.

—. "Mapping Africadia's Imaginary Geography: An Interview with George Elliott Clarke." With Maureen Moynagh. *ARIEL* 27.4 (1996): 71–94.

—. *Odysseys Home: Mapping African-Canadian Literature*. Toronto: U of Toronto P, 2002.

—. "Standing Your Ground: George Elliott Clarke in Conversation." With Anne Compton. *Studies in Canadian Literature* 23.2 (1998): 138–64.

—. *Whylah Falls*. Winlaw: Polestar, 1990.

Cogswell, Fred. "Ode to Fredericton." *Descent from Eden*. Toronto: Ryerson, 1959. 23.

Daniels, Maria, et al., eds. *Zoot Suit Riots*. 2001. 26 Sept. 2004. <http://www.pbs.org/wgbh/amex/zoot/eng_peopleevents/e_riots.html>.

Davies, Barry. "English Poetry in New Brunswick 1880–1940." *A Literary and Linguistic History of New Brunswick*. Ed. Reavley Gair. Fredericton: Goose Lane, 1985. 117–25.

Davies, Gwendolyn. "Digressions on the K-Mart Bus: Teaching Maritime Literature." Buckner 209–15.

Flynn, Kevin, ed. *Where Is Here Now?* Spec. issue of *Essays on Canadian Writing* 71 (2000).

Frye, Northrop. *The Bush Garden: Essays on the Canadian Imagination*. Toronto: Anansi, 1971.

Holmes, Robb, ed. Rude Interlude: A Duke Ellington Home Page. 1999. 25 Sept. 2004. <http://www.ilinks.net/~holmesr/duke.htm>.

Keefer, Janice Kulyk. *Under Eastern Eyes: A Critical Reading of Maritime Fiction*. Toronto: U of Toronto P, 1987.

Kertzer, Jonathan. *Worrying the Nation: Imagining a National Literature in English Canada*. Toronto: U of Toronto P, 1998.

Mannette, J.A. "Blackness and Maritime Studies." Buckner 80–95.

Nowlan, Alden. "Ancestral Memories Evoked by Attending the Opening of the Playhouse in Fredericton, New Brunswick." *Bread, Wine, and Salt*. Toronto: Clarke, 1967. 47.

Ovid. *Metamorphoses*: Books I–VIII. Trans. Frank Justus Miller. Cambridge: Harvard UP, 1999.

Pacey, Desmond. *Essays in Canadian Criticism*. Toronto: Ryerson, 1969.

Reid, John G. *Six Crucial Decades: Times of Change in the History of the Maritimes*. Halifax: Nimbus, 1987.

Roberts, Sir Charles G.D. "The City of Fredericton." Ts. The Sir Charles G.D. Roberts Fonds. MG L10, box 3, ser. 2, file 7. Archives and Special Collections, Harriet Irving Library, U of New Brunswick.

—. "To Fredericton in May-Time." Ts. The Collected Poems of Sir Charles G.D. Roberts Fonds. MG L24, ser. 1, subser. 1, #36. Archives and Special Collections, Harriet Irving Library, U of New Brunswick.

Smith, A.J.M. "The Fredericton Poets." *Towards a View of Canadian Letters: Selected Critical Essays*, 1928–71. Vancouver: UBC P, 1973. 65–76.

Spray, William. *The Blacks in New Brunswick*. Fredericton: Brunswick, 1972.

Walker, James W. St. G. "Black History in the Maritimes: Major Themes and Teaching Strategies." Buckner 96–107.

White, Shane, and Graham White. *Stylin': African American Expressive Culture from Its Beginnings to the Zoot Suit*. Ithaca: Cornell UP, 1998. 12.

The Mask of Aaron: "Tall Screams reared out of Three Mile Plains": Shakespeare's *Titus Andronicus* and George Elliott Clarke's Black Acadian Tragedy, *Execution Poems*

SUSAN KNUTSON

This study of George Elliott Clarke's award-winning *Execution Poems* in relation to Shakespeare's *Titus Andronicus* is part of a larger project that explores Canadian writers' use of Shakespeare. The project aims to sound the layered meanings of Shakespearean passages once they have found their way into Canadian poetry and fiction.[1] In *Execution Poems*, several of those layers have to do with Canada's colonial history, and with the ways that Shakespeare has been a key building-block of the British Empire.[2] Others have to do with the particular resonance of Shakespeare, and history, for generations of African Nova Scotians, or, as Clarke has named them (and himself), the Africadians. At the end of the eighteenth century and the beginning of the nineteenth they came to Canada from the USA to escape slavery and the Fugitive Slave Laws, only to experience generations of economic, social and educational discrimination.[3]

One such resonance traced by Clarke's poetic suite is the deep and spontaneous identification between his character, Rufus Hamilton, and Shakespeare's dramatic villain, Aaron the Moor—an identification that has an historical counterpoint in the enthusiastic reception of Aaron by black audiences in South Africa, as reported by Anthony Sher and Gregory Doran, and discussed by Ania Loomba, in *Shakespeare, Race and Colonialism*.[4] In *Execution Poems*, Clarke's Africadian character identifies with Aaron and speaks in the rhetorical tropes of Shakespeare's *Titus Andronicus*. The rhetorical excess and violent action place *Execution Poems* in the tradition of the revenge tragedy, of Marlowe and Seneca and also of the African American literary tradition that followed on the heels of Nat Turner's bloody revolt in Southampton County, Virginia, in 1831.[5] The mask of Aaron is worn in the pursuit of revenge and social justice. In tracing the intertextual labyrinth that binds Clarke's *Execution Poems* to Shakespeare's *Titus Andronicus*, I glimpse an Africadian Shakespeare and a Shakespearean George Elliott Clarke, and so understand something of the Classical and European patrimony to which George Elliott Clarke and his black, African Nova Scotian speakers are the legitimate heirs. I align my efforts here with the work of African-Canadian scholar David Sealy, who notes the "diverse ways in which Black diasporic subjects have selectively appropriated, incorporated, European ideologies, culture, and institutions, alongside an 'African' heritage."[6]

The poems narrate the short and bitter lives of Clarke's first cousins, Rufus and George Hamilton, who were hanged for the murder of a Fredericton taxi driver in New Brunswick, in 1949. The crucial intertext linking the poems to Shakespeare's *Titus Andronicus* both supports and complicates Clarke's social justice argument, which is articulated rhetorically in his poetry as the chiasmatic linking between the brothers' act of violent murder and their subjection to acts of murderous violence carried out by the society in which they lived. Such a structured and rhetorical performance of violence is as typical of *Titus Andronicus* as it is fundamental to *Execution Poems,* which in this way announce their poetic genealogy, reaching through Shakespeare to Christopher Marlowe's *Jew of Malta* to the "heightened rhetoric" of Seneca's typically gruesome tragedies.[7] Textual kinship is further attested to by the cheerfully brutal style shared by the Clarke and the Shakespeare texts, for example, in this well-known alliteration from *Andronicus*:

> Alarbus' limbs are lopp'd[8]

Or this cheery antanaclasis (the repetition of a word in two different senses) from *Execution Poems:*

> I'll draw blood the way Picasso draws nudes, voluptuously.[9]

The excessive literariness of this language opens up a field of dense signification that is both glorious and brutal, celebratory and indeterminate; morally and ethically deferred. As Bart Moore-Gilbert writes in his discussion of Dennis Porter's "*Orientalism* and its Problems," "the excess of the signifier over the signified at such moments produces a complex of meanings which cannot be stabilized … in any easy or straightforward way."[10]

The characterization of the brothers articulates two distinct responses to questions of language and of ethical or political action as they are framed in the postcolonial situation, urgently counter-posing creole or patois to Shakespearean English, and violence to counter-violence, moral righteousness, and revenge. Clarke invokes paradox and oxymoron even as he introduces "George & Rue: Pure, Virtuous Killers," and summarizes their shared story:

> They sprouted in Newport Station, Hants County, Nova Scotia, in 1925 and 1926.
> They smacked a white taxi driver, Silver, with a hammer, to lift his silver.
> ...
> They had face-to-face trials in May 1949 and backed each other's guilt.
> ...
> They were dandled from a gallows in the third hour of July 27, 1949, A.D.[11]

The young men's contrasting characters and contrapuntal confessions help to structure the story and ground the multiple voicing of the poems as a whole:

> George Albert Hamilton confessed—to theft—and mated the Sally Anne.
> Rufus James Hamilton polished his refined, mint, silver-bright English.[12]

George Hamilton is both less guilty and less interesting than his brother. He is the good victim of racism and discriminatory violence. His story, that he only *robbed* the taxi driver, and that, because he was hungry and in need, is elaborated in the following poem, "Ballad of a Hanged Man":

> ... See, as a wed man,
> I don't care if I wear uglified overalls.
> But I ain't going to hear my child starve.
> ....

> I had the intention to ruck some money.
> In my own heart, I had that, to rape money,
> because I was fucked, in my own heart.
> ....
> Have you ever gone in your life, going
> two days without eating ...?
>
> I ain't dressed this story up. I am enough
> disgraced. I swear to the truths I know.
> I wanted to uphold my wife and child.
> Hang me and I'll not hold them again.[13]

George "mated the Sally Anne" in the sense that he regained the moral high ground in relation to the Salvation Army, by claiming that he only wanted to be able to eat and to support his wife and children. George Hamilton makes this appeal to liberal humanist values using the non-standard variety of English known to linguists as African Nova Scotian English, or simply Black English. ("I ain't dressed this story up ..."), which is characterized by the use of the subjunctive and by retentions from nineteenth-century, or older, English.[14] Throughout *Execution Poems*, George Hamilton speaks in this popular language variety and, fittingly, he states his case here using the popular literary form of the ballad. This does not mean, however, that his language is unsophisticated, for George Hamilton's speech—like the language of the book as a whole—displays a very wide range of classical rhetorical tropes and figures. Two examples here would be *anthimeria*, the substitution of one part of speech for another, as in the phrase, "But I ain't going to hear my child starve"; and *paronomasia*, words alike in sound but different in meaning, in "I wanted to uphold my wife and child. / Hang me and I'll not hold them again."[15]

It is Rufus James Hamilton, on the other hand, who identifies most deeply with Aaron. Rufus does not deny his responsibility for the murder. Instead, this bi-dialectal linguistic virtuoso celebrates his crime and spits out his rage and anger in varieties of English ranging from the Shakespearean to the rural Black Nova Scotian, as he pleases. George asks for forgiveness, but his brother sees the act as righteous revenge:[16]

> *Rue:* Here's how I justify my error:
> The blow that slew Silver came from two centuries back.
> It took that much time and agony to turn a white man's whip
> into a black man's hammer.[17]

Rufus denounces the bloody history of African slavery and looks for vengeance against the society that abused him. His character is based on the historical Rufus Hamilton who, as George Elliot Clarke explains, spoke so articulately during his trial that his prosecutor, unable to 'shake' or 'flap' him, commented on his excellent command of English.[18] The character of Rufus is also Shakespearean. In "Reading *Titus Andronicus* in Three Mile Plains, N.S.," Rufus tells how he came to identify with one of Shakespeare's most unredeemed villains, Aaron the Moor:

> *Rue:* When Witnesses sat before Bibles open like plates
> And spat sour sermons of interposition and nullification,
> While burr-orchards vomited bushel of thorns, and leaves
> Rattled like uprooted skull-teeth across rough highways,
> And stars ejected brutal, serrated, heart-shredding light,
> And dark brothers lied down, quiet, in government graves,
> Their white skulls jabbering amid farmer's dead flowers –
> The junked geraniums and broken truths of car engines,
> And *History* snapped its whip and bankrupted scholars,

School was violent improvement. I opened Shakespeare
And discovered a scarepriest, shaking in violent winds,
Some hallowed, heartless man, his brain boiling blood,
Aaron, seething, demanding, "Is black so base a hue?"
And shouting, "Coal-black refutes and foils any other hue
In that it scorns to bear another hue." O! Listen at that! [19]

The intertextuality linking *Execution Poems* and *Titus Andronicus* rests here on the bedrock of an explicit identification between Rufus and Aaron, founded on Aaron's defense of blackness as he turns on the nurse to protect his newborn son. His baby is described as a "devil",[20] "A joyless, dismal, black and sorrowful issue /... as loathsome as a toad / Amongst the fair-faced breeders of our clime." [21] Aaron responds with rhetorical argument—"Is black so base a hue?" [22]—and with his sword.

Clarke also quotes, a few lines later, and in the epigraphs to the poems as a whole, a passage from Seneca's *Hippolytus* which Shakespeare wove into *Titus Andronicus*, where the lines are spoken by Demetrius as he readies himself to assault Lavinia:

Sit fas aut nefas, till I find the stream
To cool this heat, a charm to calm these fits,
Per Stygia, per manes vehor.[23]

The Latin translates into English as: "Be it right or wrong / I am borne through the Stygian regions among shades." Clarke writes, in Rue's voice:

Sit fat aut nefas, I am become
Aaron, desiring poisoned lilies and burning, staggered air,
A King James God, spitting fire, brimstone, leprosy, cancers,
Dreaming of tearing down stars and letting grass incinerate
Pale citizen's prized bones. What should they mean to me?

> A plough rots, returns to ore; weeds snatch it back to earth;
> The stones of the sanctuaries pour out onto every street.
> Like drastic Aaron's heir, Nat Turner, I's natural homicidal:
> My pages blaze, my lines pall, crying fratricidal damnation.[24]

Locating both hell and apocalyptic vengeance in the human world, these lines may remind us of Marlowe's Mephistopheles, who famously turns up in Gutenberg to declare, "Why this is hell, nor am I out of it." [25] Damnation, Marlowe taught, is a state of mind, and the bloody violence of Clarke's "Original Pain" elaborates on Rufus's life as one of the living damned, and further underpins the Old Testament referents of fratricidal murder and original sin. Rue's final speech, which claims, "We'll hang like Christ hanged," [26] goes one better than Aaron's last words, pronounced as he is literally being buried alive for his sins:

> If one good deed in all my life I did
> I do repent it from my very soul.[27]

At the least, both characters are in unqualified rebellion against the imperial power which would negate them.

While Aaron's calligraphy of social vengeance is acted out as murder and rape within the play itself, at the level of the literary text Aaron models the counter-discourse of the post-colonial writer, as Clarke suggests:

> The smartest, wiliest character in TA is black Aaron, and his malice toward Titus and the whole Roman power structure is driven in part by his lust for revenge against a civilization that considers him barbarous. Aaron is the model of the frustrated and embittered black (minority) intellectual who uses his mastery of the codes of the opposing civilization to wreak endless havoc within it—with a smile … He is Othello as if played by Iago.[28]

In keeping with this interpretation, we should note that literary experience is signified as such both in Shakespeare's play and in *Execution Poems*. For just as Rufus, for better or for worse, discovers a way to navigate through the violence of his childhood world via an identification with Shakespeare's Aaron, so Lavinia's rape and mutilation is communicated to her father, nephew and uncle through their reading of Ovid's account of the story of Tereus, Philomena, Procne and Itys. When Titus communicates with Tamara's sons by sending them a quotation from Horace, it is Aaron who is able to decode this literary sign and who understands and acts on the message of the text. *Titus Andronicus* and *Execution Poem*s are both explicitly concerned with poetry and the place of poetry in relation to the struggle for social justice. It is no accident, then, that in his prefatory poem, "Negation," Clarke introduces himself in terms that appear to deliberately recall Aaron's determination to act, early on in *Titus Andronicus*:

> Away with slavish weeds and servile thoughts!
> I will be bright, and shine in pearl and gold[29]

Clarke writes:

> I mean
> To go out shining instead of tarnished,
> To take apart poetry like a heart[30]

Aaron's determination to voice "the venomous malice of his swelling heart,"[31] is expressed appropriately, as a rhetorical question—"Ah, why should wrath be mute and fury dumb?"[32] His sentiments could easily be those of Rufus Hamilton, or even those of Rufus's poet cousin, George Elliott Clarke who, like Shakespeare, has employed both his voice and his rhetorical virtuosity in the service of wrath and fury.

Titus Andronicus himself is also a writer, whose response to the bloodbath in this family is to retire to his study to compose "crimson lines"[33]:

Who doth molest my contemplation?
Is it your trick to make me ope the door,
That so my sad decrees may fly away,
And all my study be to no effect?
You are deceived, for what I mean to do
See here in bloody lines I have set down;
And what is written shall be executed.[34]

It is Titus, too, who articulates the topographical boundaries of his world that conform to the traditional three levels of the Heavens, the Earth (made up of Rome and of the Country of the Goths) and Hell. When Lavinia writes in the sand the names of Chiron and Demetrius, identifying them as her tormentors, Titus cites Seneca to accuse the heavens of looking passively on as crimes are committed: *Tam lentus audis scelera, tam lentus vides?*" ["Ruler of the great heavens, dost thou so calmly hear crimes, so calmly look upon them?"][35] The heavens are disengaged and passive. Later, as he plots to cast the net of vengeance for Tamora and her sons, Titus comments that Justice has fled the earth, so that he and the remnant of his family must turn to hell for help in their distress:

Terras Astraea reliquit [Justice has fled the Earth]:
Be you remembered, Marcus, She's gone, she's fled.
Sirs, take you to your tools. You, cousins, shall
Go sound the ocean, and cast your nets;
Happily you may catch her in the sea;
Yet there's as little justice as at land.
No, Publius and Sempronius, you must do it,

'Tis you must dig with mattock and with spade,
And pierce the inmost centre of the earth.
Then, when you come to Pluto's region,
I pray you deliver him this petition.
Tell him it is for justice and for aid,
And that it comes from old Andronicus,
Shaken with sorrows in ungrateful Rome.[36]

When hell responds, through Publius, that Revenge is in Hell but that Justice must be hiding in the heavens, Titus' thoughts again turn skyward, and he does a remarkable thing: he initiates a new dynamism within his topographical field through the comedic device of firing many arrows, burdened with writing and appealing for justice to Jove, Apollo, Mars and Pallas, to the end that, "There's not a god left unsolicited"[37]:

And sith there's no justice in earth nor hell,
We will solicit heaven and move the gods
To send down justice for us to wreak our wrongs.[38]

His solicitation, his attempt to move another through the power of language is, of course, the province of rhetoric.

Clarke's *Execution Poems* likewise voices a rhetorical appeal for justice, overlaying a Canadian Maritime geography onto the three-tiered world of the Elizabethan stage. A very specific sense of Maritime places accentuates the dynamic address of "Tall screams reared out of Three Mile Plains," from the poem "Original Pain," creating the striking figure of the suffering boys' cries rising to the heavens.[39] The geography is specific and the relationship is dynamic, as the appeal—not one but many "tall screams"—is one that demands to be heard. In this, we may choose to see a parallel to Titus's soliciting scream "to move the gods to send down justice for us to wreak our wrongs."[40] But in the Canadian Maritimes the heavens are equally indifferent, it seems, as the lofty over-view of "Haligonian Market Cry" moves indifferently from the "hallelujah watermelons!—virginal pears!—virtuous corn!" to "sluttish watermelons!—sinful cucumbers!—jail bait pears!—/ Planted by Big-Mouth Chaucer and picked by Evil Shakespeare!"[41]

To conclude, the Shakespearean intertext, based on the identification between Rufus Hamilton and Shakespeare's Aaron the Moor, extends further to engender both the rhetorical language and dynamic address of Clarke's poems which, like Titus's arrows, are fired into the heavens as an appeal for justice. They are addressed to the Gods but reach only as far as another bloody act of human retribution. They are fired out of the depths of hellish human cruelty towards a heaven mistakenly imagined as the site of transcendent and absolute justice. The arc of the arrows' trajectory transcribes the boundaries of the human universe within which the characters in these stories must act and, in this way, Clarke's *Execution Poems* brings home the message of the ongoing struggle for social justice.

Endnotes

1. George Elliott Clarke, *Execution Poems: The Black Acadian Tragedy of "George and Rue"* (Wolfville, Nova Scotia: Gaspereau, 2001). *Execution Poems* was awarded the Governor-General's Literary Award for Poetry in English.
2. Michael Neill writes: "Shakespeare's writing was entangled from the beginning with the projects of nation-building, Empire and colonization; [… and] the canon became an instrument of imperial authority

as important and powerful in its way as the Bible and gun"; Neill, "Post-Colonial Shakespeare? Writing Away from the Centre," in *Post-Colonial Shakespeares*, ed. Ania Loomba & Martin Orkin (London: Routledge, 1998): 168–69. For a recent discussion of Canada's postcolonial status, see *Is Canada Postcolonial? Unsettling Canadian Literature*, ed. Laura Moss (Waterloo, Ontario: Wilfrid Laurier U.P., 2003).

3. Most Africadians trace their arrival in Canada to one of the two waves of immigration following the American Revolution and the war of 1812, when the "Black Loyalists" supported the British against the Americans, but, as Clarke points out, there have been persons of African origin in the Atlantic region since the early seventeenth century. See *Odysseys Home: Mapping African-Canadian Literature* (Toronto: U of Toronto P, 2002): 18n3. The Africadians' history in Canada thus begins at the same time as that of the French Acadians; in other words, at the beginning of the European colonization of North America. See esp. "The Birth and Rebirth of Africadian Literature" in *Odysseys Home*, 107–25.
4. Ania Loomba, *Shakespeare, Race and Colonialism* (London: Oxford UP, 2002), 75.
5. See *The Confessions of Nat Turner, and Related Documents*, ed. and introd. Kenneth S. Greenberg (Boston MA & New York: Bedford Books of St. Martin's Press, 1996); Frank Lambert, "'I Saw the Book Talk': Slave Readings of the First Great Awakening," *The Journal of Negro History* 77.4 (1992), 185–198; Jeffery Ogbonna Green Ogbar, "Prophet Nat and God's Children of Darkness: Black Religious Nationalism," *The Journal of Religious Thought* 53–54 (1997): 51–71.

6. David Sealy, "'Canadianizing' Blackness: Resisting the Political," in *Rude: Contemporary Black Canadian Cultural Criticism*, ed. Rinaldo Walcott (Toronto: Insomniac Press, 2000), 91.
7. Harold Bloom, *Shakespeare: The Invention of the Human (*New York: Riverhead Books, 1998): 80. See also Jonathan Bate's discussion of the structured violence in *Titus Andronicus,* in 'Introduction' to William Shakespeare, *Titus Andronicus,* ed. Bate (Arden Shakespeare; London: Methuen, 2002): 4–21.
8. *Titus Andronicus* I.ii.143.
9. *Execution Poems*, 32.
10. Bart Moore-Gilbert, *Postcolonial Theory: Contexts, Practices, Politics* (London: Verso, 1997): 55.
11. *Execution Poems,* 12.
12. *Execution Poems,* 12.
13. *Execution Poems*, 13–14.
14. "The Career of Black English in Nova Scotia: A Literary Sketch," in *Odysseys Home,* 86–106.
15. *Execution Poems*, 14.
16. *Execution Poems*, 41.
17. "The Killing," *Execution Poems*, 35.
18. George Elliott Clarke comments: "To turn to Rufus in *Execution Poems* [...] his English is 'concocted' BUT it is also meant to correspond deliberately to a beautiful 'oddity' in both his and general Afro-North American experience: the tendency of black autodidacts to compose/speak either an extremely 'correct'/poised English, or to deconstruct the hell out of it! The 'real' Rufus spoke well enough that his prosecutor, unable to 'shake' or 'flap' him, commented, during the trial, on his excellent command of English. (My poem, "Malignant English," is based on this episode.)

At the same time, chronicles of black settlers on The Prairies a hundred years ago gave me ideas about how to fashion Rufus's English, and I should also mention that my own father, who achieved only Grade 10, as a relatively self-taught adult, possesses the lexicon of a lawyer and the confident ease in utilizing standard English that one could expect of a politician or a professor. To sum up, Rufus's English is partly invented, and he probably never read Shakespeare, BUT I did/do see his character as exemplifying the tendency among 'out-group' speakers of a more powerful group's language to treat it practically as putty—to use it for ornamentation. (See also "Haligonian Market Cry" in this regard.) Clarke, Email interview with Susan Knutson, March 20, 2002.

19. *Execution Poems,* 25.
20. *Titus Andronicus*, IV.ii.66.
21. *Titus Andronicus*, IV.ii. 68–70.
22. *Titus Andronicus*, IV.ii. 71.
23. *Titus Andronicus*, II.i.133–135.
24. *Execution Poems, 25.*
25. Christopher Marlowe, *Christopher Marlowe's Dr. Faustus: Text and Major Criticism*, ed. Irving Ribner (New York: Odyssey, 1966): I.iii.76.
26. "Famous Last," *Execution Poems*, 41.
27. Titus Andronicus, V.iii.189–190.
28. Email Interview, 2 May 2002.
29. *Titus Andronicus*, II.i.18–19.
30. *Execution Poems*, 11.
31. *Titus Andronicus*, V.iii.13.
32. *Titus Andronicus,* V.iii.183.
33. *Titus Andronicus*, V.ii.22.
34. *Titus Andronicus*, V.ii.9–15.

35. *Titus Andronicus,* IV.i.80. Seneca, Hippolytus, II.671–72.
36. *Titus Andronicus,* IV.iii.4–17.
37. *Titus Andronicus*, IV.iii.60.
38. *Titus Andronicus*, IV.iii.50–53.
39. *Execution Poems,* "Original Pain," 15.
40. *Titus Andronicus,* IV.iii.53.
41. *Execution Poems*, 18.

Works Cited

Bate, Jonathan. "Introduction." In Shakespeare, William. *Titus Andronicus.* Ed. Jonathan Bate. London: The Arden Shakespeare, 2002.

Bloom, Harold. *Shakespeare: The Invention of the Human.* New York: Riverhead Books, 1998.

Clarke, George Elliott. *Execution Poems: The Black Acadian Tragedy of "George and Rue."* Wolfville: Gaspereau Press, 2001.

—. *Odysseys Home: Mapping African-Canadian Literature.* Toronto: University of Toronto Press, 2002.

—. Email interview with Susan Knutson, conducted between January 12 and 3 May, 2002.

Corbett, Edward P.J. *Classical Rhetoric for the Modern Student.* 3rd Edition. New York: Oxford University Press, 1990.

Greenberg, Kenneth S., Ed. *The Confessions of Nat Turner, and Related Documents.* Introd. Kenneth Greenberg. Boston and New York: Bedford Books of St. Martin's Press, 1996.

Lambert, Frank. "'I Saw the Book Talk': Slave Readings of the First Great Awakening." *The Journal of Negro History*, 77, 4 (1992), 185–198.

Loomba, Ania. *Shakespeare, Race, and Colonialism.* London: Oxford University Press, 2002.

Marlowe, Christopher. *Christopher Marlowe's Dr. Faustus: Text and Major Criticism.* Ed. Irving Ribner. New York: The Odyssey Press, 1966.

Moore-Gilbert, Bart. *Postcolonial Theory: Contexts, Practices, Politics.* London: Verso, 1997.

Moss, Laura, Ed. *Is Canada Postcolonial? Unsettling Canadian Literature.* Waterloo: Wilfrid Laurier University Press, 2003.

Neill, Michael. "Post-colonial Shakespeare? Writing away from the Centre." *Post-Colonial Shakespeares.* Eds. Ania Loomba and Martin Orkin. London : Routledge, 1998, 164–185.

Ogbar, Jeffery Ogbonna Green. "Prophet Nat and God's Children of Darkness: Black Religious Nationalism." *The Journal of Religious Thought.* 51–71.

Sealy, David. "'Canadianizing' Blackness: Resisting the Political." In Rinaldo Walcott, Ed. *Rude: Contemporary Black Canadian Cultural Criticism.* Toronto: Insomniac Press, 2000.

Shakespeare, William. *Titus Andronicus.* Ed. Jonathan Bate. London: The Arden Shakespeare, 2002.

Sher, Anthony and Gregory Doran. *Woza Shakespeare! Titus Andronicus in South Africa.* London: Methuen, 1996.

Some Aspects of Blues Use in George Elliott Clarke's *Whylah Falls*

H. NIGEL THOMAS

It is necessary to come to George Elliott Clarke's *Whylah Falls* with a head stocked with creeds concerning language use, literary genres, poetic diction, mimesis, and whatever else—if only to see what falls on the blades of his creative talents and gets transformed, protean-like, into literary products and effects for which present literary terms are inadequate. Equally, for a full appreciation of Clarke's text, one needs to be familiar, perhaps intimate, with the blues, jazz, spirituals, and the black folk church. *Whylah Falls* is exemplary in the way it fuses African diasporic and European Hellenistic and Judaeo Christian traditions. Conversely, it is also essential to abandon such knowledge temporarily to facilitate the seduction that Clarke's highly experimental composition can effect.

This is not to say that *Whylah Falls* is one hundred percent diachronic. No readable work can be. Nevertheless, *Whylah Falls* privileges diachronism over synchronism. The critic's first challenge is to identify the work's genre, but Clarke's iconoclasm soon renders this a foolish exercise.[1] There are times when the work resembles the

Homeric epic. Sometimes, in its portrayal of the travail and survival of a people, its creeds, ministers, enemies, and folk wisdom, *Whylah Falls* is reminiscent of the Jewish Old Testament. Its somewhat dissimulated but very valuable chorus, in the form of a sometimes identifiable omniscient narrator who speaks for the passive actors in the narrative or adds summarized detail—in formal poetry, prose poetry, and prose—to the unfolding story, makes us think of Greek tragedy. There are elements of tragicomic opera, sermons, detailed descriptions of setting that sometimes merge with and sometimes define the characters in them, occasional standard dialogue, and newspaper clippings. If in appearance *Whylah Falls is* a miscellany of genres, the sort of work that is now termed postmodern, in effect it is anything but miscellaneous: each of its several aspects is integral to the work's meaning and wholeness. To simplify this discussion I shall call *Whylah Falls* a poetic narrative or, paraphrasing Dryden somewhat, dramatic poetry, since, if one were to quantify Whylah Falls, it is the poetic genre that is pre-eminent.

And as regards the poetry in *Whylah Falls*, it is achieved by recombining in very novel ways (altering the function of certain rhetorical forms: the argument, for example) poetic experiments and practices from Homer to Walcott and further enriching them with techniques adapted from prose narratives, stagecraft, cinematography, and certainly the oral arts of the African diaspora. What Maria Corti observes about change and constancy in literature applies appropriately to Clarke's *Whylah Falls*: literature "is at once organic and dynamic" and "is well adapted both to catch the structural changes … from one era to another and to individuate, through that which does not change, that which changes" (4).

The blues constitute an essential part of the work's macrostructure, are, in fact, one of its synchronic poles, even if their use is at times highly diachronic. One could successfully argue that the work is driven by a blues impulse, manifest in the first paragraph of the preface: "Wrecked by country blues and warped by constant tears [Whylah Falls] is a snowy, northern Mississippi, with blood spattered, not on magnolias, but on pines, lilacs, and wild roses" (7). Sometimes it appears that this vernacular form[2] is in competition with the erudite European and Euro-American poetic traditions from which the poet-narrator frequently draws technical inspiration. But inasmuch as two (three if one includes Shelley) of the work's seventeen characters are poets, two of them definitely schooled in Western poetic tradition, this fact is intrinsic to some of the characters.

I will be limiting the rest of this paper to the role of the blues in *Whylah Falls*. Evoked blues music and music-making by the characters, not to mention the music, often blues-jazz inspired, engendered by Clarke's own subtle word combinations, furnish a considerable part of this work's texture. Clarke employs the blues sometimes in an overt, traditional, cultural way: singing and composing the blues as momentary distraction from pain or in Ellison's sense of giving form to "the chaos of living" (190). When employed thus the blues function as a sort of cultural shorthand, as metaphors that infuse the text with chronicles of pain and the exorcism of pain. Frequently, he simply implants blues diction and haunting rhythms into the lines of prose or poetry, where they function synechdocally as signifiers of the stoicism blues have come to encode for African Americans or of the troubles for which blues music is sometimes an analgesic. But inscribed in what befalls the characters are acts and experiences for which the blues have no healing power. Here Clarke's blues are more consonant with Sherley Anne Williams's explanation, one she opposes to Ralph Ellison's, of how Esther Phillips employed the blues (816–817).

Clarke's fascination with the poetic potential of African-American vernacular forms[3]—particularly the blues and spirituals—is obvious in his first collection of poems, *Saltwater Spirituals and Deeper Blues* (1986). In a sense (although I am sure it was not planned this way), this collection sketches the matrix of Africadian communities, furnishes the overview, so to speak, before Clarke focuses on the trials of a particular family—the Clemence family—struggling to survive at a particular time—the Great Depression. Clarke distils Africadian reality so that its rituals fit around the secular and sacred poles of blues and Africadian Baptist rituals, and the events that embody the forces and beliefs that frustrate Africadian aspirations occur between two springs of an archetypal year. This compression, together with various other attributes, accounts for a substantial part of the text's poetic intensity. Insofar as *Whylah Falls* portrays a Black family's attempts to survive during the Great Depression, and insofar as the blues were an institution among the unlettered Blacks, addressing their preoccupations and providing liens of psychological solidarity among the African communities scattered across North America (a fact possible because of the recent phenomenon of radio, the phonograph, and discography), all of whom were struggling against economic exploitation and virulent racism, their inscription in the text is vital mimesis.

Nineteen thirty-five, the year into which the events of *Whylah Falls* are compressed, is only a few years after the recording heyday of the legendary blues figure Ma Rainey. Moreover, in spite of the Depression—or perhaps because of it—the careers of Ida Cox and Bessie Smith were at their prime. Since these singers sang, to cite Sterling Brown's "Ma Rainey," "about the hard luck round our do'"—the devastation by the boll weevil of the cotton crops on which many southern Blacks relied, the disastrous floods of the Mississippi, as well as the penury that came with the Depression (Lieb 42)—it is logical that their lyrics became points of reference for afflicted Blacks of the period.[4] But the existential troubles of Blacks, troubles that may or may not have their genesis in but are certainly aggravated by racism, are also portrayed and deconstructed in the blues. Not least of these are the difficulties of having a satisfactory sex life, of enduring spousal abuse or spousal abandonment. Even if, as Langston Hughes eloquently informs his readers in 1926, middle class African America felt that blues and jazz reinforced the White will to discount Black humanity and would have liked to censor them (167–172), nevertheless in the years immediately preceding the Great Depression five to six million blues records sold annually, the overwhelming majority of them bought by Blacks (Cook 132). Moreover, blues composer-gospel song-writer (at one time Ma Rainey's composer and pianist) Thomas Dorsey explains that knowledge of this audience factored greatly in the blues songs he composed (Lieb 54).

Blues in *Whylah Falls*, however personalized Clarke makes them, encode both the phylogenic property that

Houston Baker ascribes to them (5) and the dialoguing between the sexes that Shirley Anne Williams so poignantly observes in them:

> I came to see that the blues is about dialogue; its story is one of frustrated union. Blues personae sought solace in lovers; part of the story of blues is this dialogue, if you will, between equals. The essence of the blues is as much a sister boasting about her man as it is her bemoaning his behaviour. Black skin was sometimes derided in the blues; time and again, singers subjected black women to alien beauty standards yet, sometimes (actually more often than not, brownskins were praised or skin color was not even mentioned) (821).

As noted above, Clarke addresses this phylogenic characteristic of the blues as early as the preface, where Whylah Falls, a composite of Africadian communities, is characterized with all the social evils for which the blues provide solace. The phylogenic trait is again reinforced in the first poem (if one discounts the preface as a poem) "Look Homeward, Exile," which functions as an overture; "Look Homeward, Exile" not only evokes the dual exile of this African Nova Scotia family—from Africa and from its United States counterpart—but summarizes the travail to which the texts that follow it are a response and an elaboration. This description, together with some of the prose passages that furnish depth to the characters, links this Africadian community with other communities of the African diaspora for whom the blues are both survival ritual and, insofar as it is recorded in song or poetry, sociopsychic history, as well as art. All the individual claims Williams makes for the blues are present in Whylah Falls—in the tense love battles between Shelley Clemence and Xavier Zachary, in Selah's travails (especially in "Jordantown Blues"), in Amarantha (the beauty and curse inherent in the word are embodied in her character) and Pablo's love affair, and in the narrator's apology to the black women whose beauty has been disparaged by black men. And as regards a circumscribing fate to which the blues respond but can neither limit nor expurgate, there are, first, the economic exploitation of Saul Clemence, an exploitation that transmogrifies him (behind which is the historic betrayal of Black Nova Scotians by the British who lured Black slaves with a promise of freedom to Nova Scotia and New Brunswick, where for the most part they were either re-enslaved or forced into being white people's menials (Walker 1–63)); and, second, the senseless murder of Othello, whose humanity the white court fails to recognize.

First, let us consider some of the work's traditional blues, for which Clarke derived inspiration from published blues lyrics.[5] An entire section of *Whylah Falls*, section III, "The Witness of Selah," is an improvisation on and sometimes an imitation of traditional blues. In every respect it examines, or adds fresh lyrics to that perennial blues theme of frustrated or abandoned love. The emotions follow something of the progress of love, from rapture to disillusionment, for both of the protagonists, X and Selah, and borrow heavily from the traditional symbols of youth and unfettered reality (essentially illusion) early on, abandoning them later for those of weariness, disillusionment, stagnation, and death. The section begins with an epigraph from famed blues singer Ida Cox, but goes on to dispute the advice to women in the Cox epigraph, for Selah, while no "angel," cannot successfully be "wild woman," has the blues, is lonely, and must employ the blues sounds the group has invented to help dissipate it. In this respect, Clarke employs the blues as cultural signature.

The first poem following the argument is a traditional blues ballad into which the ego of the singer dissolves. X the protagonist boasts about his philandering exploits, employing the allegorical conventions typical of the form. One needs to remember that he is there to court Shelley. Inasmuch as his attentions are now given to Selah her sister, the philandering component is self-explanatory (perhaps Selah should have listened to Ma Rainey's "Trust No Man"). Many blues ballads are boasts of the protagonists' sexual exploits and attributes, and, in many of the ballads by female blues singers (we'll see an example of this in the discussion of Cora's blues), the female protagonists bemoan the maltreatment received from their lovers but justify enduring it because of their men's sexual proficiency. But "King Bee Blues" also inscribes in the work a celebratory note which is a vital part of the blues, one often overlooked in the popular understanding of them. Unfortunately the boasting is at the expense of the women whose "pollen" "King Bee" delights in. The song is not about commitment but about sampling women, and there is much embodied in the word "sting," especially if we think of the swelling and pain that usually follow it, for the woman, in this case Selah, at least.

The next blues song addressed to Selah from her adorer comes after a poem that portrays her as bringing spring to Whylah Falls, thus as a fertility goddess: a Demeter in the Greek tradition, an Ani in the Ibo tradition. I cite "To Selah" in its entirety so that we can later compare it with X's and Selah's final responses to these outbursts of unmitigated passion.

The butter moon is white
Sorta like your eyes;
The butter moon is bright, sugah,
Kinda like your eyes.
And it melts like I melt for you
While it coasts 'cross the sky.

The black highway uncoils
Like your body do sometimes.
The long highway unwinds, mama,
Like your lovin' do sometimes.
I'm gonna swerve your curves
And ride your centre line.

Stars are drippin' like tears,
The highway moves like a hymn;
Stars are dripping like tears, beau'ful,
The highway sways like a hymn.
And I reach for your love,
Like a burglar for a gem (57).

This is a blues composition that would win the blues laureate for its author. It reminds us of the best of Langston Hughes' compositions in this mode. One may be inclined to hear in Clarke's metaphors echoes of the Renaissance-Elizabethan conceit (and they may well be there since Clarke possesses a doctorate in English literature), but there is really nothing here to grate the ear of the unlettered bluesperson, except the sinister connotations and false note perhaps of the final couplet. Here "high" art and folk art blend.

This poem also falls within the purview of earlier traditions of courtship in the African diaspora. In seeking to win over the beloved's affection one did not use prosaic language. Zora Neale Hurston's Lucy Potts and John Pearson engage in this ritual in *Jonah's Gourd Vine*, employing some of the conventional rhymes that had evolved for the purpose; and August Wilson uses it in burlesque in *The Piano Lesson*. This poem and Selah's response (below) can be termed courtship blues. Clarke employs them for purposes of cultural individuation as well as individual characterization.

In "Blues for X" Selah replies on X's own terms. She trills to his twangs on her strings. In this poem she is all spring, a true innocent:

> I'm your lavish lover
> And I'm slavish in the sack.

or

> My bones are guitar strings,
> And blues the chords you strum.
> My bones are slender flutes
> And blues the bars you hum.
> You wanna stay my man,
> Serve me whiskey when I come (61).

The statement-response pattern here is not presented strictly in dialogue fashion but is nonetheless analogous to the bantering dialogue that often preceded some blues songs. Ma Rainey was famous for this (Lieb 54–55).

One might call this the naive blues, of which there are in the tradition many examples. Generally they invest the moment with disproportionate value. Selah's response to X's overtures, when compared to her sister Shelley's, points to her gullibility and justify the literal meaning of her name—pause or exclamation. Every one of X's metaphors for her is replete with ambiguity. Certainly at the time X wrote highways were not cleared in winter, and when the "butter moon" is not there, what does he see? Indeed the poem focuses on the visible, which after habitual looking soon loses its novelty. The metaphors themselves presage the failure of their relationship.

When sexual passion is sated, the treachery in words and the intrinsic emptiness of symbols one's passion can no longer fill become evident. This is the theme of many of the female blues songs. It is then that the struggle begins, usually on the woman's part, to hold on to one's partner, often to the point of resorting to desperate measures. In "Ecclesiastes," appropriately titled since in it passion cedes to reflection, X's depression-disillusionment blues are voiced. It is both fall and X's fall, his examination of the ashes of sexual fire. Appropriately the poem dispenses with the metrics of ritual and the lyrical quality of rhyme—its tone is elegiac but devoid of the comforting sentiments of the elegy—for at this phase the naive confidence of youth and the reassurance of ritual are absent.

> I am tired of gold sunflowers with jade leaves.
> The Sixhiboux River, almost fainting,
> Weeps through the dull, deaf hills. Behind all words
> Burns a desert of loneliness. Sunlight
> Dulls to vulgar gold. Once I believed
> Selah's passion would seed sunflowers and yield
> Skull honey—ineluctable bees' dreams
> But all is gilt sorrow and gleaming pain:
> The heavy sunflowers droop, brightness brushes
> The earth; wisdom is late and death is soon (66) [6]

And Selah too must face without mitigating masks the exigencies of time and existence. No longer able to be "slavish in the sack" or yield music from her bones, she can in "How Long Can Love Go Wrong?" face the lies in courtly love poetry, as well as the gender limitations of the men who author such poetry, who, calling her "serif,/ lacy curlicues,/ a baroque belladonna/ critical men hallow" (67), can never imagine her destroyed either by uterine cancer or the vapid promises of Casanovas. And like the X of "Ecclesiastes," and her sister Shelley, who refuses to be deceived by poetry—having seen her father's love transmogrify into the fist that strikes her mother into unconsciousness—she finally knows that no poem can picture her beauty, certainly not those that X writes.

Appropriately "The Witness of Selah" concludes with what one might call "real" blues, not the ritualized songs, not the boasts, not the rationalizations of beaten but sexually-fulfilled women, but the horror of those for whom life has been one long string of deceptions. Clarke derives much of his inspiration for this poem from the classic blues. "Jordantown Blues" can be read as a condensed amalgam of several classic blues songs in which women express their harrowing experiences with their menfolk, songs for which Ma Rainey was especially noted (Lieb 80–128). By the 1930s blues songs about abused women were so abundant that Sterling Brown could remark: "It is a popular misconception that Blues are merely songs that ease a woman's longing for a rambling man. Of course, this pattern has been set, especially by certain priestesses of the Blues cult"[7] (373). "Jordantown Blues" thus furnishes the missing dialectic—or provides a conclusion for the stories begun—in "King Bee Blues" and "Blues for X." It even improvises on, expands on, such relationships as Cora and Saul Clemence's (in part II "The Trial of Saul"). In fact, because Selah's experience with men is as bitter as her mother's, the narrative embodies the notion that connubial blues are passed on from generation to generation.

The poem reads:

At Jordantown, Selah practises love –
Hot apple pie, country and western woe,
Lash of the man away all night,
Whip of the man at work all day,
Fists of the man drunk to numbness,
His yellow eyes flailing at nothing,
While life sags to extremes, bloodstreams, pinched, squeezed,
By his diet of white Tory rum, pig tails,
And her diet of fear, tea, and aspirin.
Tonight, this gospel, this sermon, of a man,
Delivered by liquor, staggers, stumbles,
To their small home, chokes on a prayer of blood –
His repentance of a three-day wine binge –
And topples, comatose, to buckled knees.
He is sped, gagging to a hospital
Where he ends, where he dies, where he stops breathing,
For Jesus comes for him through the rooftop,
Leaving Selah to practise love alone (68)

There is an uncompromising portrayal here of life's ugliness compared with which the earlier blues ballads appear trivial.

Here I would like to focus on a fascinating aspect of *Whylah Falls*, its blues poems written in a non traditional blues style. It is simply impossible to write a book, let alone a paper, that compares the hundreds of African-American poets (formal and folk), fiction writers, and playwrights who improvise on the blues. Suffice it to say I shall only mention a couple for comparative purposes.

If we look again at "Jordantown Blues," we note that Clarke puts his poetic expertise to full use. Note, for example, the onomatopoetic violence captured in "Lash of the man ..." "Whip of the man ..." "Fists of the man ...": words carefully chosen and arranged (in dactyls) for their force and consequently their subliminal semantic value. Note as well the succinct, dramatic contrasts between Selah's needs and behaviour and those of her mate. Such intensity of sound and economy of language are rare in the blues, which reflect the lassitude of the depressed state, and where repetition creates partial stagnation, or at least some form of spiralling or circular movement. Moreover, those who write blues-inspired poetry generally seem to want it to reflect many of the formal properties of the sung blues. Langston Hughes' best known blues poem "The Weary Blues" is a good case in point. Not only does the poem replicate the "lazy sway" and moans of the blues, it also pays close attention to blues meter and rhymes, ensuring that they generate blues emotions and reflect the traits of their progenitors: "With his ebony hands on each ivory key/ He made that poor piano moan with melody./ O Blues! / Swaying to and fro on his rickety stool/ He played that sad raggy tune like a musical fool./ Sweet Blues!/ Coming from a black man's soul./ O Blues! ..." (33).

Sterling Brown's "Ma Rainey" is another very good example. Brown's poem deliberately reproduces the colloquial speech of Ma Rainey's spectators. Undoubtedly, the poem is a heartfelt tribute to Ma Rainey's ability to minister to the African-American audiences she performed for. Brown does his own experimentation with the blues form, writing section I and all but the final quatrain of section III in trimeter, section II in hexameter, and section IV in a variable meter, ranging from tetrameter to hexameter. Brown, while letting the poem rhyme, ensures that the rhymes do not become repetitive. While the rhyme scheme of the first five and the last five lines of section IV is aaabb, that of section II is abcbdbaefege. The long vowels and trochees of section III create the "invocative" sound Brown desires: "O Ma Rainey,/ Sing yo' song;/ Now you's back/ Where you belong,/ Git way inside us,/ Keep us strong …" (ellipses in the original). But section IV, despite its rhyme, imitates conversational prose: "I talk to a fellow, an' the fellow say,/ She jes' catch hold of us, somekindaway./ She sang Backwater Blues one day:/ '*It rained fo' days and' de skies was dark as night,/ Trouble take place in de lowlands at night …*'" (Harper 62–63).

The citations from Hughes and Brown exemplify the ways blues poets make their poetry echo the form. Setting aside those poems where Clarke simply but justifiably imitates the blues, his approach to the blues is dialogic. If we take another look at "Jordantown Blues" we will see that Clarke puts blues content in his own very personalized form. The balladic repetiton and the rhymes are not there; the lazy pace is supplanted; only the pain remains. With the difference that Cora employs folk speech, speaks in her own voice, the same is true of "Cora's Testament":

> Mean-minded Saul Clemence, ugly as sin,
> Once pounded, punched, and kicked me 'cross the floor;
> Once flung me through the second-storey glass:
> My back ain't been right for clear, twenty year.
> But I bore it, stuck it out, stood his fists.
> He be worms now. How'd I forget … (42)

To contextualize this poem it would be useful to examine a conventional blues song that explores the theme of wife abuse. Ma Rainey's "My Sweet, Rough Man" is ideal for this purpose:

> I woke up this morning
> My head was sore as a board
> I woke up this morning
> My head was sore as a board
> My man beat me last night
> With five feet of chopped up cord
>
> He keeps my lips split
> Got eyes as black as day
> He keeps my lips split
> Got eyes as black as day
> But the way he love me
> Make me soon forgit (Henderson 111)

Both "Cora's Testament" and "My Sweet, Rough Man" explain why the brutality is/was endured. Rainey's version, the traditional answer, is that the man possesses attributes—usually of a sexual nature—that compensate for the brutality. Cora, shaped by Clarke's post-feminist sensibility, endures because she is powerless to do otherwise, or because the alternative—at the very beginning—succumbing to incest, is more horrific. But meaning in "Cora's Testament" is enlarged because the poem as microtext conjoins with and relies on the other parts of the marcotext (*Whylah Falls*) for its full meaning. For example, we know from the advice that Cora gives to Missy (in "The Symposium," two poems before this one) that not only has she become a cynic about connubial relationships but that she possesses a great deal of wisdom in managing them.[8] This wisdom, however, imbues her with a certain pathos and is ironic, since in spite of it she loses Saul to Missy, the stepdaughter to whom she imparts this wisdom. Clarke's fabling here is in character with the blues; instead of the female blues protagonist who is unable to trust her best friend with her man, it is the mother who cannot trust her stepdaughter with her husband. But the extreme gravity of the situation evokes the comic, the tragic burlesqued, reminding us, in tone at least, of such blues lyrics as in this Richard M. Jones song, recorded in 1926: "I'm all alone at midnight/ And my lamp is burning low./ Never had so much trouble in my life before./ I'm gonna lay my head/ On that lonesome railroad track,/But when I hear the whistle,/ Lord, I'm gonna pull it back" (192). Jones' blues would be considered to be hokum. Cora's can hardly be thus characterized.

Nor do we rely on Cora for our full knowledge of Saul Clemence's behaviour. Clarke telescopes over two hundred years of Black racial oppression in Nova Scotia into the economic exploitation that dehumanizes Saul Clemence (and probably Cora's "uncle" too) and shows him and the other Africadian characters as still seeking the "liberty"—still reeling from the cruel joke played on them—the British promised their ancestors back in 1783.

We see that while "Cora's Testament" (as opposed to testimony) employs the brutal diction of the blues and the vernacular speech of its narrator, Clarke here tempers the lyrical quality which invests the blues with a de facto ritual quality and eliminates the double-entendres (present in, for example, a poem like "My Sweet, Rough Man") characteristic of such blues. This represents a formal deviation from traditional blues lyrics. In "Cora's Testament," "Jordantown Blues," and "The Wake," which we shall look at shortly, Clarke eschews the repeated lines or any of the traditional rhyme schemes. Instead he relies on alliteration, internal rhyme and the faintest of slant rhymes, as in, for example, "floor," "fists," "forget," to create the desirable musicality.

If the brutality Saul Clemence subjects Cora to gives rise to "Cora's Testament," the cheapness with which official White Nova Scotia holds Africadian life engenders "The Wake," which follows Scratch Seville's murder of Othello. "The Wake" is comprised of Cora's emotions conveyed in the diction of the erudite narrator X. On this occasion words fail her, and she "stammers her pain in a white poem/ Of rum more eloquent than speech." Only after the expulsion of part of the pain via violent acts can she find a vent in ululation, i.e., the howling out of her pain, which is all the intelligible sound she is able to utter until her face is tear-glazed—"glistens like the sea." In this poem Clarke depicts experiences for which the exorcising function of blues is ineffectual. And after we have read the jurors' verdict of "self-defence" in what is shown to be the cold-blooded murder of Othello ("self-defence" bears the freight of centuries of injustice—all the broken promises to the Black Loyalists have been excused with that one word),[9] we understand better her abject grief.

Blues use in *Whylah Falls* is diverse—from imparting a cultural distinctness to the community, to equipping the characters with a language in which to communicate their sorrow and occasionally joy, to furnishing Clarke with novel linguistic possibilities. However, except where Clarke wants the ritual use of the blues to mirror their historic use, as, for example, in courtship and *camaraderie*, he places on them his personal stamp. As metaphors the blues come laden with so much meaning and prior use that the poet who chooses to use them risks being repetitive. That Clarke manages to make them function in novel ways is proof of his poetic talent.

Endnotes

1. Clarke says that, when he reads for high school students, he tells them that *Whylah Falls* is a novel written in poetry (in conversation with this writer).
2. I am well aware of Albert Murray's contention, in *Stomping the Blues,* that the blues are a highly sophisticated art, that successful blues artists have studied the form carefully and left their stamp on it. Indeed, using Duke Ellington as an example, he points to the sophistication a "folk form" can attain in his argument that Ellington is the only authentic American voice among famed American musicians like Aaron Copland, John Cage, Virgil Thomson (203–224 ff). My use of the term vernacular means employing the idiom of the unlettered folk.
3. African-American here includes African-Canadian or Africadian, the term that Clarke prefers.
4. I am relying on chapter I of Sandra Lieb's *Mother of the Blues: A Study of Ma Rainey* (1980) for much of the historical information concerning the careers of these blues singers.
5. He specifically mentions (157) Samuel Charters, *The Poetry of the Blues* (New York: Oak Publications, 1963).
6. It is interesting that Shelley, whom X courts before he is distracted by Selah, understands very early on the dynamics as well as the evolution of passion. Indeed in a genial gesture, she places the 100 roses sent by X as a testimony of his love in vinegar, a highly symbolically appropriate act, for passion, like roses, soon wilts. But the flavour of roses distilled in vinegar lasts, long after the love has died or has itself turned to vinegar. Although she is the youngest of the Clemence daughters and

several years younger than X, she is the wisest character in *Whylah Falls*. Hers is a mind that strips reality to its essence in order to distinguish between the ephemeral and the durable. At the end of *Whylah Falls*, she invites X to invent with her the beauty that will unite them and outlive decay and the permutations symbolically embodied in the seasons of the year.

7. First published in B.A. Botkin, ed. *Folksay* (University of Alabama Press, 1930), 324–339.
8. While Clarke's is the richer, far more comprehensive, informative, and aesthetically pleasing text, it is quite possible that he found the germ for it in Lillian Hardaway Henderson's "Trust No Man":

   I want all you women to listen to me,
   Don't trust your man no further'n your eyes can see;
   I trusted mine with my best friend,
   But that was the bad part in the end.
   ...
   Just feed your daddy with a long-handled spoon,
   Be sure to love him morning, night and noon,
   Sometimes your heart will ache and almost bust,
   That's why there's no daddy good enough to trust.
   (Lieb 125–126)

   However, if he did not, his composition points to the similarity of attitudes and responses to phenomena by communities separated by thousands of miles.
9. I am thinking of self-defence in the sense of tribal sentiment, especially when the tribe in question refuses to see immorality in its supremacist sentiments. In this case "self-defence" could mean that it is perfectly justifiable to kill any Blacks by whom one feels in any way threatened. Such practices therefore keep Blacks

living with the certitude that the principles of justice that white Nova Scotians take for granted do not apply to them.

Works Cited

Baker, Houston A., Jr. *Blues, Ideology and Afro-American Literature: A Vernacular Theory*. Chicago and London: University of Chicago Press, 1984.

Brown, Sterling A. "The Blues as Folk Poetry." 1930. Reprint. *The Book of Negro Folklore*. Langston Hughes and Arna Bontemps, eds. New York: Dodd, Mead and Co., 1958. 371–386.

—. *The Collected Poems of Sterling A. Brown*. Selected by Michael S. Harper. New York: Harper Colophon Books, 1983.

Clarke, George Elliot. *Whylah Falls*. Winlaw, British Columbia: Polestar, 1990.

—. *Saltwater Spirituals and Deeper Blues*. Porters Lake, Nova Scotia: Pottersfield Press, 1983.

Cook, Bruce. *Listen to the Blues*. New York: Charles Scribner's Sons. New York, 1973

Corti, Maria. *An Introduction to Literary Semiotics*. Bloomington and London: Indiana University Press, 1978.

Ellison, Ralph. "Living with Music." *Shadow and Act*. New York: Vintage, 1964. 187–198.

Hughes, Langston. *Selected Poems of Langston Hughes*. New York: Vintage, 1974.

—. "The Negro Artist and the Racial Mountain." 1926. Reprint. *The Black Aesthetic*. Addison Gayle, ed. New York: Doubleday, 1973. 167–172.

Hurston, Zora Neale. *Jonah's Gourd Vine*. 1934. New York: Harpers Perennial Library, 1990.

Jones, Richard M. "Trouble in My Mind." *Early Down Home Blues*. Jeff Todd Titon, ed. Chicago: University of Illinois Press, 1971. 192.

Lieb, Sandra R. *Mother of the Blues: A Study of Ma Rainey*. Amherst, Massachusetts: University of Massachusetts Press, 1981.

Murray, Albert. *Stomping the Blues*. New York: Vintage, 1982.

Rainey, "Ma" (Gertrude Pridgett) "My Sweet, Rough Man." *Understanding the New Poetry: Black Speech and Black Music as Poetic References*. Stephen Henderson, ed. New York: Morrow, 1973. 111.

Walker, James. St. G. *The Black Loyalists: The Search for a Promised Land in Nova Scotia and Sierra Leone, 1783–1870*. Toronto: University of Toronto Press, 1992.

Williams, Sherley Anne. "Returning to the Blues: Esther Phillips and Contemporary Blues Culture." *Callaloo* 14:4 (Fall 1991). 816–828.

Wilson, August. *The Piano Lesson*. New York: Plume, 1990.

"This history's only good for anger": Gender and Cultural Memory in *Beatrice Chancy*

MAUREEN MOYNAGH

National narratives are, willy nilly, acts of cultural memory, if we understand cultural memory to be about identity, values, and recollections of the past that serve the needs of the present.[1] National narratives are also, as we know, profoundly gendered.[2] Taking my cue from Lauren Berlant, who asks what it would mean "to write a genealogy of sex … in which unjust sexual power was attributed not to an individual, nor to patriarchy, but to the nation itself" (221), I want to ask what it would mean to stage an act of cultural memory in which unjust sexual power is indeed attributed to the nation and where the identity at stake is both national and diasporic. Cultural memory is a tool of the powerful as well as of the disenfranchised, and if, as Marita Sturken has argued, cultural memory "is a field of cultural negotiation through which different stories vie for a place in history" (1), it is also the case that the terms of negotiation are prejudiced in favour of the dominant group. Yet among the consequences of undertaking a genealogy of sex in the nation, Berlant argues, would be the exposure of the importance of sexual underclasses "to national symbolic and political coherence" and the establishment of an alternative historical archive, "one that claimed the most intimate stories of subordinated people as information about *everyone's* citizenship" (221). The promise, then, of articulating cultural memory with gender and race is the contestation of hegemonic narratives of nation, a splitting open of the historical sutures that close out stories of racial terror and sexual injustice, relegating them to a space beyond the body of the nation.

In this essay, I would like to transpose Berlant's inquiry to Canada and to undertake a genealogy of sex in the nation via a reading of the scripting of cultural memory in George Elliott Clarke's verse drama and opera *Beatrice Chancy* (1999). The drama is set in Nova Scotia in 1801 and combines a tale about incest and patricide with the history of slavery in the province. The title character is the daughter of a white Loyalist planter and one of his slaves; she has been raised in her father's household, educated in the ways of white folk, and treated like a prized possession. When Beatrice declares her love for another slave, however, her father's "love" is abruptly transformed: he rapes her. Beatrice, in turn, murders her father and is hanged, but not before sparking a revolt among the other slaves on the plantation. Another installment in Clarke's mythopoetic elaboration of "Africadia,"[3] *Beatrice Chancy* shares with Clarke's other poetic works and much of his literary criticism an abiding concern with the erasure of the history and, more broadly, the lived experiences of African Nova Scotians and African Canadians from the national imaginary. In contesting that erasure, Clarke has created works in a range of media, from the printed page to theatre, radio, film, and most recently opera. In many of these works Clarke has undertaken to restore the lives of black women to their proper order of importance, but nowhere in so far-reaching and fundamental a manner as in *Beatrice Chancy.*

As Clarke engages in the process of what Toni Morrison in *Beloved* called "re-memory," constructing a history of slavery in a nation actively invested in forgetting that slavery was ever practiced there, he seduces his audiences into an uncomfortable intimacy with public violence and compels them not only to denounce that violence but to acknowledge their complicity in it. In choosing to make his heroine the mulatta daughter of a slaveholder and the victim of incestuous rape, moreover, Clarke exposes the nation's reliance on sexual underclasses in a way that has far-reaching implications for national self-understanding. Clarke's commemoration of the experiences of slaves in Canada is not only an effort to "maintain at the center of national memory what the dominant group would like to forget" (Singh, Skerrett, and Hogan 6), it also writes African Canadians into national narratives in a way that refuses patriarchy together with racism. In staging a drama about incest, Clarke impresses on his audiences the extent to which cultural memory work that redresses sexual and racial violence is necessarily about "everyone's citizenship." His heroine, Beatrice, performs what Berlant calls an act of "diva citizenship," staging "a dramatic coup in a public sphere in which she does not have privilege" and "calling on people to change the social and institutional practices of citizenship to which they currently consent" (223). In "indigenizing" (Findlay) a diasporic narrative, Clarke interrupts the national imaginary, disrupting its coherence with a drama that lays bare the nation's intimacy with racial and sexual violence.

Technologies of memory

Literature is but one of the technologies of cultural memory, but as a technology of memory literature resonates in multiple ways in *Beatrice Chancy.* Not only is literature Clarke's chief medium for cultural memory work, it is also arguably his medium for, as it were, communing with the dead.[4] In writing about memory and the art of memoir, Morrison observes that slave narratives represent the beginnings of black literature in the United States ("The Site of Memory" 85). Not surprisingly, memoirs and slave narratives are at the foundation of African-Canadian writing as well, as Clarke attests (*Fire* 1: 12, *Eyeing* xiv), citing John Marrant's *Narrative of the Lord's Wonderful Dealings with John Marrant, a Black (Now Going to Preach the Gospel in Nova-Scotia)* (1785); David George's *An Account of the Life of Mr. David George, from Sierra Leone in Africa …* (1793); Boston King's *Memoirs of the Life of Boston King, a Black Preacher, Written by Himself …* (1798); and Josiah Henson's *Life of Josiah Henson, formerly a Slave, now an Inhabitant of Canada* (1849). As the records of slavery and of the experiences of New World Africans more generally, these memoirs are the literary foundations of cultural memory in the African diaspora. The dual function of representing a life and speaking to injustice that characterized the slave narratives also characterizes the cultural memory work that Clarke undertakes in *Beatrice Chancy.* Clarke draws directly on this body of diasporan writing; he acknowledges Harriet Jacobs' *Incidents in the Life of a Slave Girl: Written by Herself* in particular. Yet like Morrison, Clarke's interest in these texts arguably has to do with more than the historical information that they can yield. Morrison suggests that her interest in recreating accounts of slavery in fiction is to remember what the authors of the slave narratives were compelled to forget. Where for the sake of decorum the authors and editors of slave narratives scrupled to suppress the harshest details of slavery, Morrison understands her task as finding a way to "rip that veil drawn over 'proceedings too terrible to relate'" (91). Connected to this task is that of imagining an interior life, also suppressed in the slave narratives, and claiming the agency historically denied African Americans as a people. Clarke, too, tears down the veil over not only the most graphic acts of exploitation but over slavery itself. In imagining a life for Beatrice and endowing her with agency, moreover, Clarke is effectively doing double duty: remembering slavery in behalf of African Canadians and in behalf of the nation. In *Beatrice Chancy* cultural memory is performed as countermemory.

There is another way in which literature serves Clarke as a technology of memory in *Beatrice Chancy.* Not only does Clarke draw on and indigenize African diasporan works like Jacobs' *Incidents in the Life of a Slave Girl* and Frances Harper's *Iola Leroy* (1892), he borrows a story from European history and literature as well and indigenizes it twofold, making it African and Canadian. In choosing the story of Beatrice Cenci, Clarke effectively makes decorum a central preoccupation. For there can scarcely be an act more usually veiled in secrecy than incest or a figure more apt for blurring the line "between personal and national tyranny" (Berlant 232) and exposing the nation as agent of unjust sexual power. Incest is an indecorous act, but as an intimate transgression taking place "in private" it is frequently veiled in the public code of decorum that will not admit of (or to) it. The drama effectively deconstructs decorum, exposing its endless deferral of the ethical behaviour in the name of which it differentiates between classes, genders, and races. A masquerade of seemliness and propriety, decorum is the guise adopted by those who would justify acts of violence and oppression conducted according to the terms of a patriarchal and racist social code. Decorum is also the refuge of those who would not see or hear of such acts but allow them to continue. Beatrice, in rising up against her violator, violates the terms of decorum, refuses its morality, and claims the justice of her actions. In this rising up, Beatrice Chancy performs an act of "diva citizenship."

In reading *Beatrice Chancy* as an act of cultural memory, as I aim to do, I am also compelled to consider the conditions of its performance. That is to say, under what circumstances does it enter into the public sphere to offer its counternarrative, to deconstruct the decorum of Canadian national narratives? One might well expect, in the case of a verse drama and opera, that performance is, quite literally, the chief mechanism for intervention. Yet the matter is not at all straightforward. To begin with, there are effectively two "versions" of *Beatrice Chancy.* The opera is not a performance of the verse drama but a production of a separately published libretto.[5] The verse drama, on the other hand, while clearly a dramatic text, is not necessarily a theatrical text.[6] There is abundant textual evidence suggesting that the drama is to be read as poetry rather than performed as a play: stage directions scan, descriptions of the characters are similarly poetic, there are photographs scattered through the volume, and the arrangement of the words on the page is frequently key to meaning. As cultural memory work, then, *Beatrice Chancy* is transmitted both by textual and performative means. Yet, if features of the verse drama are literally unperformable, they are nonetheless arguably performative in another sense. I contend that it is possible, even crucial, to speak of performance with respect to both versions of *Beatrice Chancy.*

In his elaboration of performance as a medium for cultural memory, Joseph Roach cites Richard Schechner's definition of performance as "restored behavior" or "twice-behaved behavior" and conjoins it to the theatrical concept of surrogation ("Culture" 46, *Cities* 3). Key for Roach is the constitutive impossibility of restoring behaviour, for "no action or sequence of actions may be performed exactly the same way twice; they must be reinvented or recreated at each appearance," and thus "in this improvisatory behavioral space, memory reveals itself as imagination" ("Culture" 46). For Roach, surrogation supplements Schechner's understanding of performance in its "uncanny" emphasis on reinvention, on theatrical doubling, and on "the doomed search for originals by continuously auditioning stand-ins" (*Cities* 3). There is much in Roach's elaboration of surrogation, of "the three-sided relationship of memory, performance, and substitution" (*Cities* 2), that I find suggestive for a discussion of *Beatrice Chancy,* not least his interest in how surrogation operates between cultures in what he calls the "circum-Atlantic world." Yet where Roach positions memory and performance largely outside of textual modes of cultural transmission, I would like to suggest that in the verse drama, quite as much as in the opera, Clarke is engaged in acts of surrogation.

W.B. Worthen argues persuasively that "although Roach tends to frame performance surrogation as a form of resistant remembering that is opposed to the oppressive forgetting he associates with textual transmission, the power of this sense of surrogation lies in how it reflects the transformative nature of the cultural transmission of meanings, textual as well as performative" (1101). In other words, texts and their cultural meanings are also reiterated, reinvented, and remade as they are circulated; textual studies, too, is "doomed" in its search for originals. Worthen is particularly interested in the ways that a dramatic performance may be understood as a form of surrogation, "as an act of iteration, an utterance, a surrogate standing in that positions, uses, signifies the text within the citational practices of performance" (1102). Not only are these insights helpful for understanding the significance of *Beatrice Chancy* the opera, Worthen's extension of surrogation to textual transmission offers another way of thinking about the workings of cultural memory in the verse drama as well.

Not only does Clarke reiterate and reinvent Percy B. Shelley's *The Cenci* and other literary, dramatic, and filmic versions of the Renaissance tale; not only does he reiterate slave narratives like Jacobs' *Incidents in the Life of a Slave Girl*; and not only does he refunction historical texts to his purposes, Clarke cites and signifies (on) theatrical and poetic form in his poeticized stage directions and self-conscious referencing of theatrical performance and canonical literary works throughout. While each reference has its own contextual resonance, taken together they comprise a citational practice that, like the theatrical mode of doubling, holds copy and "original" up together. This citational practice, moreover, shares with Roach's notion of surrogation the sense of cultural and ethnic difference for, as Clarke has attested on numerous occasions, "part of [his] strategy as a writer, in responding to [his] status as the scribe of a marginal and colonized community, is to sack and plunder all those larger literatures … and to domesticate their authors and their most famous or noted lines" (Compton 143). Clarke's work, moreover, underscores what Roach describes as the mutually constitutive relationship between literature and orature, "the range of cultural forms invested in speech, gesture, song, dance, storytelling, proverbs, customs, rites, and rituals" ("Culture" 45), insofar as Clarke cites not only literary canons but what he calls "Africadian" poetry, by which he means the poetry "rooted in the voice and in [the] shared jokes, stories, proverbs" (140) of Black Nova Scotian communities. Performative in the sense of "*draw*[*ing*] *on and cover*[*ing*] *over* the constitutive conventions by which it is mobilized" (Butler 51), Clarke's poetic drama draws on conventions both of literary texts and of the ritualized practices of everyday life and speech that Roach sees as the realm of "living memory as restored behavior" (*Cities* 11). In what follows, I analyze the surrogation, the resignifying of historical and literary archives in *Beatrice Chancy*, and I then explore the citational practices that mobilize both the verse drama and the opera as technologies of cultural memory.

History, countermemory

Beatrice Chancy is set in the Annapolis Valley of Nova Scotia in 1801, where slavery remained legal, as it did in the rest of British North America, until 1834, when it was officially abolished throughout the British Empire. Both the French and English settlers practiced slavery in the colonies that were eventually to become Canada, although slavery was not to become the economic cornerstone in these northerly colonies that it was elsewhere in the Americas. In 1783 an influx of 3,000 free blacks in the wake of the American Revolutionary War, together with the more than 1,000 black slaves who accompanied white Loyalists to Nova Scotia, both augmented and destabilized what was effectively a slave society in the province. If the presence of free blacks made things easier for fugitive slaves, the practice of slavery represented a constant threat to free blacks (Walker 41). As far as white Loyalists were concerned, all blacks were fit for slavery, and a provincial social formation that slotted blacks as labourers for whites only reinforced that ideology (Mannette 111; Walker 42). Barry Cahill observes: "Like the *ante-bellum* United States, Loyalist Nova Scotia could not endure half-slave and half-free. Either the slaves would have to be emancipated, or the free Blacks would have to emigrate" ("*Habeas Corpus*" 186). In effect, something of both these alternatives came about. In 1792, a large number of free black Nova Scotians left for Sierra Leone, and from then until the arrival of black refugees between 1814–16, "Nova Scotia's residual black population was largely unfree and was concentrated in Annapolis County" (Cahill, "Slavery" 43). Meanwhile, from the late 1790s into the early 1800s, successive non-Loyalist chief justices waged what Cahill terms a "judicial war of attrition against slavery in Nova Scotia" ("*Habeas Corpus*" 182). Unable to rule on the legality of slavery as an institution, judges sought by other legal means to free those blacks jailed as fugitives even as Loyalists sought, unsuccessfully, through the Provincial Assembly, to create statutes affirming and extending slavery as a practice.

The play and the opera are historically resonant with this struggle over slavery, as well as with the broader diasporan experience of slavery in the Americas. In this way, Clarke confronts the national amnesia about slavery with the diasporan linkages the nation prefers to deny or displace to the late twentieth century. The national significance of this representation of Loyalist Nova Scotia, moreover, has in part to do with the place of the Loyalists in what historian Daniel Francis has dubbed the "myth of the master race" (52–87). One of the foundational narratives of Canada as a nation, "the myth of the master race" has to do with the fundamentally British and imperial character of Canada. Without its ties to Britain and the empire, Canada counted for little, according to the terms of this narrative, "but as part of a union of Anglo-Saxon nations, and an Empire which embraced a quarter of the world's population, Canada could participate in the great mission of spreading justice, freedom, and prosperity around the world" (Francis 63)—not to mention ensure its independence from the United States. According to the imperialist narrative of Canada as a nation, the Loyalists were "'the real makers of Canada': they were the best and the brightest that the American colonies had to offer" (56). Given that the "real makers of Canada" were frequently staunch defenders of slavery, there is an irresolvable contradiction at the heart of the national vision of Canada as a land of justice and freedom.

Gradually, as Britain's colonies claimed their independence around the world and Canadian immigration policies opened up, the myth of the master race came to be displaced by another, the myth of the Canadian mosaic, which itself evolved into the myth of multiculturalism in the wake of Prime Minister Pierre Elliott Trudeau's official 1971 policy.[7] Consistent in all of these narratives, despite the nominal embrace of diversity in the postwar and particularly post-1971 period, is a foundational racism and sexism. If the "myth of the master race" was clearly a myth about whiteness in which there was simply no place in the nation for racial others—not First Nations, not blacks, not Chinese, the postwar myths of inclusiveness could still, for different reasons, not admit of the existence of slavery. The myth of multiculturalism, on the other hand, makes claims about the cultural freedom of all Canadians, irrespective of ethnic origin, and pronounces an end to discrimination and forced assimilation.[8] According to the terms of this myth, slavery is a U.S. phenomenon; Canada's only acknowledged connection with the institution is as the terminus for the underground railway, as the geopolitical locus of the North Star and freedom. Testimony to the endurance of this popular understanding of Canada's role in the history of slavery is to be found in the Canadian Broadcasting Corporation's television series, "Canada: A People's History" (CBC-TV and Radio Canada 2000–2001), which passes over in silence the practice of slavery in early settlements and among Loyalist immigrants but explicitly dramatizes the arrival of black refugees under the auspices of the underground railway.

Clarke tackles the occlusion of blackness in these myths of nation both in his writing and in his critical work. "If Canada itself is a residual America," Clarke observes in a recent essay, "old-line black Canadians form a kind of lost colony of African America. The American Revolution, the War of 1812, and abolitionist agitation forged the first major African-Canadian populations" ("Contesting" 2). Yet African Canadians are a "lost colony" in another sense—lost from view. It is no exaggeration to claim that African Americans figure more frequently in the Canadian national imaginary than African Canadians, for, as Clarke notes, Euro-Canadians reference "African-American culture ... to buttress Canadian moral superiority vis-à-vis Euro-American culture" (3). In particular,

Euro-Canadians are keen to see themselves as reflected in what Clarke terms "a classical African-American discourse on Canada [that constructs] the nation as the promised land, or Canaan, for fugitive African Americans" (2). Significantly, this is a vision of Canada post-1850, as opposed to Canada pre-1834, when slavery was legal. The myth of nation that represents Canada as a place of refuge, tolerance, and equality is dependent on the careful erasure of that earlier history. Clarke's cultural memory work addresses a crisis in the discourse of multiculturalism that has dominated the last quarter of the twentieth century, and his intervention is nowhere more effective than in *Beatrice Chancy,* which explicitly challenges the historical erasure at the heart of this narrative of nation.

Beatrice Chancy is dedicated to Marie-Josèphe Angélique and Lydia Jackson, two African-Canadian women who were enslaved, one in New France, the other in Nova Scotia.[9] Their lives are recorded, however elliptically, in the archives, if not in popular histories, but the meaning of those lives is just beginning to be accounted for through the cultural memory work of African-Canadian writers like Lorena Gale (2000), Sylvia Hamilton (1994), and Clarke. Jackson's story, in particular, is germane to my discussion of the place of sexual injustice in the formation of the nation and to the function of cultural memory work that is centered on these acts. *Beatrice Chancy* is not patterned on the events of Jackson's life, but it is faithful to the history of the social formation that oppressed her. Because the occluded history of slavery in Canada is so much at stake in redressing the racism of contemporary myths of nation, and because sex and race were articulated in particularly oppressive ways in that historical moment, Jackson's story is particularly instructive. Jackson, I would go so far as to suggest, is Beatrice Chancy's historical correlate.

Jackson was a free black woman living in Nova Scotia who, having been abandoned by her husband and having no recourse under the law, found herself in dire economic straits. Her situation was exploited by a man named Henry Hedley, who "hired" her as a companion to his wife, then persuaded her to sign a contract that, in her understanding, indented her to him for a period of one year. The unscrupulous Hedley, knowing Jackson was illiterate, had in fact made the contract out for thirty-nine years. He then promptly sold Jackson to Dr. John Bulman (Bolman) of Lunenberg, Nova Scotia, for £20. Bulman was a particularly vicious master who beat Jackson frequently and raped her. Even while she was under Bulman's control, she attempted to resist this treatment, managing to file a complaint with an attorney in Lunenberg. Bulman was a powerful man, however, and successfully used his influence when the case went to court. After some three years of slavery under Bulman, Jackson managed to escape and flee to Halifax, where she again sought to obtain justice. In accordance with contemporary practices, she had a "memorial," or statement of grievances, drawn up and presented to Governor Parr, who ignored it. Some time later, she approached Chief Justice Thomas Strange, who promised to look into the matter. Strange was the first of the two successive chief justices who sought to battle slavery in the courts, to the extent that it was possible. Jackson then also met with John Clarkson, an abolitionist who was in Halifax organizing a mission to Sierra Leone of those free blacks who were dissatisfied with conditions in Nova Scotia. Clarkson took up Jackson's case himself for a time, but he decided that it could not be resolved while he was in the province and recommended that she "give it up and leave Bulman to his own reflections" (Clarkson 90). It is Clarkson's report on his mission that provides the fullest archival account of Jackson's experiences.

In her memorial and in her appeals to Strange and Clarkson, Jackson undertakes a kind of diva citizenship. Faced with the intransigence of the Loyalist Ascendancy, which Bulman represented, Jackson did not obtain the redress she sought and in all likelihood abandoned Nova Scotia for yet another "promised land," Sierra Leone. Bulman's "private" acts of sexual and racial injustice go unpunished, if not undiscovered, because of the "public" political sanction for sexual and racial inequality. Jackson's public testifying against Bulman, her repeated efforts to obtain redress for the offenses committed against her, are acts of courage in a society that scarcely acknowledged her "right" to speak. Her assumption of agency and her exposure of the connection between public and private tyranny make her an appropriate figure for comparison with Clarke's heroine. In his verse play, Clarke chooses as his vehicle for memory work another story about violence and ethics, the story of Beatrice Cenci.

Twice-told tales and surrogate acts

At the core of the original story are two acts of violence, two crimes: incest and parricide, crimes that, so named, resonate even more deeply than when they are called rape and murder because they are crimes not only against society but against the most intimate kinship structures on which patriarchal, capitalist, Western societies have been built. The incest taboo is commonly understood as the basis for the creation of social ties beyond the family unit. For Claude Lévi-Strauss, the incest prohibition is "the supreme rule of the gift" that creates mutual obligation among families. These social relations are of course gendered: in patriarchal, capitalist societies, men forge social ties through the exchange of women; that is to say, fathers give their daughters in marriage to other men in exchange for social, economic, and political gain.[10] That father-daughter incest is the most common breach of the incest taboo in patriarchal societies underscores, according to Judith Herman, the extent to which "the rights of ownership and exchange of women within the family are vested primarily in the father" (60). Francesco Cenci, in taking his daughter (for) himself, violates but also exercises a fundamental social law. In murdering her father, Beatrice also violates social law, not only by killing a member of her society but by striking at the kinship structure itself and its gendered organization. For in rising up against her father, Beatrice does the unimaginable: the object of exchange becomes an agent in her own behalf. In many tellings of this tale, the audience is asked to think differently about this act of murder, this parricide, than social law dictates. We are asked to think about Beatrice Cenci as a tragic heroine and to regard her act of parricide as a symptom of society's crime against this female individual. These are the elements of the original history and some of its literary versions that Clarke exploits in *Beatrice Chancy.*

In adapting this tale to slave-holding Nova Scotia in 1801, Clarke sets up the kinship narrative in order to tear it down. For as scholars writing about slavery have shown, this story of gender and kinship was rewritten under slavery. Not only were black families separated during the course of the notorious Middle Passage, but plantation societies throughout the Americas fundamentally disrupted African kinship relations. Hortense Spillers describes the plantation system in this way: "In effect, under conditions of captivity, the offspring of the female does not 'belong' to the Mother, nor is s/he 'related' to the 'owner,' though the latter 'possesses' it, and in the African-American instance, often fathered it, and, as often, without whatever benefit of patrimony" ("Mama's Baby" 74). Of course, this is not to say that slaves did not construct family relations anyway, imagining alternative family relations that were very powerful, but Spillers' point, and mine, is that the dominant society did not recognize those alternative family relations, and thus slaves were officially outside of kinship structures. Black women slaves were, at the same time, subjected to a process of "ungendering,"[11] first, by being assigned the same kinds of work as the men and subjected to the same acts of brutality and torture, and second, by being placed outside of a gendered moral code. Slavery as a system placed its captives outside an ethical framework by representing slaves as commodities equivalent to so many pounds sterling. At the same time that the captive body is reduced to a thing, "provid[ing] a physical and biological expression of 'otherness,'" the very otherness of the captive body "translates into a potential for pornotroping" (Spillers, "Mama's Baby" 67) that means black women can be subjected to rape without any breach of decorum.

That decorum in slavery societies depended on a deferring and differing of racial and gendered constructs is nowhere so clear as in that particularly pervasive moral discourse during the nineteenth century, the discourse of "true womanhood" (Jones; Carby). The markers of "true womanhood" were virtue, chastity, physical frailty—and whiteness. In fact, the achievement of "true womanhood" was absolutely dependent on the existence of black women slaves, who performed the strenuous physical labour that permitted white plantation mistresses to be delicate and fragile and whose stereotyped sexuality (few black women slaves had the luxury of chastity) served to guarantee the purity of their white counterparts (Carby 30). Merely to survive rape, the common lot of black women under slavery, was to contravene "true womanhood," for if the sentimental novels of the era are to be believed, no "true" woman would survive sexual assault (34). The removal of black women, under slavery, from the patriarchal kinship system was another guarantee that the category of womanhood would inevitably be bound up with whiteness, for, as Spillers observes, "the 'reproduction of mothering' [among black slaves] in this historic instance carries few of the benefits of a *patriarchilized* female gender, which, from one point of view, is the only female gender there is" ("Mama's Baby" 73). In fact, if we consider the way that this moral discourse, with its particular articulation of gender and race, depends on patriarchy, we might conclude that under slavery in North America, decorum begs the question not only of a raced and gendered morality but of kinship itself. In using father-daughter incest as a figure for unjust sexual and racial power in *Beatrice Chancy*, Clarke uses guerrilla tactics to stage an insurrection from within the structures of kinship, confronting the nation with its violence and the shame of its hypocrisy.

Another figure "restored" and reimagined in *Beatrice Chancy* is the mulatto/a, and once again we have to do with a decorous masquerade of sexual and racial injustice. Spillers argues that "the mulatto in the text of fiction provides a strategy for naming and celebrating the phallus;" that is to say, "the play and interplay of an open, undisguised sexuality are mapped on the body of the mulatto character, who allows the dominant culture to say without parting its lips that 'we have willed to sin'" ("Notes" 179). That this sexual mapping tended to conjoin "the new taboo of miscegenation" and "the old taboo of incest" (Sollers 302) makes the mulatto/a particularly apt for Clarke's cultural memory work. Spillers reads this figure for what it reveals about "gender as a special feature of racialist ideology" (181). Located between the white lady, who is maternal and reproductive but, paradoxically, "chaste," and the black woman, who is female pleasure without womanhood, the mulatta allows "the male to have his cake and eat it too, or to rejoin the 'female' with the 'woman'" (183). A figure or, in Spillers' words, an "idea-form" emanating from the perverse desires of the dominant culture, the mulatto/a has a substantial textual and performance history in the African diaspora.[12] Yet Spillers notes that "the thematic of the 'tragic mulatto/a' seems to disappear at the end of the nineteenth century" (176). It is appropriate, then, that at the end of the twentieth century, Clarke's surrogation of the theme in *Beatrice Chancy* is a rewriting that makes explicit what had, for the dominant narrating of this fiction, always to be silenced, obscured. For Spillers, the mulatto/a represented "an accretion of signs that embod[ied] the 'unspeakable,' of the Everything that the dominant culture would forget" (177), and in this respect also the figure is an appropriate one for representing the national "forgetting" of slavery. In *Beatrice Chancy,* the "idea-form" of the mulatto/a and the mixed-race historical subject are held together via a particular form of surrogation: Beatrice wears two masks, standing in at once for the historical subject and the idea-form. Her complicated agency lies in this dual status, for as historical subject she speaks and acts out against the violence and perversity of the idea-form, even as her fate (incestuous rape, murder, and hanging) is largely controlled by it.

What better way to make the point that slavery was an intimate part of the formation of Canada (however much myths of nation have sought to forget it) than to represent it as a family affair? In *Beatrice Chancy,* Beatrice is slave and daughter, and it is her ambivalent status as both that proves so troubling. The story of kinship is rewritten in the drama as Beatrice's symbolic value as Francis Chancy's daughter (and not merely the biological fact of her relation to her master) is acknowledged. In fact, as the play opens, it is her status as daughter that seems to be winning out. We learn that she is about to return home from a convent school in Halifax where she has been sent "to copy / White ladies' ways" (17). Reminiscent of the pattern laid out in *Iola Leroy,* where Eugene Leroy sends Iola's mother Marie north to be educated before he manumits and marries her, this trope in *Beatrice Chancy* becomes a means of exposing Chancy's perverse white male fantasy, his desire to eat his cake and have it too, as we shall see presently. Beatrice's status as daughter is irrevocably bound up with the acquisition of whiteness but also, as the play makes clear, with her female gender. The overseer Dice, who is also rumoured to be Chancy's offspring, has no chance of being acknowledged as Chancy's son. As Chancy himself asserts: "My son must be white and known to be white" (28). Beatrice, on the other hand, is most useful to Chancy as a daughter whom he can exchange for political gain. As he tells Reverend Peacock, when the latter suggests he sell Beatrice: "She's too expensive to waste. I'll graft her / On some slavery-endorsing Tory / To fat my interests in the Assembly" (28). The ambiguity of Beatrice's status emerges in the contradiction between Chancy's plans for her, which position her as daughter, and the language he uses to convey those plans, which is at once crudely biological ("I'll graft her") and economic—more appropriate to a slave, in other words. Strictly speaking, under slavery any child of a black mother was black. Thus Chancy's efforts to remake Beatrice in his own image ("I dispatched Beatrice to Halifax / To shape her more like us—white, modern, beautiful" [52]) suggest a deliberate reworking of kinship in a way that exposes its racial subtext.

The ambiguity of Beatrice's status, in other words, allows Clarke to expose and indict the workings of the system of slavery and the social system that condoned it. Nova Scotia, one of the slaves tells us early in the play, is a whorehouse (14). The commodification of sexual relations is the political economy of a province that allowed slavery to exist and that bartered its daughters for political patronage. The language of commodification pervades the play, informing both the slaves' understanding of their position in a plantation economy—"Father," Beatrice demands in a sharp reminder of the difference between daughters and slaves, "would you barter me like a hog, / Or wood, or a piece of machinery?" (56)—and the discourse of white society. Reverend Peacock and the Hangman both regularly remind Chancy that Beatrice is his property to dispose of as he sees fit, and they both make clear that it is more fitting that he sell her as a slave than marry her off as a daughter. These representatives of the church and the judicial system—for the Hangman will ultimately carry out Beatrice's death sentence—lend institutional support to Chancy's patriarchal power. Chancy's first speech tells of traffic in women slaves as he gives his overseer and would-be son, Dice, a shopping list:

> Buy a hogshead of stomach-stabbing rum,
> H.W.L.'s tragic Natchitoches tobacco,
> A puncheon of molasses, a keg of nails,
> One purebred *nègre* heifer and her calf
> (Pay £70 for the lot, not a *sou* more),
> And fifty-two yards of *Hobbes*-forged chains. (23)

The parenthetical injunction to limit costs that divides the "*nègre* heifer" from the chains in this casually rhymed-off list underscores the crude economy governing the life of bondage. The bonds of kinship form a startling contrast. When Chancy expresses surprise that Dice makes no attempt to escape bondage, the latter responds: "You've played the only father I've loved" (24). Once again, however, Chancy denies this kinship: "Your complexion's like night-exhausted stars / But go as if you could sue to be my son" (24). Chancy characterizes his slaves, stereotypically, as "childish cattle / That need unflinching mastery" (26). Paradoxically, the adjective "childish" serves to remind us once again of the question of kinship at the center of this play, and the fact that "cattle" is so close to "chattel" reminds us that at least one and probably two of Chancy's chattel are in fact his children. The lines between property and kin refuse to remain clearly drawn. Chancy's infertile wife Lustra, who sees herself ambivalently as Beatrice's stepmother and as her rival, alternately objects to Beatrice's commodification and subscribes to it. "My only child's not for sale to your likes!" (56) she declares when the Hangman offers to buy Beatrice; later, when speaking to Beatrice, she observes sardonically: "For a piece of property, you quarrel much" (72). As it turns out, Beatrice's dual status is a threat to the system that produced her, and through her actions, tragic heroine that she is, she brings that system crashing down on herself.

If, in the context of the play, her gender gives her access to whiteness, Beatrice's mixed racial heritage imposes strict limits on that access. "True womanhood," it turns out, is not within her purview, for the virtue that characterizes "true womanhood" hangs on whiteness, as we have seen. Appropriately then, Chancy declares Beatrice chaste on her return from the convent school in Halifax, where she has been sent to acquire whiteness. That virtue is a sign of whiteness is also underscored by Chancy's overt description of the role that slaves play in the moral economy of the province, where blackness is needed to define whiteness. "How can we be beautiful, free, / Virtuous, holy, pure, *chosen*," Chancy demands, "If slaves be not our opposites?" (26). Beatrice's mixed heritage, though, makes Peacock skeptical of her proclaimed chastity. In expressing his doubts, he proffers the stereotypical view of black female sexuality: "Is Beatrix Cincia sacred? No, no. / . . . / She'll batten on hardness like any whore. / Black slave hussies are only born / To nasty, baste, breed and suckle" (38). That the slaves read the question of Beatrice's virtue very differently provides another level of commentary on the dominant discourse. Here the concern is that her convent experience might have altered her allegiances. Lead worries: "What if her heart's frostbit? / What if she craves to bed down a white boy?" (18). As it turns out, of course, Lead has nothing to worry about. But Beatrice's loyalty, her desire for Lead, makes impossible her borrowed whiteness. For while the rape of female slaves by white planters reinforced the system of slavery through what amounted to an exercise of power and control over the slave population as a whole, the notion that a white woman might actually desire a black man was inadmissible. Thus when Chancy discovers that Beatrice wishes to marry Lead, he punishes her by demoting her to slave status, declaring that "my daughter can't love some bull-thighed nigger!" (55) and treating her accordingly, first by locking her up and then by raping her.

Until Beatrice spurns his desires through her decision to marry Lead, Chancy indulges in a fantasy facilitated by Beatrice's mixed racial heritage, which makes her a candidate for the acquisition of whiteness in the first place. Beatrice's lighter skin allows Chancy to pretend that bondage is indeed kinship. "My power isn't violation, it's love" (27), he attempts to persuade Peacock on the eve of Beatrice's return from the convent school in Halifax. Peacock attempts to force Chancy into a decision about Beatrice's dual status: "Do you want Beatrice to fear or love you?" he asks, pointing out: "She is equally your daughter and your slave." Chancy persists in his equivocation: "I've sponsored her convent school for three years—/ An unusual blessing for a slave. / But she's my daughter" (27). Chancy appears to favour her filial status here, but he simultaneously affirms her status as slave. Moreover, on Beatrice's return "home," we begin to suspect Chancy's "love" for her may be more conjugal than paternal after all. He remarks, "Regard: rare, Demerara skin—mare's skin. / Look how she denominates her mother" (53). A lighter-skinned version of her mother, Beatrice might just have other uses than fatting his interests in the Assembly. That decorum, whether conjugal or paternal, is quickly abandoned when Beatrice declares her love for another slave, which exposes the sham as well as Beatrice's real vulnerability. As mulatta, Beatrice is subjected both to white male fantasies and to the rule of sexual availability that applies to all black women under slavery. Chancy's use of rape as punishment is a sign that, for him, she is no longer "white," no longer his daughter.

It is Beatrice who emphasizes her status as daughter at this point, vowing to Chancy: "Tenderly, I love you, as your daughter" (69). Chancy, no longer willing to recognize Beatrice as white, insists on reading her love as lust, as evidence of her blackness: "All your lyricism, love speech, is dress / For the nakedness of longing" (70). For Chancy, such a reading is sanction for his act of rape, hardly even a crime under slavery, let alone incestuous. His meditation on the act of violence he is about to perform transfers culpability to Beatrice, who, in the terms of yet another racist fantasy, is seen as seducing her rapist:

> I tempt my brain—or she lures me—to grave
> An organ in a fresh, unscabrous cleft,
> To be darkly traduced, a prize, vicious,
> Sap-eating triangle, housing noxious
> Buzzing of incestuous insects busy
> At sex, dumping blood—swank, nervous—like Christ's. (81)

Yet this speech also acknowledges Chancy's guilt and his betrayal, as he speaks of her sex as both smooth and pure, the opposite of scabrous, and of his penetration as a misrepresentation, a defilement. The imagery of insects engaged in "noxious" activity marks the incestuous act as unnatural, the bloodletting a martyrdom, a crucifixion. Still later in his soliloquy, Chancy shifts back to the language of commodification, as he represents Beatrice as "a costly, well-kept diamond" about to be "cracked by a jeweller's chisel—/ A soft, ebony jewel, split tenderly, / Then vomiting priceless ruby facets" (82). Her punishment is to move across the bar of her dual status, from daughter to slave: "My hands will speak horror to her body. / She'll learn what it means to be property" (82). But Beatrice, in insisting on her status as daughter, on the injustice of Chancy's discounting of her as merchandise (70), makes possible the moral condemnation of Chancy's act by defining it as incest as well as rape. In this way, she rewrites the moral code operative under slavery, making black women the agents of moral authority rather than its negated objects.

Significantly, it is when Chancy treats Beatrice most as an object that she emerges most fully as agent, and her agency lies in her ability to expose the operations of the moral code of slavery. She indicts the false Christianity of the slaveholders even as, against the Easter setting of the play, she takes on the role of crucified Christ. More significantly, through Beatrice, Clarke makes poetry the means of rending the veil of decorum historically dropped over the most violent and gruesome acts of slavery. It is, ironically, Chancy who describes Beatrice's way with words:

> Wantonly, I'll discover her verse—
> Wet, shining, under a black bush, a language
> That is flesh webbing us, the mouth feel of poetry,
> The Word in her mouth—like salt water,
> Malicious, sad, like Clemence orchards
> Torn apart by hail. (81–82)

If the Word is phallic mastery, Beatrice swallows it up, using it to create a different language, one that speaks of the crimes committed against her. Chained and imprisoned by Chancy once she declares her love for Lead, lashed by Dice who finds her in her lover's arms, Beatrice complains to Lustra of Chancy's crimes: "he makes thieves and harlots of his slaves" (72). When Lustra chastises her for the impropriety of her speech—"To hear a woman speak thusly—so close to shame" (72), Beatrice lashes out: "Would my words stab! I'm molested / By white men's words and black men's eyes" (72). Delineating her situation in a gendered and raced system that deems her speech indecorous, Beatrice vows to use her words as a weapon in her defense. She refuses the perverted ethics of a system that justifies racial terror by blaming violation on its victims—"Your lean thighs justify your mother's slavery" (86), Chancy tells Beatrice moments before he rapes her in the chapel. Here the decorum that conventionally cloaked the worst violence of slavery is represented as censorship: as Chancy rapes her, Beatrice's speech registers a terrible silencing: "I hurt [*two words garbled*] my throat / [*Several words whited out*] a knife" (87). Decorum as whitewash, literally. What remains of Beatrice's speech after this violation—"I hurt," "my throat," "a knife"—combines pain with the source of speech and a weapon ambiguously positioned, perhaps *at* her throat, or perhaps we are to understand that her throat *is* now a knife, a weapon. In subsequent scenes, Beatrice does not hesitate to articulate the violence done her in "blunt talk." When Lustra attempts to silence her by reminding Beatrice that Chancy is her father—in a hollow appeal to the kinship system that Chancy himself destroyed—Beatrice responds: "Call him as you like. I call him my raper." And when Lustra admonishes: "These words aren't poetry, Beatrice: They canker," Beatrice gives her what she asked for, if not exactly what she wants: "You like poetry, so here's sweetheart poetry: / He wants me for his piece of brown sugar, / And he wants you to watch him licking it" (109). Poetry is at once what Chancy attempts to destroy and the means of representing his crimes.

Verbal niceties are the representational equivalents of the racist and sexist kinship system in the name of which Beatrice is enslaved and violated. Barred from her tenuous position as daughter, yet suffering as a daughter, Beatrice embraces the role of outlaw in order to indict the false morality of slave societies: "White men, you took away my freedom / And gave me religion. / So be it: I became a devout killer" (140). Thus, she assumes agency in another, terrible guise: she becomes Chancy's judge and executioner. That we are able to read Beatrice's act of murder as the symptom of a slave society's crime against her is again due to Clarke's careful manipulation of the historical subtexts. One of the other clear limits to Beatrice's temporary and limited access to whiteness as Chancy's daughter is her inability to summon anyone to her defense. Thus, when she proposes to protect her status as daughter by summoning colonial soldiers, telling Lustra "I require that Wentworth / Field troops to warranty my father's love" (77), her stepmother quickly admonishes her: "Beatrice, you forget your low place. Troops shield / White women" (77). Having no other recourse, Beatrice acts in her own behalf, but also in behalf of the other slaves. In signing her own death warrant through her illicit act, Beatrice nonetheless succeeds in dealing a blow to slavery itself by sparking a revolt. In effect, Beatrice derives her agency from the system that oppresses her. Spillers points out that "the powers of domination succeed only to the extent that their permeation remains silent and concealed to those very historical subjects ... upon whom the entire structure depends" ("Notes" 185). In *Beatrice Chancy,* we witness the breakdown of this system, insofar as Beatrice, as historical subject, becomes only too aware of how domination works and refuses to remain silent, exposing her father's actions and renaming him her "raper."

In imagining this conclusion for *Beatrice Chancy*, Clarke not only rewrites the story of the Cenci, he transforms the history that Lead early in the play deems "only good for anger" (17). Lead is responding specifically to the story of Beatrice's mother, and with her story Clarke encapsulates a diasporan history and centers it on the combined racial and sexual exploitation that was the lot of black women under slavery:

> Her name was Mafa. Thefted from Guinea,
> She washed ashore when that slaver, *Fortune,*
> Splintered off Peggy's crushing Cove, sinking
> Three hundred Africans. Bought as bruised goods
> By Massa, next seven years his forced wife,
> She died when I was seven, Bee was four,
> And she was herself just twenty-one years. (17)

"Fortune" is not merely the name of the ship but a synonym for the economic system that created the slave trade that "thefted [Mafa] from Guinea." Conversely, Mafa's fortune, not to mention that of her shipmates, founders in Nova Scotia where she is sold and raped. In *Beatrice Chancy*, this diasporan history is brought home, as it were, and is made to confront hegemonic national narratives that would seek to stop it at the Canada-U.S. border. In attributing unjust sexual and racial power to the nation, Clarke makes "this history [that]'s only good for anger" a testimony to the suffering of subordinated people, and in the transformation of Beatrice from commodity to agent, we can read a representation of subaltern insurgency, a claim to citizenship in the name of those historically denied it and those who continue to be asked for their passports.[13]

(Re-)Staging public memory

It remains to take account of the ways that this representation of subaltern insurgency is made to speak to the living as well as communicate with the dead. In addition to the citational practices specific to textual and operatic transmission that work to signify *Beatrice Chancy*, there are broader discursive structures that condition the reception and circulation of both. Paradoxically, in light of its support for the anodyne visions of multiethnic and interracial harmony that have helped to occlude the history of slavery in Canada, multiculturalism may be said also to offer a larger discursive structure for the entry of *Beatrice Chancy* onto the public stage in Canada.[14] That there are effectively two versions of *Beatrice Chancy* (or two formal variants, to be more precise, since cultural transmission clearly makes for a potentially infinite number of "versions") must also be taken into account, for the opera and the verse drama function as surrogates, one for the other, thus extending and reinforcing *Beatrice Chancy*'s performative possibilities. Its success as a chamber opera has led to its reproduction in other media, specifically CBC (Canadian Broadcasting Company) Radio and CBC-TV, venues that not only increase its audience considerably but, in their role as national, publicly funded media, perform the task of representing the nation to itself. That *Beatrice Chancy* is "the first Canadian opera [to be] broadcast on television in more than 30 years" (Bernstein B4) suggests, at the very least, that its impact in the public sphere has not been negligible.

Let us begin with the matter of textual transmission. While reading is most often a solitary activity, the transmission of literary texts is in fact a collective and collaborative process, thus affording a text entree into the public sphere. Via reviews in the press as well as literary magazines and academic journals, via interviews with Clarke on radio and television, via educational organizations and institutions, and via public "readings," literary texts come to have a place in the public sphere in ways that can legitimately be described as performative insofar as each of these modes of reception and circulation offers "an elaborate reiteration of a specific vision of social order" (Worthen 1097) in which the text is made to signify.[15] To date, although it was only published in 1999, *Beatrice Chancy* has enjoyed a fairly remarkable reception—remarkable because of its extent, and remarkable in view of the challenge this text poses to the dominant vision of social order in the nation.

As an opera, *Beatrice Chancy* has perhaps made an even greater impact. It opened to rave reviews in 1998 and has had three more stage productions since then, a fact that is regarded as something of a feat given that new operas are rarely revived. Clarke's libretto, with its insurgent testimony about the unjust racial and sexual power of the nation, is here mobilized by the citational practices of chamber opera performance. If, as Worthen suggests, performance "regimes can be understood to cite—or, perhaps subversively, to resignify—social and behavioral practices that operate outside the theater and that constitute contemporary social life" (1098), it is worth taking note of the social preoccupations that have surfaced in contemporary Canadian opera. Linda Hutcheon and Michael Hutcheon argue that although they do not always address explicitly Canadian themes, "the Canadian operas written in recent years go to the heart of the nation's concerns about such things as the ethics of power and the definition of the nation and of the self" (6). *Beatrice Chancy,* then, may be said to have found a national(ist) medium for its repatriation of a diasporan history.

James Rolfe's composition, described as "citational in ways which make it both resolutely contemporary and historically resonant" (Hutcheon and Hutcheon 7), quotes extensively from spirituals, gospel, the blues, and jazz, as well as Scottish strathspey and reels in an effort to evoke the historical and cultural terrain encompassed in Clarke's libretto. The music is a collage of twentieth-century operatic colours in a minimalist setting. It is scored for two violins, a viola, a cello, bass, piano, and percussion. In the primacy accorded the libretto and the theatrical elements of operatic performance, the composition resonates clearly with U.S. musical theatre in the tradition of George Gershwin, Kurt Weill, and Leonard Bernstein. It also exhibits the stylistic influences of Alban Berg and Benjamin Britten. The harmonic language, thinly orchestrated, alludes to compositions by Igor Stravinsky, Arvo Pärt, and Gershwin and occasionally offers glimpses of an older operatic style through references to Henry Purcell.[16] The opera opens with a ring shout, during which the singers play percussion instruments, and closes with the singers and the musicians standing together on the stage singing the spiritual "Oh, Freedom!" thus according prominence to the African diasporan narrative at the heart of the libretto.

The production by Queen of Puddings Music Theatre Company underscores the tensions between subaltern history and hegemonic narratives of nation that Rolfe's music and Clarke's libretto articulate.[17] The musicians are also costumed as slaves and perform at the side of the stage, in view of the audience. For one critic, this "blurring of boundaries ... encourages us to contemplate our own complicity in injustice" (Bernstein B4); for another, it represents "a gesture of unity that embrace[s] the audience as well" (Kareda 89). For Bernstein, the relationship of score to libretto is also potentially conflictual: "Rolfe's deft assimilation and fusion of musical styles ... seems to offer the possibility of plurality and understanding between races and classes that the story itself grimly withholds" (B4). The power of surrogation, in this instance, lies precisely in these unresolved tensions. Where the finale strives for transcendence, what emerges is perhaps best understood in terms of the ambiguous transcendence offered in the spiritual form, itself a resonant vehicle of cultural memory, where visions of a peaceful realm of freedom beyond the world of slavery present a powerful critique of the strife and lack of freedom in that world.

Through operatic performance and the collective modes of literary reception, not to mention radio and television broadcasts, *Beatrice Chancy* has entered onto the national stage and, via its eponymous heroine, undertaken an act "of risky dramatic persuasion" (Berlant 223). The tension between national narratives and subaltern memory that is, in one way or another, a feature of all citations of the work threatens to foreclose any intervention that it might make into a national self-understanding about slavery. Beatrice Chancy's performance of countermemory consists in her assumption of agency on behalf of historic and contemporary African-Canadian women, speaking of past injustice in order to call upon the nation in the present. It is a fleeting agency, to be sure, derived from suffering and the lived contradictions of her status as daughter and slave and aptly conveyed through the character's surrogation of the mulatta as both type (which, by definition, is entirely without agency [Spillers, "Notes"]) and historic subject. Yet in her performance of the wronged mixed-race daughter and the avenging spirit, Beatrice effects a kind of intervention, claiming a citizenship historically denied her.

With *Beatrice Chancy*, Clarke contributes to the growing body of contemporary African diasporan literature engaged in the process of representing the pain and trauma of the experience of slavery. In works ranging from Morrison's *Beloved* (1987) to Maryse Condé's *I, Tituba, Black Witch of Salem* (1992), from Octavia Butler's *Kindred* (1979) and Gayl Jones's *Corregidora* (1975) to Dionne Brand's *At the Full and Change of the Moon* (1999) and Lorena Gale's *Angélique* (2000), the ethical impulse to renew the self-understanding of New World Africans and to rewrite their relationship to dominant society is enacted through an abiding concern with gender, with the particular place of the black woman in the sexual economy of slavery. The peculiar national refractions of that diasporan history entail distinct mnemonic devices. In choosing the story of Beatrice Cenci, a tale of incest and parricide, Clarke strives to awaken the nation to its own repressed intimacy with racial and sexual violence. "My country needs me, and if I were not here, I would have to be invented," Spillers once observed in commenting on the overdetermined construction of black womanhood in the U.S. context ("Mama's Baby" 65). Yet in a national context that can barely conceive of an African-Canadian female subject, the need for inventing one has more to do with an overdetermined absence. In this context, what better story could one tell of unjust sexual relations than a story of incest? In effect, the national relation to slavery in the Canadian context is incestuous, not only by virtue of being a family affair but by virtue of being taboo, silenced, absent from the national imaginary. But Beatrice refuses to be silenced and, in a virtuoso performance, compels our sympathy and elicits our outrage in her behalf. That she is aiming at a diva performance is clear from her response to Deal, who advises her to play Moses to Massa's Pharaoh: "I'll play Beatrice. I'll play her beautifully" (62).

Endnotes

1. See, e.g., Jan Assmann's definition of cultural memory.
2. A sample of the extensive feminist research on nationalism would include work by Kumari Jayawardena (1986), Nira Yuval-Davis and Floya Anthias (1989), Deniz Kandiyoti (1991), and Anne McClintock (1995).
3. *Africadian* is a word coined by Clarke as an alternative to *African-Nova Scotian, Afro-Nova Scotian, black Nova Scotian,* or other possible appellations. A fusion *of Africa* and *Acadia,* this term is evocative of an imagined community. Clarke's most important poetic works to date, which in other respects are very different, have centered on "Africadia": *Whylah Falls* (1990), *One Heart Broken into Song* (1999), *Beatrice Chancy,* and *Execution Poems* (2000). Clarke was born and grew up in Nova Scotia, where, as he puts it, his "bloodlines run deep ... to 1813 on [his] African-American / Mi'kmaq mother's side and to 1898 on [his] African-American / Caribbean father's side" ("Eyeing the Northern Star" xii).
4. I have in mind here not only *Beatrice Chancy* but Clarke's poems about Lydia Jackson and Africville (1992), his commemoration of the hanging of his cousins George and Rufus Hamilton in *Execution Poems,* his commemoration of Graham Jarvis in *Whylah Falls,* and the novel *George and Rue* (2005).

5. See "*Beatrice Chancy*: A Libretto in Four Acts" (Clarke). The full opera premiered at the Music Gallery in Toronto in 1998 and has subsequently been remounted at the Du Maurier Theatre in Toronto (June 25–26, 1999), at Alderney Landing Theatre in Halifax (August 12, 14–15, 1999), and at the Citadel Theatre in Edmonton (February 8, 10–11, 13, 2001), and it was broadcast on CBC Radio (October 25, 1998) and CBC Television (February 8, 2001).
6. There was a "dramatic reading" of *Beatrice Chancy* at Theatre Passe Muraille in Toronto, July 10–11, 1997.
7. The myth of the mosaic, typically counterposed to the concept of a melting pot, which is held to be American, conceives of Canadian ethnic diversity in terms of a constellation of distinct groups living amicably side by side. As Francis (1997) points out, the concept of the mosaic originates with the Euro-Canadian mainstream, its benign vision of ethnic relations masking racism and social stratification along ethnic lines.
8. There are important differences between the discourse of multiculturalism, as it developed in the U.S. academic context in the 1980s and 1990s, and the ways that the concept of multiculturalism resonates in Canada in light of its origins in Liberal government policy and the concomitant federal funding that continues to be made available to ethnic groups across the nation. For a comparison of the discourse in the United States and Canada, see Huggan and Siemerling. Critics of the policy have argued that it creates a two-tiered funding system that continues to marginalize the work of ethnic minorities. See Philip, Kamboureli, Wilson, Gunew, and Li.
9. Angélique had an illicit affair with a young Frenchman at a time (1730s) when concubinage was explicitly

proscribed under the Code Noir. Angélique's affair was discovered and condemned. Shortly thereafter, a fire broke out in a section of Montreal; Angélique was blamed for the fire and hanged in a public square for her crime.

10. Gayle Rubin's careful elucidation of these issues remains an important source.
11. See Davis, Jones, Carby, and Spillers ("Mama's Baby").
12. A partial list would include Dion Boucicault's *The Octoroon* (1859); the novel by Mayne Reid, *The Quadroon* (1856), on which Boucicault's play is based; Richard Hildreth's *The Slave; or, Memoirs of Archy Moore* (1836); Lydia Maria Child's "The Quadroons" (1842); Elizabeth Livermore's *Zoe; or, The Quadroon's Triumph, A Tale for the Times* (1855); as well as Harper's *Iola Leroy,* Nella Larsen's *Passing* (1929); and Jessie Fauset's *Plum Bun* (1929).
13. Both Clarke and Adrienne Shadd have written about how regularly in Canada, African Canadians are assumed to be from somewhere else, usually either the United States or the Caribbean. See Shadd and Moynagh.
14. Press notices and television reports of the opera have assiduously referred to "Canada's dirty little secret" (Clarke, Rolfe, and Hess) or "Canada's invisible history" (CBC-TV, "Opera"), in what seems an almost obligatory gesture of expiation.
15. For reviews, see, e.g., Beaton, Burns, Wiwa, McNeilly, Sandiford, Sealy, and Sugars. Interviews with the author include the CBC Radio interview by Tom Allen (Clarke); the CBC-TV interview, together with James Rolfe and John Hess (Clarke, Rolfe, and Hess), by Linda Griffin; and a spot on CBC-TV's national

news program, "Opera Sheds Light on Canada's Invisible History."

16. I am grateful to Daryl Burghardt of the Music Department at St. Francis Xavier University for his assistance in describing these musical styles.
17. Queen of Puddings has mounted all the productions of *Beatrice Chancy* to date, and the same singers, including Measha Brüggergosman in the role of Beatrice, have performed each time.

Works Cited

Assmann, Jan. "Collective Memory and Cultural Identity." *New German Critique* 65 (Spring-Summer 1995): 125–33.

Beaton, Virginia. "*Beatrice Chancy* resonates with poetic grace." Review of *Beatrice Chancy*, by George Elliott Clarke. *Sunday Herald* 11 July 1999: C7.

Berlant, Lauren. *The Queen of America Goes to Washington City: Essays on Sex and Citizenship*. Durham, NC: Duke UP, 1997.

Bernstein, Tamara. "A Canadian Opera Worth Cheering About." *National Post* 8 February 2001: B4.

Burns, Kevin. Review of *Beatrice Chancy*, by George Elliott Clarke. *Quill and Quire* 65.5 (1999): 35.

Butler, Judith. *Excitable Speech: A Politics of the Performative*. New York: Routledge, 1997.

Cahill, Barry. "*Habeas Corpus* and Slavery in Nova Scotia: *R. v. Hecht ex parte Rachel*, 1798." *University of New Brunswick Law Journal* 44 (1995):179–208.

—. "Slavery and the Judges of Loyalist Nova Scotia." *University of New Brunswick Law Journal* 43 (1994): 73–134.

Carby, Hazel. *Reconstructing Womanhood: The Emergence of the Afro-American Woman Novelist*. New York: Oxford UP, 1987.

CBC-TV. "Opera Sheds Light on Canada's Invisible History." *National*. 5 October 1999.

CBC-TV and Radio Canada. "Canada: A People's History." Produced by Mark Starowicz, Hubert Gendron, and Gordon Henderson. Television series. 2000–2001.

Clarke, George Elliott. *George and Rue*. Toronto: HarperFlamingo, 2005.

—. *Execution Poems*. Wolfville, NS: Gaspereau, 2000.

—. *One Heart Broken into Song*. Digital Betacam, 90 minutes. Toronto: Telefilm Canada. 1999.

—. Interview by Tom Allen. *This Morning Sunday*. CBC Radio. 25 July 1999.

—. *Beatrice Chancy*. Victoria: Polestar, 1999.

—. "Contesting a Model Blackness: A Meditation on African-Canadian African Americanism, or the Structures of African Canadianité." *Essays on Canadian Writing* 63 (Spring 1998): 1–55.

—. "*Beatrice Chancy:* A Libretto in Four Acts." *Canadian Theatre Review* 96 (Fall 1998): 62–77.

—, ed. *Eyeing the North Star: Directions in African-Canadian Literature*. Toronto: McClelland & Stewart, 1997.

—, ed. *Fire on the Water: An Anthology of Black Nova Scotian Writing*. Vol. 2. Lawrencetown Beach, NS: Pottersfield, 1992.

—, ed. *Fire on the Water: An Anthology of Black Nova Scotian Writing*. Vol. 1. Lawrencetown Beach, NS: Pottersfield, 1991.

—. *Whylah Falls*. Vancouver: Polestar, 1990.

Clarke, George Elliott, James Rolfe, and John Hess. Interview by Linda Griffin. *Opening Night*. CBC-TV. February 8, 2001.

Clarkson, John. 1792. *Clarkson's Mission to America, 1791–1792*. Ed. Charles B. Ferguson. Halifax: Public Archives of Nova Scotia, 1971.

Compton, Anne. "Standing Your Ground: George Elliott Clarke in Conversation." *Studies in Canadian Literature* 23.2 (1998): 134–64.

Davis, Angela. *Women, Class, and Race*. New York: Random House, 1981.

Findlay, Len. "Always Indigenize! The Radical Humanities in the Postcolonial Canadian University." *ARIEL: A Review of International English Literature* 31.1 (1999): 307–26.

Francis, Daniel. *National Dreams: Myth, Memory, and Canadian History*. Vancouver: Arsenal Pulp, 1997.

Gale, Lorena. *Angélique*. Toronto: Playwrights Canada, 2000.

Gunew, Sneja. *Framing Marginality: Multicultural Literary Studies*. Melbourne: Melbourne UP, 1994.

Hamilton, Sylvia. "Naming Names, Naming Ourselves: A Survey of Early Black Women in Nova Scotia." *"We're Rooted Here and They Can't Pull Us Up": Essays in African Canadian Women's History*. Ed. Peggy Bristow. Toronto: U of Toronto P, 1994. 13–40.

Herman, Judith Lewis. *Father-Daughter Incest*. Cambridge, MA: Harvard UP, 1981.

Huggan, Graham, and Winfried Siemerling. "US/Canadian Writers' Perspectives on the Multiculturalism Debate." *Canadian Literature* 164 (Spring 2000): 82–111.

Hutcheon, Linda, and Michael Hutcheon. "Opera and National Identity: New Canadian Opera." *Canadian Theatre Review* 96 (Fall 1998): 5–8.

Jayawardena, Kumari. *Feminism and Nationalism in the Third World.* London: Zed, 1986.

Jones, Jacqueline. *Labor of Love, Labor of Sorrow: Black Women, Work and the Family from Slavery to the Present.* New York: Basic, 1985.

Kamboureli, Smaro. "Of Black Angels and Melancholy Lovers: Ethnicity and Writing in Canada." *Feminism and the Politics of Difference.* Ed. Sneja Gunew and Anna Yeatman, Boulder, CO: Westview, 1993. 143–56.

—. "The Technology of Ethnicity: Law and Discourse." *Open Letter* 8th ser. 5–6 (1993): 202–17.

Kandiyoti, Deniz. "Identity and Its Discontents: Women and the Nation." *Millennium: Journal of International Studies* 20.3 (1991): 429–43.

Kareda, Urjo. "The Little Company That Could." *Toronto Life*. December 1999. 81–90.

Lévi-Strauss, Claude. *The Elementary Structures of Kinship.* Boston: Beacon, 1969.

Li, Peter. "A World Apart: The Multicultural World of Visible Minorities and the Art World of Canada." *Canadian Review of Sociology and Anthropology* 31.4 (1994): 365–91.

Mannette, Joy A. "'Stark Remnants of Blackpast': Thinking on Gender, Ethnicity and Class in 1780s Nova Scotia." *Alternate Routes* 7 (1984): 102–33.

McClintock, Anne. *Imperial Leather: Race, Gender, and Sexuality in the Colonial Contest.* New York: Routledge, 1995.

McNeilly, Kevin. "Word Jazz 2." Review of *Beatrice Chancy,* by George Elliott Clarke. *Canadian Literature* 165 (Summer 2000): 176–8l.

Morrison, Toni. *Beloved.* New York: Knopf, 1987.

—. "The Site of Memory." *Inventing the Truth: The Art and Craft of Memoir.* Ed. William Zinsser. Boston: Houghton Mifflin, 1987. 85–102.

Moynagh, Maureen. "Mapping Africadia's Imaginary Geography: An Interview with George Elliott Clarke." *ARIEL: A Review of International English Literature* 27.4 (1996): 71–94.

Philip, Marlene NourbeSe. "Why Multiculturalism Can't End Racism." *Frontiers: Selected Essays and Writings on Racism and Culture, 1984–1992.* Stratford, ON: Mercury, 1992. 181–86.

Roach, Joseph. *Cities of the Dead: Circum-Atlantic Performance.* New York: Columbia UP, 1996.

—. "Culture and Performance in the Circum-Atlantic World." *Performativity and Performance.* Ed. Andrew Parker and Eve Kosofsky Sedgwick. New York: Routledge, 1995. 45–63.

Rubin, Gayle. "The Traffic in Women: Notes on the 'Political Economy' of Sex." *The Second Wave: A Reader in Feminist Theory.* Ed. Linda Nicholson. New York: Routledge, 1997. 27–62.

Sandiford, Robert Edison. "Acts of Fact and Fancy." Review of *Beatrice Chancy,* by George Elliott Clarke. *Antigonish Review* 120 (Winter 2000): 161–63.

Sealy, David. Review of *Beatrice Chancy,* by George Elliott Clarke. *Canadian Review of American Studies* 30.1 (2000): 116–18.

Shadd, Adrienne. "'Where Are You Really From?' Notes of an 'Immigrant' from North Buxton, Ontario." *Talking about Difference: Encounters in Culture, Language and Identity.* Ed. Carl E. James and Adrienne Shadd. Toronto: Between the Lines, 1994. 9–15.

Singh, Amritjit, Joseph Skerrett, Jr., and Robert E. Hogan, eds. *Memory and Cultural Politics: New Approaches to American Ethnic Literatures*. Boston: Northeastern UP, 1996.

Sollers, Werner. "'Never Was Born': The Mulatto, an American Tragedy?" *Massachusetts Review* 27.2 (1986): 293–316.

Spillers, Hortense. "Mama's Baby, Papa's Maybe: An American Grammar Book." *Diacritics* 17.2 (1987): 65–8l.

—. "Notes on an Alternative Model: Neither / Nor." *Year Left 2*. Ed. Michael Sprinker, Mike Davis, and Manning Marable. New York: Verso, 1987. 176–94.

Sturken, Marita. *Tangled Memories: The Vietnam War, the AIDS Epidemic, and the Politics of Remembering*. Berkeley: U of California P, 1997.

Sugars, Cynthia. Review of *Beatrice Chancy*, by George Elliott Clarke. *Books in Canada* 29 (February 2000): 13–14.

Walker, James W. St. G. *The Black Loyalists: The Search for the Promised Land in Nova Scotia and Sierra Leone*. Toronto: U of Toronto P, 1992.

Wilson, Seymour. "The Tapestry Vision of Canadian Multiculturalism." *Canadian Journal of Political Science* 26.4 (1993): 645–69.

Wiwa, Ken. "Unveiling Canada's Hidden Slave History." Review of *Beatrice Chancy*, by George Elliott Clarke. *Globe and Mail* 3 July 1999: D16.

Worthen, W.B. "Drama, Performativity, and Performance." *PMLA* 113.5 (1998): 1093–1107.

Yuval-Davis, Nira, and Floya Anthias, eds. *Women-Nation-State*. New York: St. Martin's, 1989.

Rewriting Violent Histories: Transcultural Adaptation in *Beatrice Chancy*

AMANDA MONTAGUE

With the advent of the internet there is growing discussion about the nature of original creativity in comparison to translation and adaptation of pre-existing texts. George Elliott Clarke's play, *Beatrice Chancy* and his opera, *Beatrice Chancy* are provocative examples of the adaptation of the old Cenci legend to a new social context, historical period and geographical location. In this essay I will focus on Clarke's opera, *Beatrice Chancy* and briefly compare it to Shelley's verse drama, *The Cenci* (1819). In her theorization of adaptation, Linda Hutcheon contends that adaptations are re-imagined works based on a previous text but never exact replications of that text: "Literary adaptations are their own things—inspired by, based on an adapted text but something different, something other" (Hutcheon 5). As a process of both restoration *and* reinvention, "works adapted *from* literature [become] part of our readerly experience *of* that literature" (5). The past five centuries have generated extensive narrative treatment of the Cenci legend. But as Hutcheon recounts in her examination of Cenci adaptations, Clarke contends: "These creators have dallied with Beatrice Cenci, but I have committed indiscretions" (1).

The history of the Cenci family dates to sixteenth century Rome where, in 1577, Beatrice Cenci was born to the violent and sadistic Roman nobleman, Francesco Cenci. Throughout Beatrice's life, Cenci subjected her, her siblings, and her stepmother Lucretia, whom Cenci married in 1595, to ongoing persecution. This oppression took the form of various degrees of mental and physical abuse, including the alleged incestuous rape of Beatrice. In a radical act of rebellion in response to this subjugation Beatrice, with the assistance of her family, orchestrated the murder of the corrupt patriarch. But the family's conspiracy was subsequently discovered, leading to their execution by papal decree in 1599. The history of Beatrice Cenci became an integral part of Italian national consciousness, while the tragic and sensational elements of her story served to catapult it to mythic status. Moreover, Beatrice's victimization and ultimate execution by autocratic authority served to figure her as a martyr.[1] It has been claimed that "the 'legend of Beatrice' was born on the day she died" (Ricci 271), by the spectacle of her funeral that "resemble[d] a popular demonstration" and "an equivocal report of the case and execution" (v). As a legend, the tragic themes of patriarchal tyranny, incest, personal and social corruption, and systemic exploitation of disenfranchised bodies have garnered global interest in Beatrice's story. It has traversed centuries and nations and has incurred dozens of translations, adaptations, and remediations.

While visiting Italy in 1818, Percy Bysshe Shelley encountered a manuscript account of the history of the

Cenci family. Upon reading her story, Shelley was initially moved by the pathos of Beatrice, whom he saw as "violently thwarted from her [gentle] nature by the necessity of circumstance" (727). A year later, inspired by the story's themes of domestic and social injustice under patriarchal authority, Shelley composed a verse drama entitled *The Cenci,* with the object of bringing Beatrice's tragedy "home to [the] hearts" of the British people (729). More than a century and a half later, in 1992, the Canadian poet George Elliott Clarke encountered Shelley's verse drama while studying at Queen's University. His interest in the play instigated a collaboration with composer James Rolfe that led to the creation of the chamber opera, *Beatrice Chancy*. Their adaptation relocated Beatrice's story to the Annapolis Valley, Nova Scotia in the year 1801, and introduced themes of Canadian slavery and racial violence. In doing so, Clarke brings the violent history of Beatrice Cenci "home" to Canada by using it to reveal a history of racial oppression that has been carefully suppressed in Canadian national discourse.[2]

By re-imagining Beatrice as the mixed-race daughter of white slave owner Francis Chancy, Clarke's narrative recontextualization employs a European history of social and domestic violence in order to expose Canada's historic intimacy with racial violence and oppression. Not only was *Beatrice Chancy* influential in unveiling the censored history of slavery in Canada, it also proved to be groundbreaking in the world of new Canadian opera.[3] In "Embracing *Beatrice Chancy*, or In Defence of Poetry," Clarke delivers a candid reflection of the creative process he and Rolfe embarked upon with the opera. He expresses his frustration with the textual restrictions of the operatic form (primarily the need for brevity, as it takes longer to sing lines than to speak them). Clarke vented these frustrations in the form of a verse drama, or what he refers to as the opera's "evil twin," which he composed alongside the libretto (16). The verse drama, also entitled *Beatrice Chancy,* was written in Bellagio, Italy in 1998 while Clarke was on a Rockefeller Foundation Fellowship, and published in 1999 by Polestar Books in Victoria, British Columbia. This act of multimodal narrative (re)creation is an instance of what Hutcheon calls the various "afterlives" and "pre-lives" of adaptation: "Works of literature can have afterlives in their adaptations and translations, just as they have pre-lives, in terms of influences and models" (5). In terms of the "pre-lives" of *Beatrice Chancy,* Clarke cites both Shelley's play and the legend upon which it is based as primary sources for the opera, but then appends the libretto with a list of more than fifty additional influences, twenty-six of which are textual adaptations of the Cenci legend, including six plays, three operatic adaptations, a screenplay, and a sculpture. Clarke also sources other Beatrices, including Dante's Beatrice in *La Vita Nuova* and Shakespeare's Beatrice in *Much Ado About Nothing,* as well as Harriet Jacobs' slave narrative, *Incidents in the Life of a Slave Girl,* and two Beatrice restaurants. The sheer extent of this list of sources evinces the complex dialogue among multiple texts that is a central part of the creative process behind *Beatrice Chancy* both as an opera and as a verse drama.

Moreover, the process of textual recreation and reinterpretation is also part of Clarke's narrative effort to rebuild and reclaim an archive of Africadian identity within Canada's discourse of nationhood. The relegation of African-Canadian experiences to the margins of national narrative has occurred, in part, because of the selective nature of Canada's archives.[4] These archives strategically position the black body by including images that depict subordination while contradictorily silencing the nation's violent exercise of despotic power and racial privilege.[5] The narrative of *Beatrice Chancy* challenges this positioning in an attempt to re-narrate the history of a group that has lived *sotto voce* in Canadian national consciousness. A similar discourse of suppression characterizes the Cenci legend. Shelley addresses this in a footnote to the preface of his play where he reveals, "the Papal Government formerly took the most extraordinary precautions against the publicity of facts which offer so tragical a demonstration of its own wickedness and weakness; so that the communication of the [manuscript] had become, until very lately, a matter of some difficulty" (728). In emphasizing the past suppression of the Cenci story, Shelley calls attention to the silences that have been imposed on Beatrice's history and then employs these silences thematically throughout the play.

Shelley's *The Cenci* explores a system of patriarchal power where the male voice is sanctioned by a firmly entrenched network of tyrannical power relations, rooted in religious authority. Consolidated on three levels (the divine, the papal, and the domestic), this network of socio-political patriarchal control systematically silences the female voice. This tripartite structure of patriarchal power is particularly toxic as it allows tyrannical contagions to permeate all aspects of life, making it difficult for the marginalized to breathe, let alone speak. Throughout the play, Beatrice struggles to achieve vocal and physical liberation from patriarchal oppression. Yet her attempts to gain visibility in the system in which she is marginalized are constantly stymied, first by her father, and later by the system that sentences her to death for parricide. In the world of *The Cenci*, the authority of the father indicates a clear distinction between voices that are publically permissible (the voice of the patriarch) and those that are not (voices of subjugated individuals—usually women, though not exclusively as poor, unemployed men, like Giacomo, who are also marginalized within this discourse). But at the same time, the authority of the father suggests an essential link between the public and the private as it points to the reciprocal sanctioning of fathers within the system. In other words, if the domestic father is dependent on the Holy Father for socio-political power in the same way that the Holy Father depends on God the Father for the sanction of his power, it follows that the stability of the father's control in the home comes to represent the stability of the papal government. Therefore, the papal authorities will, for the right fee, publically sanction private acts of abuse and abjection, such as the physical and verbal abuse Count Cenci inflicts on his wife and children, in order to maintain the socio-political. However, despite their inherent co-dependability, the prospect of the boundary between the public and the private being traversed is a key source of anxiety for those in power. This is apparent when Beatrice speaks out against her father at the banquet he sardonically holds in celebration of the deaths of his two elder sons. In this scene, which explicitly conflates the public and the private, as public dignitaries are brought into the Cenci household, Beatrice presents herself before the patriarchy as a physical and vocal challenge to the system of privilege. In appealing to the guests to relieve her and her family from Cenci's tyranny, Beatrice's attempt at vocal insurrection endangers the stability of the patriarchal order and generates anxiety for her father, driving him to quickly suppress the moment by dismissing the guests: "Goodnight, farewell: I will not make you longer spectators of our dull domestic quarrels" (1.3.162–3). Because Beatrice's voice threatens to undermine Cenci's control, he quickly diffuses the situation. But it is this act that, in part, motivates the impending sexual assault of Beatrice.

The discourse of suppression in *The Cenci* continues with an incestuous rape enacted on Beatrice by her father that is never actually named.[6] The rape of Beatrice is simultaneously an instance of action and non-action. As the climax of the drama, first alluded to by Count Cenci at the beginning of the play, the rape motivates the subsequent action—the parricide, the trial, and the execution—yet remains silenced as, concealed off stage, it is neither seen nor heard. After the act is committed, Beatrice returns to her stepmother, Lucretia, unable to name the deed that has left her "veins" "contaminated" and her "limbs" "putrefy[ed]" (3.1.26, 96). In *Justice in The Cenci*, Laurence Lockridge suggests that by "not naming the incest, [Beatrice] tries to lend it an unreality" (97) in an attempt to evade and nullify the trauma of the incestuous sexual assault. But this evasion is not sufficient as Beatrice's refusal to articulate the act in answer to Lucretia's persistent questions still leaves her mentally and physically debilitated. Lucretia notes: "Thou art unlike thyself; thine eyes shoot forth / A wandering and strange spirit. Speak to me, / Unlock those pallid hands whose fingers twine with one another" (3.1.81–84). Beatrice experiences an overwhelming response to the rape that she associates with suffocation: "The air is changed to vapours such as the dead breath in charnel-pits! Pah! I am choked!" (3.1.14–16). In this incestuous sexual defilement Beatrice encounters a kind of death, one that is engendered by blood (a blood relation), infects through blood (incest/intercourse), and one that she considers resolving through an act of blood-letting:

> Oh blood, which art my father's blood,
> Circling through these contaminated veins,
> If thou, poured forth on the polluted earth,
> Could wash away the crime, and punishment
> By which I suffer—no, that cannot be! (3.1.95–99)

But this feeling of suffocation also covertly signals the miasma of oppression that the hegemonic discourse of patriarchal power generates for those who fall outside its system of privilege. Beatrice cannot name the act because it cannot be atoned by words: "No law … can adjudge and execute the doom of that which I suffer" (3.1.135–7). Her silence suggests the difficulty that victims of sexual abuse often have in articulating their experiences and the shame involved with exposing, expressing, and reliving instances of sexual violation. But it also attests to the fact that her body lies outside of the system of legal protection and privilege. Her experience cannot be fully articulated in a social order that renders her body abject.

In *Beatrice Chancy* the discursive limitations for victims of sexual abuse are felt even more acutely under slavery. In a critique of the slave narrative of Harriet Jacobs, Martha J. Cutter suggests that in such writings, "language practices … keep slaves disempowered" (210). She contends that Jacobs' narrative exhibits "the way religious, legal, and spoken discourses are used to create a false reality which imprisons slaves in a culture of silence" (215). This practice is revealed in the opera through Deal's conviction: "We own nothin' but our breath—… An' massa even poison that" (Clarke 3.2.23–5). However, it is not until after the rape that Beatrice realizes the full extent of her imprisonment within this system and the ways in which her body is controlled by hegemonic discourses of power and entitlement. Francis Chancy's supremacy in the system of power and racial privilege that governs early nineteenth-century Nova Scotia depends upon the commodification of women and slaves as "things" (Clarke 1.2.89–90). Within the slave system, Chancy's control is not only established on the basis of servitude, but also as sexual domination. When Beatrice declares her love for Chancy's slave Lead, her father interprets this as an undermining of her whiteness, something that he has bestowed upon her (both genetically and by, as he claims, sending her to the convent in Halifax), and also of his sexual entitlement. He attempts to reclaim this entitlement (which, ironically, he already has by law) in two acts of corporeal violence: his torture of Lead and his rape of Beatrice. After her father rapes her, Beatrice is forced to contend with her status as daughter, sexual object, and slave.

This new identity is a result of the trauma that the rape engenders. According to Cathy Caruth, the traumatic encounter is an instance where something "incomprehensible outside of the self … has already gone inside without the self's mediation, hence without any relation to the self, and this consequently becomes a threat to any understanding of what a self might be in this context" (131–132, 5n). In other words, trauma elicits a double consciousness, where one's self-concept becomes incongruous to how others perceive him or her.[7] This duality of self generates a sublime, even Gothic, trauma of identity. In both *Beatrice Chancy* and *The Cenci,* the double consciousness elicited from the traumatic sexual encounter is evidenced in Beatrice's "doubled" relationship to her father after the rape. The act of incestuous rape is, quite literally, an incomprehensible, unmediated physical intrusion, or penetration, that threatens the victim's concept of self. In the act of incest, the boundaries in the familial relationship deemed natural or permissible become blurred through doubling; Beatrice is now forced to see herself through the eyes of her father who acknowledges her as both a daughter and a sexual object. The combination of a natural (familial) relationship with her father and an unnatural one (as an object of sexual abuse) propels Beatrice into a state of trauma that borders on madness. However, in both texts, Beatrice does not let this trauma destroy her. Instead, she manipulates her double-conscious state into a source of liberation and rebellion. In other words, the psychic state of double consciousness is a liminal mental place suspended between knowing and feeling. This state, as I have already suggested, can elicit psychological trauma when one's knowledge of the self becomes challenged or limited by external forces of power. But by contrast, this state of double consciousness also provides room for resistance because the ability to know one thing and feel another allows the individual to imagine alternate possibilities for the self. In this way, the individual can assert his or her value in a system where he or she is essentially valueless and can *feel* empowered despite *knowing* he or she has been socially relegated to a position of powerlessness. The resistance that double consciousness occasions allows for actions to become reactions, opening the door for insurrection. In both texts, this resistance takes the form of parricide. Through an act of self-scrutiny, Beatrice resolves to no longer submit herself, and her soul, to a determined state of social abjection. Instead, she uses the moment to image the possibility of an alternate course of action and ultimately decides to have her father murdered, an act that momentarily overturns the systems of power and privilege that have reduced her to vocal and physical subordination.

In *Beatrice Chancy*, Beatrice takes this insurrection one step further by challenging the discursive limits to which she is subjected. Before she and Lead are about to carry out the murder of Francis, Lustra reminds Beatrice that Chancy is her father. But Beatrice rejects this term stating: "Call him what you like. / I call him my raper" (Clarke 4.1.47–8).[8] By insisting, without fear and without hesitation, on the term raper, Beatrice attempts to move away from socially determined language. By using it to replace the name of father she enacts a complete disavowal of familial structure, and an implicit disavowal of patriarchy. In this moment, Beatrice reconfigures the practice of naming as an imperial tool for ownership. Particularly by using the noun form of the word, the naming becomes not a *narration* of the event but rather *identifies* Francis, making its utterance a reciprocal act of ownership through which Beatrice re-claims her body and her past. In naming Francis as her raper, Beatrice remembers and articulates the violence that has been inflicted not only upon her, but also upon her mother and her ancestors. This is an important step in the process of cultural re-narration that the opera sets out to accomplish. It is through this act of naming that Beatrice generates a counterdiscourse that testifies to the alternate national experience of those marginalized by patriarchy and racism.

Although Beatrice speaks out against oppressive hierarchies, she, like Shelley's Beatrice, is still controlled by a politically determined language that positions her outside the domain of privilege.[9] In the end, Beatrice's conviction of Chancy has no social or political credibility because the language of violation does not register on a nationally abjected body. Ultimately she, in an echo of Shelley's Beatrice, will refuse linguistic justification and "not cry out" (Clarke 4.1.109). The justification of Beatrice is a central preoccupation for Shelley in his adaptation of the Cenci legend. In his preface to *The Cenci*, Shelley evinces his preoccupation with what he calls the "restless and anatomizing casuistry" of the Cenci legend, where "men seek the justification of Beatrice, yet feel that she has done what needs justification" (731). Although Beatrice is a victim of her father's criminal acts, she too becomes a criminal by orchestrating his murder. Shelley was particularly interested in the moral complexity (and ultimately the tragic nature) of this circumstance. Can (or should) an audience exonerate Beatrice for the crime of parricide because of the abuse she suffers at the hands of her father? This is also a topical question in discourses of slavery in terms of the problems of rebellion: slaves must fight violence with violence in order to achieve freedom from their oppressors. This concept of questionable justice is part of the subtext of *Beatrice Chancy*, first alluded to in the biblical imagery of the opening ring shout and becomes a pivotal part of the finale.

Both *The Cenci* and *Beatrice Chancy* are ambivalent on the point of violence as a means to achieve liberation, for although Beatrice succeeds in the elimination of her father, she is still subjected to the violent control of the law. Yet in the opera's finale, Beatrice is able to envision a new existence of equality and freedom. In her final aria Beatrice entreats the memory of her suffering: "Remember that we craved only love, / That we were the light that blazed as love died" (4.2.18–19). Beatrice's voice projects freedom as a reality, but one that is linked to the stark reality of death, evidenced by her adoption of the status of martyr: "Belovèd Jesus, take my blood, / Use it all to scour away our sins" (4.2.20–21). It is in death that liberation is achieved. This potential freedom, although it provides hope, does not excuse or exonerate acts of the past, nor does it subvert the violence of the narrative. As Clarke contends: "History is a moral force: one that indicts—and never absolves" (Beatrice Chancy 63). As adaptations of the Cenci legend, both Clarke's opera *Beatrice Chancy* and Shelley's verse drama *The Cenci* are interested in the movement from abjection to agency through acts of physical and vocal insurrection. Through adaptation the character of Beatrice is transformed from an Italian martyr into an African-Canadian freedom fighter whose act of vocal insurrection generates a counterdiscourse that contests systemic racial and sexual injustice.

Endnotes

1. See Groseclose, Barbara."The Incest Motif in Shelley's *The Cenci.*" *Comparative Drama* 19.3 (1985): 222–39. Print.
2. Cf: "In *Beatrice Chancy* this diasporan history is brought home, as it were, and made to confront hegemonic national narratives that would seek to stop it at the Canada-U.S. border" (Moynagh 116).
3. *Beatrice Chancy* has been one of the most successful contemporary Canadian operas to date, achieving a multi-production run across Canada. The opera was first performed in Halifax in 1999, then in Toronto and Edmonton in 2001. It has aired on both CBC Radio and CBC-TV, being "the first Canadian opera broadcast on television in more than 30 years, and the first

opera of any sort broadcast on CBC-TV since 1989" (Bernstein B4). Additionally, the role of Beatrice was the debut lead performance of Measha Brueggergosman who has gone on to become one of Canada's leading internationally acclaimed sopranos.

4. See: "Opera From The Soul." *The National*. CBC. 5 Oct. 1999. Television.
5. See: Clarke, George Elliott. Interview by Herb Wyile. "We Have to Recover Their Bodies." *Speaking in the Past Tense: Canadian Novelists on Writing Historical Fiction*. Waterloo: Wilfrid Laurier University Press, 2007. Print.
6. Shelley's silence around the act of rape is due, in part, to the censorship restrictions of the Stage Licensing Act that was in effect in Britain from the 18th century to the early part of the 20th century. I argue that Shelley's conscious employment of silence in *The Cenci* is not only to appease the censor but also thematically motivated. As a letter to Thomas Love Peacock from 1819 reveals, Shelley believed he had treated the subject with "particular delicacy," so that it would be suitable for the stage (*L.* ii. 102). However, the play is immediately relegated to the closet after it is declared too "objectionable" by the manager of Covent Garden, Thomas Harris (Shelley 279).
7. The notion of double consciousness has also been used to characterize the slave experience. In *Beatrice Chancy*, Beatrice, as a mulatta, already possesses a certain degree of double consciousness: "My singed skin / Tells white men I'm their whore, / Tells black men I'm their serf" (Clarke 2.1.18–20).
8. This act of naming distinguishes Clarke and Rolfe's adaptation from Shelley's verse drama, where it is left unarticulated.

9. See: Worton, Michael. "Speech and Silence in The Cenci." *Essays on Shelley*. Ed. Miriam Allott. Liverpool: Liverpool University Press, 1982. 105–24. Print.

Works Cited

Bernstein, Tamara. "A Canadian Opera Worth Cheering About." Rev. of Beatrice Chancy by George Elliott Clarke and James Rolfe. *National Post* 8 Feb. 2001: B4. Print.

Caruth, Cathy. *Unclaimed Experience: Trauma, Narrative, and History*. Baltimore: Johns Hopkins University Press, 1996. Print.

Clarke, George Elliott. "Beatrice Chancy: A Libretto in Four Acts." *Canadian Theatre Review* 96 (1998): 63–77. Print.

—. "Embracing Beatrice Chancy, or In Defense of Poetry." *The New Quarterly* 20.3 (2001): 15–24. Print.

Cutter, Martha J. "Dismantling 'The Master's House' Critical Literacy in Harriet Jacobs' *Incidents in the Life of A Slave Girl*." *Callaloo*19.1 (1996): 209–225. Print.

Hutcheon, Linda. "In Defence of Literary Adaptation as Cultural Production." *M/C Journal* 10.2 (2007). Web.

Lockridge, Laurence. "Justice in *The Cenci*." *Wordsworth Circle* 19.2 (1988): 95–8. Print.

Moynagh, Maureen. "'This History's Only Good for Anger': Gender and Cultural Memory in Beatrice Chancy." *Signs* 28.1 (2002): 97–124. Print.

Ricci, Corrado. *Beatrice Cenci*. Trans. Bishop, Morris and Henry Longan Stuart. New York: Boni and Liveright, 1925. Print.

Shelley, Percy Bysshe. "*The Cenci*: A Tragedy in Five Acts." *The Poems of Shelley*. Ed. Kelvin Everest and Geoffrey

Matthews. Vol 2. London: Pearson Education Limited, 2000. 2 vols. 712–875. Print.

—. *The Letters of Percy Bysshe Shelley*. Ed. Frederick L. Jones. Vol. 2. Oxford: Clarendon Press, 1964. 2 vols. Print.

“I am the lyrical warrior”: George Elliott Clarke’s *Black*

GIULIO MARRA

Black (2006) is composed of eight sections united by the recurring term “black”. The starting point for the collection can be found in the preceding work *Blue* (2001) and more precisely in the lines that begin that volume:

> *History* fell upon us like the lash—
> Lacerating. (19)

In the opening section the poet poses the conflict he experiences with language and culture, as lived in all its crudeness, and the feeling of being successively disintegrated. It begins with a distressing, and at the same time, defiant celebration of a hanging. Here *Black* finds its precedence in *Execution Poems* (2001), dedicated to the hangings of George and Rufus Hamilton in 1949. The historical reality of this event furnishes the perspective. The speaker sees the world through the optics of an internal, angry disharmony. This 1949 hanging speaks of racism, of poverty, of a vindictive justice system and is constructed in *Black* in the same terms. The reader feels the painful sensations expressed by the poet when he identifies himself with: "Le nègre negated, meager, c'est moi," ("Negation" in *Blue* and in *Execution Poems*). The lamentation is so strong that it brings the poet to reformulate what in society is considered noble, beautiful and just, through a poetic journey which brings the poet to struggle to find and to redefine his own different self.

In the opening poem of *Black*, "George and Rue: Coda," the image that captures the murder of Burgundy is that of the moon: "that night: a white man's face." The punishment is public and an example, but it is not just a question of justice when we encounter a "British-accented lynching. To exterminate two germs." We see an indication of the inner conflict of the poet who, on the one hand, condemns, and, on the other, tries to explain the motivation for the murder. Here is the justification for Rue's crime in *Execution Poems*:

> The blow that slew silver came from two centuries back
> It took that much time and agony to turn a white man's whip
> Into a black man's hammer. (35)

This justification, which does not deal directly with the murder, is corroborated by a seminal episode narrated in the section "Black Mail," the last pages of *Black*, in which Clarke remembers an analogous murder committed with a hammer during slavery: "a black boy was slain by a blow from a hammer wielded by his master."

The hanged men swing in the air, "Those dangling feet, pealing"—almost the toll of a bell offered to the reader's conscience—poses the question of where justice resides. "A murmur of light, eh?" It is almost inevitable to recall the words from Milton's celebrated sonnet: "When I consider how my light is spent," a sonnet in which the poet asks God what he must do to be saved:

> "Doth God exact day-labour, light denied?"
> I fondly ask. But patience, to prevent
> That murmur, soon replies: "God doth not need
> Either man's works or his own gifts."

After the hanging, we arrive at the first reflection on poetry. In a "Letter to a Young Poet," the speaker comments on his own (?) ambition to write "a poem on Love," but he soon realizes he would poison, or has poisoned, love. The "blackness" of the hanging, placed at the beginning of *Black* and of human history (Cain's murder of Abel), has found a place in the heart and mind of the poet. What he writes from that moment is impurity: the torment of the rejection, an *ominous obsession*, sustains his words with repugnant images:

> See, the poet's body whelps carrion-insects,
> Vomit some worms, some ants, some wasps, some bees—
> Things malevolent and marvelous at once
> Their horrifically mixed-up mouths chewing,
> Ripping, devastating your heart. (17)

A new spiritual contortion follows when the poet substitutes the love in "Letter to a Young Poet" with hate. With the word "hate" we enter into the interior conflict of the poet, which is essentially a debate over language. Here the cultural and historical precedence seems to be George of *Execution Poems*, who answers questions with the irrelevant (or irreverent) aside:

> I really speak Coloured, but with a Three Mile Plains accent
> . . .
> Ma English be a desert that don't bloom less watered by rum.

Successively, in "Language," English, we learn, is:

> Balderdash and *braggadocio*
> ...
> A tongue that cannibalizes all other tongues. (18)

And in *Blue,* "III.I", Clarke uses bitter irony:

> Your black mouth ought to be elegant with snow –
> So words emerge icy, paralyzed: Britannic. (*Blue* 133)

The poet suffers an inevitable temptation for impurity. He hates the language that hate orders him to use, and halts for a moment of inaction, before the black ink that captures the words, before a subject and a colour that are prefigured like innocence, but translate into frightening words:

> Speculate on the words still bottled blackly
> In placid ink—
> Fear what may leap from the *Innocence*. (18)

Here is a first announcement of the poet's feelings towards history. Language is in itself innocent but such innocence is irretrievably lost as soon as words are brought to light. Words enter history, language is a product of history, a history read as violence. Language is therefore a testimony of an imposed and violent civilization that the black poet encounters, which he refuses and rebels against. Instead of the sweet syllables of one's mother tongue, the poet experiences the harshness of words that hurt the lips and break the jaws that pronounce them. The English language is depicted as "the tang and bray of a savage civilization" and in *Execution Poems* English is defined as "Malignant English".

From this painful awareness the poet begins, in "Language," to construct his artistic identity, by rejecting language:

> A botch of art in slovenly English
> Bad grammar, bad everything;
> It cannot perform ethically. (18)

In these poems on the inability of the poet to write in English, the recurring image is a sensation of physical repulsion:

> So I can only vomit up speech—
> Half-digested English—
> Soiling it with virulent Negro stomach juices. (19)
>
> I spit out verse—ruddy larvae, red writhing worms—
> Like a TB victim hawking scarlet phlegm into a sink.

The poet has ample space to demonstrate his political and cultural positions, which Clarke had manifested in previous poems, such as "Antiphony" and "Calculated Offensive" (*Blue*), where he expresses a strong reaction to British literature and European culture. In "For Evelyn Shockley" (*Black*) he defines himself as "A herring-choker Negro with a breath of brine," recalling both his Nova Scotia origin ("My black 'Bluenose' brogue") and the fact that his language is constructed as "A feinting langue haunted by each slave boat." Clarke justifies his linguistic choice and stylistically distinguishes it from Standard English for a compulsive use of alliteration: "My brains were brass, fucked, alloyed By alliteration" and in *Blue,* "III. I," he quotes comments on his poetic style: "They say, 'Put away all that alliteration. It's too much like jazz'"). In "IV. ii for

Andrea Thompson," Clarke summarizes what "Caucasian critics" describe as "the repercussions of black voice":

> ... our "exuberant, sing-song
> Poetry", our "sure-good Jive", "Rap rhymes",
> Our "big smiles", our big fun with "big words." (26)

His linguistic choices include puns, assonance and rhythmic play, seldom used vocabulary, strongly idiosyncratic, at times dialect, slang, and neologisms in the superabundant variety of adjectival selections. This linguistic radicalism—or deviance—is summarized in the line: "So rum-pungent Africa mutes perfumed Europe" (*Black*). The frequent polysemic word Clarke uses in his poetry is 'repercussions', meaning reactions, echoes, and also the sound of instruments like cymbals, xylophones, rattles, Caribbean steel drums; these indicate the distant sound of a "grammar scummed far, so far, of an Oxford/ or Webster disciplinary." His poetry is dedicated to a political and cultural project when he tries

> ... to lift an entire ocean into literature—
> The slaver's Atlantic, yes, Africa's sepulcher. (24)

And when he wants to recover the sound and constant chatter of the Halifax taverns, which provide him with the original language he looks for:

> I had to sing—or write out—*black* noise:
> *dat* hubbub and hurly-burly of Halifax pubs,
> girly, boyo, all *dat* hurdy-gurdy gabble,
> all *dat* dumpy, lumpy, frumpy speech! (25)

In the last poems of the section "Black Lung," Clarke confirms his ambitions. Looking back, he sees the weak side of his poetry: "Rhyming Oxonian and Negronian" and wants to find "Higher quality coal—or iron—or gold." He accepts, in "Spoken Word," a series of poetic tasks (which recall "Nu(is)ance" and "To X.X." in *Blue*):

> Invent stray, pungent lyrics,
> Callous as *jacquerie*, violent
>
> As addled presidents,
> To clap boisterousness into poetry,
>
> To collide words together,
> Go, scratch poems in frost,
>
> Daub poems in sweat.
> Ain't Shakespeare a broke-ass tongue,
>
> Mixing pig's breath of sulphur
> With hose's breath of sugar,
>
> Some unpronounceable English trash—
> Rancid, acidic, rash? Balderdash! (22)

The range of his innovations in style and content are realized in the section entitled "Black Ink" in which, after reciting the Anglo-Saxon canon in "The Canon"—from Chaucer to Milton, to Donne, to Blake, to Hopkins, to Whitman—he defines the offensive capacity of a good poem, which "stabs like a dagger now, Explodes later like a grenade" and ideally refers to his essay entitled "Let Us Now Attain Polyphonous Epiphanies," where he confesses to have been nourished by the "wanton tons of Afro-Americana, 'Negro' verse come all the way from Harlem, Chi-town and L.A.":

> I read intensively the glow-in-the-dark names: Langston Hughes, LeRoi Jones (Amiri Baraka), Gwendolyn

> Brooks, Alice Walker, and Ishmael Reed. But I most adored the sultry smoky verse of Jean Tommer (see *Cane*, the Southern-fried songs of Sterling Brown, the soul anthems of Carolyn M. Rodgers, the mystical bohemianism of Conrad Kent Rivers, the intellectual dandyism of Melvin B. Tolson, the Africanist musings of Henry Dumas, and above all, the beautiful, baroque decors, gutbucket music, and history-informed genius of Robert Hayden (1913–1980), himself a pupil of W.H. Auden—and the blues. (*Blues and Bliss* 25)

When he comes to describe the principles which inspire him, he confirms the shattering potential which poetry should have: "Ink and voice—the liqueurs of the savage—Ignite the very fire of freedom". Still the pen that gives voice to his thoughts succeeds in producing "psychological blues." There is always a tension in Clarke's poems between a poetic tradition which he would like to free himself of but which, inevitably, he feels is a part of himself and the desire to reach a goal of his own, where poetry and ethical perspective coexist, a goal, as he writes in "Language," that will enable him to "perform ethically":

> All true songs acknowledge Pain,
> But Love is everything.

This is to say that Clarke's poetic itinerary tends to abandon well-trodden paths to proceed towards the affirmation of ideal values such as love, beauty and justice. In the realm of justice—both in the poetry and in plays such as *Whylah Falls* and *Beatrice Chancy*—we find that beauty, or the aesthetic, nourishes itself with the lost voices of history and with the foul breath of real people; people of colour who died in transatlantic voyages, or were condemned by white justice, whether they committed crimes or were victims of crime. Or they are fellow poets of whom we read in the most tormented poems of the section "Black Ink": "À Edgar Mittelhölzer" (a Guyanese novelist and suicide) and "À Arthur Nortje" (a South African poet who died from an overdose). Here Clarke bewails precisely the fatal roles played by injustice, by social alienation, and by human misery. Here we read of the difficulty encountered by Mittelhölzer in course of his life; and his *angst* is realized in a ferocious attack against a myth of white literature, the innocence of Miranda threatened by Caliban:

> A delicious rape, eh? Caliban tupping Miranda.
> The white whore whelps a black child: poetry.
> But it's not Britannia's, it's yours. (42)

The wounds of history become the blood of poetry, as the subject of spirituals, of proverbs, of the blues, of sermons, of Gospels, and of newspapers. The voice of the poet who wants to become a poet, even if he hears mothers' howls multiplying like cockroaches, is distinguished from the annoying and fussy English poets, and from the screaming American writers:

> The English poets tut-tut; the Yankee poets yap:
> But the true Negro poet sings and drums and cries. (42)

The song of revenge that Clarke articulates before the image of Mittelhölzer, who sets himself on fire (a fire which shatters him like a mirror), collects the ashes that Clarke mixes with the earth until they become ink, "fresh India ink," with which he forms the outline of his thoughts:

> A black flag of ink
> Proclaiming anarchy—in piracy—in a white desert.
> Your ashen heart reveals this ashen prophecy:
> All ex-colonial speakers of English be liars. (44)

Arthur Nortje is also associated with the use of a language and a grammar that is born of suffering, which erases the white grammar of existence:

> Your vernacular sops and oozes black ink
> The color of drool out a smashed mouth,
> Stammering, dyeing all those white grammars,
> Blotting the air. (45)

In the section "Black Earth," Clarke seems to become discursive and his verse echoes a Wordsworthian "recollection in tranquility." The first piece, "Towards a Geography of Three Mile Plains, N.S.," begins with an act of memory: "Remember the well and its water encrusted by ice." But why should we expect the figure of "Bill" Wordsworth to remain a fleeting apparition? This is a land of strong odors from urine and excrement, where the only pear tree has been burned by lightning, where the Ten Commandments are read on the windows of an "abandoned, dead-minister-owned house", where ugly weeds sprout from abandoned pianos. The moral condemnation is spread over the whole landscape, including apples that are "gangrenous blossoms" and bulrushes that are set alight. A carnal love is pictured in "kinky ink" and takes place among steel railway tracks, mosquitoes, railways ties and gravel, in "funk and honey slime." The poet in "VI, i for Walter M. Borden, C.M." is "A gardener in a graveyard," an assertion written during a visit to gardens, where the poet digresses into an experience which recalls "The Garden" of Andrew Marvell, but here we meet the ambiguous sensations of a seventeenth-century *Et in Arcadia Ego*. Deception is ever present even in this paradise, where there is no freedom to let nature flourish; instead, it hides a serpent and poison. The air is full of perfume from roses, but it also smells "like a bordello." Insects flit among the juicy red pears, but the fallen fruit is "teeming/ Also with maggots as fierce as asps." And so the sky is the color of sapphire, "But the round stinks of dying apples, berries"; stagnant water in "Annapolis Royal's Historic Gardens" sits as quiet "As lethal flowers" and, walking among the trees, one scents "the reek of rot under a thrusting tree." These powerful contrasts are muted in the "Italian poems" such as "À Bellagio" ("I" and "II"), where memory becomes delicate and sentimental and we observe a tender farewell to a place loved by the poet.

The natural world appeals to Clarke; he dedicates to it marvellous observations. But at the end of the first stanza of "Nisan" (a period in the Hebrew calendar which corresponds to March-April), he describes the April rain as "polishing lenses/ Of water in fields" and returns to political condemnation: "Could such charged endless/ Churn even scour away Parliament's filth?" A Parliament in "III, iv" (*Blue*) is described as "The Great Greasy Way." In the "Imperial Rose Garden," the geometrical design "mirrors triangulated, assassins' gunfire," and the marvellous complexity of colours suggest "A political party of Machiavellian intent."

In the last section, the anger is calmed before the tomb of Pound in Venice. I would say that the rest of the collection experiments with a new sensibility that abandons anxious tones and focuses on constructing, reconstructing, or describing feeling and actions always at the centre of a black poetics. This presupposes that nature, the places, the meetings, and the loves resonate with history and human courtesy. Love, in particular, appears as the major discourse that Clarke follows. It is a love that does not disdain sarcastic or erotic tones, the ideal or explicitly carnal, and at times recalls the bitter satire that Swift uses in his meetings with his own beloved, Celia. In other poems, particularly those dedicated to Geeta he offers an ideal and noble representation of love.

In these poems nature and human passion prevail, especially in the recollection of feelings of love, almost always painful and lost as in the poem, "La Vérité à Ottawa." Here the description of the city is pointed, almost technical and accompanied by the memory of "acidic love that seeped/ Into all the sutures and silences of the marriage." In "La Vérité à Ottawa (II)," there are references to other fickle, amorous experiences more fictional than real, more word constructions than concrete acts:

> I suffered vicious visions
> Of that Bible-toting tease, than hymn-singing quim,
> That wriggle of a woman in a squiggle of a dress. (73)

This is followed by notations on "Their scented *émail* of baby powder and sweat", "Pythagorean obscenities" and the evocation of a "unique queen, Apricilious"; a rendering of linguistic word play of a sexual act: "In a lush organ grinding of plush organs", or an example of mythical labour: "Augean cock plunging into Stygian—o Sisyphean—pussy, sapping." Then we arrive at the dominant section, "Black Eye," which to me constitutes a kind of purgatory in which the poet declares (as in "A Beautiful Plague") his wish to navigate through "The dark fog of *amour*." In reality, he seems to want to liberate himself of obsession or to liberate an eroticism ever-hungry and cosmic. He dreams in a pastiche of sounds "how to escalate from conjecture to ejaculate joy" or imagines a woman who falls like a star on the velvet of black fur:

> Let her tumble like a star against velvet black,
> Her morals crumbling mine all night. (82)

Or he imagines seeing, in "Watch," a woman with a sensuous pace whom he erotically desires to transform from a silly girl into a "snorting bitch":

> Her breasts jousting with her blouse:
> Nipples startingly, vividly rigid. (83)

In the erotic universe of Clarke, we find space for a liberated spirit that borders on machismo, if it was not for Clarke distinguishing between reality and imagination when he says in "Gynography": "Only the dream of Africadia is written here," or when, in "Beautiful Plague," he turns to the fairytale:

> When Peeping Tom eyes Sleeping Beauty
> Despair parades through *Paradise* (84)

He also reduces the erotic dream to a black ink well: "Ink copulates with Intellect; Poetry cries out."

This is a glorification of love, of poetic joy more than a real manifestation of eroticism. It is a vision of the world that rises from verse with assonance, alliteration, and even in descriptions of nature as in "Nisan":

> Then lightning
> Punches down through clouds, while rain's lush push
> Rush, and gush, a crushing inundation,
> Flushes out snow, but foundations first flowers. (68)

Or he uses natural images to describe the desires of love:

> Craving to ply gold lacquer upon her limbs
> To be that brassy sunlight gilding her snow. (89)

The main sections, "Black Ice" and "Black Cloud," I find less suggestive and more explicitly political. We move from "Moral Maxims" to brief reflections on the history of the twentieth century and evocations on the assassinations of J.F. Kennedy and Malcolm X, "Black star having wings." He recalls the attack and fall of the twin towers in "IX/XI," and the antithesis between the ill-treated Jean Chrétien and Pierre Elliott Trudeau, to whom Clarke has devoted a major dramatic play.

The two last sections, "Black Light" and "Black Velvet" seem to me to constitute points of arrival. Here the initial anger of one looking for a usable identity denied him as a man and as a poet, seems to have evaporated and lead to a consciousness that, first of all, has to come to terms with family and the places of his origins. Secondly, it must deal with the amorous sentiments here quite removed from the erotic threats that I focused on earlier. It is here that the dichotomy signalled at the beginning takes shape, leaving clear evidence of the ideal tension, the desire for truth and beauty, which characterizes the entire opus of Clarke. If we were to adopt a Dante-like structure, Dante being a poet that Clarke knows well, we could say that Clarke begins in an "inferno," crosses a "purgatorio," and arrives at a "paradiso." In these last two sections we meet a pacified man, one who digs deep within himself and becomes conscious of his origins and his humanity. In "A Discourse on My Name" he speaks of the man Clarke, while in "À Geeta" (cf. "Discourse on Pure Virtue" in *Blue*) he speaks about the man and the poet. Notwithstanding that the name George Elliott Clarke signifies a triple, British ancestry: English, Scottish and Irish, he declares himself Africadian, since his name denounces "our utter subjection," or else exacts "a most curious revenge" and it is this last which the poet will execute.

His irony is ready when he translates the name Elliott with its Hebrew meaning as "Man of God." Notwithstanding that he finds himself "amongst the bleakest, blackest sinners" he nevertheless finds in his name:

> My constant admiration of virtue
> My constant desire for redemption (125)

Here is the first truth about the poet and the man, that he asserts himself etymologically, being a "religious man" (Elliott), a scholar (Clarke) and a farmer (George). Behind the projection of etymological fantasies, there emerges the reality of Clarke's family and human history. George is the name of his great-grandfather, "George Johnson, / A Mi'kmaq still living when I was born." Elliott is from the protagonist Elliott Ness from the TV series *The Untouchables*. And so we arrive at Clarke, the name that carries the pain of Black history:

> The site of my bondage to African slavery
> In its Caribbean phase. (127)

The poet proudly reclaims his Caribbean origins and at the same time feels the weight of history on his shoulders:

> But I feel that Clarke is too much a part of clanking history—
> Anchors, chains, leg-irons, fetters, horseshoes—(128)

In the following poem, "Morality Sonnet," Clarke changes tone and enters a very intimate phase. First there is a reflection on death, on the inevitable unstoppable invasion of the enemy of veins, arteries, nerves, muscles, tissue and organs, even to the heart which "calcifies to bone." Clarke turns to the Horatian ode, *Exegi monumentum aere perennius,* the idea that poetry conquers time and is more enduring than bronze:

Flagging, I hurl these words
To shout down Time
Just as it becomes Eternity. (130)

But at the same time, *à la manière d'Ovide*, he describes himself in "III. Iv" (*Blue)* with terribly ironic self-recognition:

Like some sad fool pissing against the hurricane
I fling these words against eternity. (138)

It is in the intimate dimension that prevails in "Black Velvet" that we find the two concluding poems of the collection. I would say that "À Geeta" constitutes the exact conclusion of the images of beauty represented by the photographs of Ricardo Scipio that Clarke places as the introduction of each section, a celebration of black beauty which oscillates between literary creation and reality. In "Gynography" Clarke compares real girls to the beauty celebrated in *Whylah Falls*, a poetic collection and a drama:

Among all the beautiful girls down here,
Only that one from Whylah Falls is beautiful. (86)

The ideal girls are realized in the figure of Geeta. We are reading an erotic and passionate poem to the woman he loves:

Call yourself, glancingly
"A small, brown woman"
for the phrase is exact:
You are diminutive, Indian, and a *femme*. (136)

He wishes to give to the reality of the woman he loves a mythical dimension and he lets himself go (as in "IV. ii for

Andrea Thompson") with "big words," a kind of apotheosis for the "just five feet tall" Geeta:

> But your mind encompasses God
> And your heart compasses the world,
> And you overwhelm even towering fools. (136)

The figure of Geeta oscillates between the eroticism of her appearance ("whose skin is alive with the night-undressing sun") to a mythical apotheosis:

> Ah Pomona of Mauritius
> Kali of Ile Maurice. (136)

This eroticism is manifest even in the errors that issue from voluptuous lips: "Even our English errors are erotic!" The spiritual apparitions along the beaches of North Carolina, Barbados, and Mauritius are "some crimson bird-of-paradise erupted/ From amid slippery greenery," and the veils which she wears are "just a breeze," light like the moon after a rain. In her, Clarke finds the end of his amorous travels, a moment of pacification in a woman who, under the guidance of John Donne, he describes "[a]s a country no one has colonized." And so his love poems may be able to "even out-race you, Time!" And in "III.iv" he imagines a public of lovers who,

> Will love and make love and marry
> With some of my words on their lips (*Blue* 140)

The poetry that concludes the collection is presented like a human and poetic testament. Perhaps following "Au Tombeau de Pound" and "Le Tombeau de Bishop" in *Blue* and "Au Tombeau de Pound (II)" in *Black*, Clarke imagines that he has arrived at the end of the temporal arc of life and reassesses what is most valuable in his experiences.

The poem appears to be a natural continuation of "A Discourse on My Name." Here Clarke speaks about himself within the context of his family and their locations. In "Will" he speaks about himself and it is inevitable that he also speaks about death. *Black* begins and ends with striking images of death, an execution and a contemplation on death, which in reality allows us to interpret life. There are no heroic ideas in this poem; first there is the desire about where and how to conduct his life:

> I would like, if possible,
> An oasis beside the Atlantic (139)

He sees ample flowerbeds of lilies and lilacs, "a stone bench for lovers," volumes of black berries in August, books to remember, rum, and a place to wait for the return of April flowers. The same expectations are resumed in "For my funeral": a white shroud, wild flowers, the pillow his mother made for him when he was a child, music, a lot of music, and above all,

> The Choir doing "Pass Me Not"
> Mournful, *mournful*! (141)

He wants poems read beside his tomb in Windsor, Nova Scotia, and "someone, please plant Lombardy poplars nearby."

Works Cited

Clarke, George Elliott. *Beatrice Chancy*. Vancouver: Polestar Book Publishers, 1999.

—. *Black*. Vancouver: Polestar Book Publishers, 2006.

—. *Blue*. Vancouver: Polestar, 2001.

—. *Execution Poems*. Wolfville, N.S.: Gaspereau Press, 2001.

—. *George & Rue*. Toronto: Harper Collins, 2005.

—. *Whylah Falls*. Vancouver: Polestar, 1990.

Marvell, Andrew. "The Garden." *The Norton Anthology of English Literature*. 6th edition. M.H. Abrams. Ed. New York: W.W. Norton, 1996. p. 817.

Milton, John. "When I Consider How My Life Is Spent." *The Norton Anthology of English Literature*. Op.cit. p. 661.

George Elliott Clarke's *Othello*

DIANA BRYDON

"After Howlin' Will Shakespeare, Blind Jack Milton,
and Missouri Tom Eliot, I'm just one more dreamer
to hoist a guitar and strum Sixhiboux Delta Blues. Oh yes."
(Clarke 1990: 53)

Although "Howlin' Will Shakespeare" leads Clarke's list of precursor-dreamers and blues jazzmen, he is far from alone. Some might think it perverse to single Shakespeare out from among the crowds of famous writers who jam Clarke's work.[1] Indeed, my first reaction on reading *Whylah Falls* was to imagine Clarke as a PhD student in English literature who had spent far too much time cramming for comprehensives and drunk far too much coffee in the process. That effect, the anxiety of influence that haunts modernism and postcolonialism in different but related ways, emerges as one note within the polyphonic structure of the whole, but it is often drowned out by the exuberance and inventiveness of Clarke's play with the different traditions that he has inherited. Published interpretations of *Whylah Falls* have paid little attention to the Shakespearean intertext as such, preferring to focus on elements of the poem's formal constitution or its thematic engagements with Nova Scotian place and history. Ultimately, I do not see the "anxiety of influence" strongly marking Clarke's aesthetic.[2] Far more powerful is Clarke's desire to write his people and his place into historical memory, through creating a literature that proclaims itself as conscious mythology. The urgency of this task is palpable: "I feel I am constantly writing against our erasure, and yet the erasure continues" (Moynagh 73). Part of this task involves writing against "received notions of blackness" (Moynagh 75). Some of the most powerful of these are articulated in Shakespeare's *Othello*. But another part of that erasure is the forgetting of what Clarke sees as an important fact: "African-Canadian literature has always been international" ("Eyeing" 1997: xv).

In *Whylah Falls*, one might easily conclude that the citations of other writers drown out the sole note signalled by the naming of a single character "Othello." Most articles on the text barely discuss it. Yet I will argue that this naming and the story of Othello Clemence lie at the heart of this book and its later transformation into drama. In attending to the function of invoking *Othello* in *Whylah Falls*, I am acutely aware of Chris Bongie's doubled set of warnings: against "spasms of high seriousness" and against yielding to postcolonial anxieties about popularity and value, without investigating their fraught relations to the canon and to questions about the role of art in community. Clarke himself addresses these issues in interviews, suggesting that his work exists "in two different modes": the "print-oriented" and the "speech-oriented" but that he tries to mesh the two to reach a wider audience (Foster and Ruprai 20), thereby satisfying Canadians' unfulfilled desire for "some kind of public speech that has true resonance" (Ibid.15).

How do Clarke's invocations of Shakespeare's Othello create such speech? What do they reveal about the local uses of Shakespeare in creating communal identities under contemporary conditions? Where does Canada fit within the international dialogue now developing between Shakespeare studies and postcolonial studies?[3] For the critic working on Canadian dialogues with black Atlantic traditions, further questions emerge. How does one talk about belonging in a multicultural nation and within contexts of diaspora, which may homogenize more than differentiate different origins and trajectories of movement? George Elliott Clarke, Dionne Brand, Marlene NourbeSe Philip and Rinaldo Walcott, among others, have been influential in bringing such questions to a national audience, and another generation of scholars is now emerging with an expanded set of questions.[4]

At an earlier stage in postcolonial criticism, during the 1980s, critics were tempted by Salman Rushdie's notion of a postcolonial "writing back" against the monuments of empire. That model is now complicated by Babelian investigations of the ambivalences and complicities of such citations, investigations particularly appropriate to the fraught contexts of settler-invader societies, an insight that Clarke makes much of in all his work. The "ghosts of slavery" (Sharpe) further challenge the discourse of civility embraced by Canadian settler nationalism, but in Clarke's analysis, less to discredit it than to hold it to its promise.

Language is Clarke's site for negotiating these realignments. Although Clarke readily embraces the postcolonial model of "answering back," he incorporates it within a "polyphonic poetics" (Fiorentino) which mixes Shakespearean echoes with those of various black cultural traditions. About his use of Elizabethan language in *Beatrice Chancy*, Clarke says: "I don't apologize for using Elizabethan language in a work about Canadian slavery ... I see the flavour as absolutely appropriate. I felt compelled to go there. I am answering back to Shakespeare and to Dante and to Shelley" (Nurse 30). But what does it mean to answer back to Shakespeare in *Whylah Falls*?

For Clarke, it seems partly a matter of self-validation, partly homage and partly a way of writing his own place into the great tradition, but on his own terms. As Ted Davidson suggests, he writes himself into the lineage of "father-poets" (206) who form the canon, and he writes "against the threat of white cancellation" (267), the fate of every poet confronted by a blank page but one with special resonance for the black poet who sees white cancellation as manifesting a potent but sometimes silent racism. *Whylah Falls'* form of answering back, then, recovers Canada's active moments of white cancellation and the voices it silences, redefining home and exile, the erotics of desire and epithalamium, and weaving them into a narrative that teaches the apparently universal lesson of "How Beauty honeys bitter pain" (152). The death of Clarke's Othello forms the pivotal moment in his text, making erasure visible and delaying, possibly indefinitely, the realization of desire. Michael Bristol's chapter, "Race and the comedy of abjection in *Othello*," can be read in dialogue with Clarke's *Whylah Falls*, to illuminate the Canadian readings of Shakespeare's *Othello* that each author provides. Bristol situates *Othello* within a tradition of great stories that "express the collective bad conscience of our civilization" (175). *Whylah Falls* invokes that collective bad conscience but shifts the terms of address from Shakepeare's implied English audience to a multicultural and contemporary Canadian one. In the process, much of the painful challenge of the original story is softened, yet echoes remain. Bristol reads *Othello*, less as a tragedy than "as a comedy of abjection that depends on a background of racial hatred and violence" (175–6). One might say the same of *Whylah Falls*. I read *Whylah Falls* as an anti-modern and romantic text in the Canadian Red Tory tradition, celebrating the survival of a beleaguered community in a context of racial hatred and violence, which accuses the state of failing to guarantee its promise of "peace, order and good government" to all its citizens.

In interpreting "*Othello* as a carnivalesque text in the Bakhtinian sense" (179), Bristol suggests that the play may be read "as the carnivalesque derangement of marriage as a social institution and of the contradictory role of heterosexual desire within that institution." I find this focus on the institution of marriage a helpful complement to Dorothy Wells' examination of Clarke's revisions of Petrarchan and Elizabethan sonnets and of pastoral poetic conventions in *Whylah Falls*. Clarke describes the derangement of marriage, most notably through the tragic figure of Saul Clemence and his incestuous affair with his stepdaughter Missy, which contributes to Shelley's distrust of men and the language of love, but as Maureen Moynagh argues, Clarke's love story appears to have a happy ending, with X and Shelley together once more (2000: 217). Clarke celebrates heterosexual desire and particularly the beauty of black women as the object of black men's desire through the twinned courtships of X and Shelley and Pablo and Amarantha, and through the brief affair that X enjoys with Selah before returning to Shelley. Yet there is also a thread of homosocial desire linking the poem's three male poets, X, Pablo and Othello, forming a strong undercurrent to the poem's explicit courtship story. One might argue that the violated body of the dead Othello forms the true heart of this tale.

Clarke's story is set during an economic depression. He pays close attention to the material realities of his characters' lives. In speculating about how a contemporary audience might have received Shakespeare's play, Bristol suggests that *Othello* may have functioned "as an adaptation of the social custom, common throughout early modern Europe, of charivari" (180). This same social custom, still practiced in rural communities in Canada today, is immortalized in such Canadian texts as Susanna Moodie's *Roughing it in the Bush* and Lawrence Hill's *Any Known Blood*, where it is explicitly employed to police interracial marriages. Through invoking charivari, and Moodie's account of it, Bristol reads *Othello* as staging "a ceremony of broken nuptials" and "the unmasking of a transgressive marriage" (180). Clarke's writing back to *Othello* may be clearest here. Although charivari is not explicitly evoked in *Whylah Falls*, I think it haunts the text's delicate negotiation of communal taboo, reinforced by its images echoing scenes of lynchings. But by redefining Othello's character, the circumstances of his betrayal and especially of his death, and by placing his murder in the middle of the narrative rather than at the end, Clarke succeeds in enabling Whylah Falls, that "ebon Muse/ Whose Word is Liberty" (72), to triumph over the "chronic violence of the envy-jealousy system," and of its racist permutations, as invoked by Shakespeare's play.

Like Djanet Sears in *Harlem Duet*, Clarke takes on Shakespeare's Othello "to exorcise this ghost" but while her "rhapsodic blues tragedy" (14) tells the absent black woman's story, Clarke's text takes up the challenge of redefining and rearticulating the black man's desire, through the living voices of X, Pablo (who is described as "Moorish" [93] and more easily fits the role of Shakespeare's "extravagant and wheeling stranger" [I.i.135]) and Othello, and through the post-death testimony of Othello and those affected by his murder. Indeed, Clarke's O is described as "muscled Othello, Shakespeare of song" (83)—clearly a figure of desire. If Shakespeare's *Othello* concerns "a black man isolated from other black people" (148), as Ania Loomba, among others, argues, then Clarke's rewriting reinstates Othello among his people. Relations within the black community become more important to Clarke than relations between black and white, as Clarke takes the actual story of the unpunished murder of a black man and embeds it within the broader dynamics of the Whylah Falls community and its larger black Atlantic connections, explicitly placing this rural Nova Scotian community within circuits connecting black experience in Paris, Cuba and Birmingham, Alabama, throughout the twentieth century.

This global context is highlighted even more explicitly in the play, which begins in Paris, with the chorus and then Pablo remembering "how Othello got killed and how his killer got away" (223) and with X explicitly addressing the black man's dilemma: "My father's life insurance is freedom,/ But my name's still 'Coloured,' 'black,' 'nigger,'/ So, wincing, I crawl, this barbed globe of pain" (226). Othello too speaks lines in the play that more clearly reference Shakespeare's imagery:

> Mary had a little sheep
> She took it to bed with her to sleep.
> The sheep turned out to be a ram,
> And Mary had a little lamb (227).

A defiant reshaping of Iago's notorious speech to Desdemona's father in Shakespeare's *Othello*, "Even now, now, very now, an old black ram/ Is tupping your white ewe" (I,I, 88–89), the rewritten nursery rhyme "signifies," in troping black tradition on this persistent stereotype, as does the bluesy "King Bee Blues" (but without explicitly invoking *Othello*) in the poem.[5] The play reshapes the poem's material for dramatic focus, so that, perhaps especially when read in light of the play, the poem's engagement with *Othello* becomes clear.

Bristol notes that "Something real is at stake for the audience of *Othello*, even though the actual performance of the play depends on recognition of its status as fiction" (199). Clarke too addresses the real through foregrounding the performative qualities of language. Bristol's analysis helps make sense of the ways in which *Whylah Falls* weaves the story of the murder of Othello Clemence into the other plot strands, centred on heterosexual desire, that bind this community, threaten its survival and link it to the natural and human worlds. When seen in this light, all the variants of desire and the ways in which they shape community and isolate from it, become frames built around the murder of Clarke's Othello and the failure of the authorities to punish the murderer. The racial identity of the murderer may be less important (although his whiteness is heavily stressed in both poem and script) than the failure of the justice system to punish the crime. (Clarke is reported to have changed the identity of the murderer from a white man to a black man, for financial reasons, in a Halifax stage production, declaring "My poetry is about what beautiful black people have done, not what awful white people have done to us" [Workman C9].) Nonetheless, Clarke's "Preface" to the poem invokes a setting of oppression and struggle, describing Whylah Falls as "a snowy, northern Mississippi, with blood spattered, not on magnolias, but on pines, lilacs, and wild roses." His "Admission" declares: "These poems are fact presented as fiction. There was no other way to tell the truth save to disguise it as story." A memorial to Graham Cromwell, murdered in Weymouth Falls, follows, suggesting the centrality of the unpunished murder to the poem. Cromwell's unavenged death, Clarke implies, can only be told through Shakespeare's *Othello* and the exorcism of its legacy. The success of this exorcism may explain the poem's victory in the 2003 CBC Radio Canada Reads competition. Clarke's story, like Shakespeare's, expresses "the collective bad conscience of our civilization," disguising truth as story, by resituating the murder of Graham Cromwell within an earlier time period (the 1930s) and reimagining it through the lens of Shakespeare's *Othello*. Clarke was profoundly affected by the failure of the justice system to convict Cromwell's killer. His article describing the case, "The Birmingham of Nova Scotia: The Weymouth Falls Justice Committee vs the Attorney General of Nova Scotia," declares: "Consider this a blues cry, a Black witness, for Justice" (17). The article begins and ends with lines of poetry from *Whylah Falls*, suggesting the intimate twinning of the two. Yet the real that is at stake in this poem depends on its recognition as performative fiction.

In *Whylah Falls*, the renaming of the murder victim as Othello, invokes broader western cultural traditions beyond the political events played out in the southern United States and echoed in Nova Scotia. (Although it is interesting to note that W.E.B. DuBois' maternal grandfather was also named Othello [Johnson 143]). Whereas certain commentators locate the tragedy of Shakespeare's

Othello in his desire for whiteness until he actually begins to forget that he is black (Johnson 155), Clarke's poem is suffused with extravagantly articulated expressions of a desire for blackness. Othello Clemence is comfortable in his blackness, belligerent in his defence of his sister Amarantha's honour, and an artist who expresses himself through music. In Clarke's story, the threat of a black man having sex with a white woman becomes merely a vicious lie, but a lie powerful enough to prompt a murder, which Clarke explicitly terms a "martyrdom" (89). (Such imaginings, rumour suggests, infected the popular folk interpretation of Cromwell's murder as well.) The poem's Iago, the Liberal politician Jack Thomson, maliciously tells S. Scratch Seville that Othello is having an affair with Seville's wife, Angel. In fact, Thomson himself is involved with Angel. He has also been threatened by Othello for approaching Othello's sister, Amarantha, and finds the lie a convenient way to combine revenge with camouflage. The complexities of Shakespeare's Iago are sacrificed here to pit artists against politicians as masters of the word. Thomson's words deal death. The poet's words live. As X claims: "My poems, thrown to the creek, gleam, wriggle, leap" (25). Suffering is transformed into beauty and survival is proclaimed: "Angered by whip and lash of joblessness, maddened by gun and jail of politics, these souls clap hands and sing, 'What did I do/ To be so black and blue?'" (126). The echoes of slavery, Yeats's late romanticism,[6] and blues vernacular combine to "blacken" the English of Clarke's inheritance while suggesting that art transcends politics and social inequities—a comforting conclusion to a troubling performance. My argument has attended to the trouble rather than its transcendence, while noting the tensions between the two.

Clarke's open letter to Derek Walcott states: "I thank you for pioneering a way of blackening English ... You cannibalize the Canon and invite your bretheren and sistren to the intoxicating, exhilarating feast" (17). I find this metaphor more appropriate to Clarke's work than to Walcott's, but as a metaphor describing Clarke's art, "cannibalizing the Canon," captures the aggression, the fraught politics, the edgy humour and the exuberant excess of his achievement, turning one of the more potent justifying metaphors for imperial racism back on itself and enabling appropriation, digestion, transformation and elimination to replace direct protest against the injustices of the world. *Whylah Falls*, unlike "those skinny, / Malnourished poems that professors love" (79), according to Clarke's sceptical Shelley, has gorged its full on the bounty that language provides and spilled it out generously with the shock of the real.

Endnotes

1. I am using the 1990 text of *Whylah Falls* for this discussion. References to the 1997 play will be indicated in my text. I am grateful to Jennifer Drouin and Susan Knutson for inviting me to participate in the ACCUTE panel on Shakespearean/Canadian Intertexts at the Winnipeg Congress in May 2004. A lengthier and revised version of the paper is being prepared for the book they are planning based on this session. Comments from participants at this session and from my colleagues, M.J. Kidnie and Taiwo Adetunji Osinubi, and the warm openness to dialogue of George Elliott Clarke are also gratefully acknowledged. Jessica Schagerl provided prompt and helpful research

assistance, as did Barbara Bruce when I first began this project. Students in my graduate course on "The Black Diaspora," especially Helene Strauss, Heather Snell and Lori Walter, also provided compelling insights.

2. Jon Paul Fiorentino identifies this concern as crucial to Clarke's aesthetic.
3. Irena Makaryk and I raised this question in our co-edited collection, *Shakespeare in Canada*, but they are far from resolved.
4. Good introductions to this foundational work and that which is following it may be found in Clarke's *Odysseys Home* and in Walcott's *Black Like Who?* as well as in their various edited collections. For a fuller discussion of this aspect of my argument see my article "Black Canadas: Rethinking Canadian and Diasporic Cultural Studies" *Revista Canaria de Estudios Ingleses* 43 November 2001: 101–117.
5. See Henry Louis Gates' *The Signifying Monkey* for an explanation of this important tradition.
6. Yeats' "Sailing to Byzantium" claims that "An aged man is but a paltry thing,/ A tattered coat upon a stick, unless/ Soul clap its hands and sing, and louder sing/ For every tatter in its mortal dress" (104). Clarke harnesses the energy of Yeats' poetic resistence to mortality in the service of a historically and racially specific protest against racism, violently shfting the visual image from the "tattered coat upon a stick" to that of a black congregation swaying in the spirit. The final lines of this stanza, "Nor is there singing school but studying/ Monuments of its own magnificence," may be considered a further comment on the ways in which Clarke has made Shakespeare's *Othello*, together with

Africadia's other international inheritances, his "singing school."

Works Cited

Bristol, Michael. "Race and the comedy of abjection in *Othello*" *Big-Time Shakespeare.* London: Routledge, 1996.

Brydon, Diana and Irene Makaryk, eds. *Sakespeare in Canada: 'A World Elsewhere'?* Toronto: U. of Toronto P. 2003.

Brydon, Diana. "Black Canadas: Rethinking Canadian and Diasporic Cultural Studies." *Revista Canaria de Estudios Ingleses. 43, November 2001. 101–117.*

Clarke, George Elliott. "The Birmingham of Nova Scotia: The Wymonth Falls Justice Commitee vs the Attorny General of Nova Scotia." *Towards a New Maritimes,* eds. Ian McKay and Scott Milson. Charlottetown: Ragweed, 1992, 17–24.

—. "George Elliott Clarke to Derek Walcott." *Open Letter* 11: 3 (2001) 15–17.

—. *Odysseys Home: Mapping African-Canadian Literature.* Toronto: U. of T. Press, 2002.

—. *Whylah Falls.* 2nd ed. Vancouver: Polestar, 1990.

—, ed. *Eyeing the North Star: Directions in African-Canadian Literature.* Toronto: McClelland & Stewart, 1997.

Davidson, Arnold E. "*Whylah Falls*: The Africadian Poetry of George Elliott Clarke." *Down East: Critical Essays on Contemporary Maritime Canadian Literature,* ed. Wolfgang Hochbruck and James Taylor. Trier: Wissenschaftlicher Verlag Trier, 1996. 265–76

Fiorentino, Jon Paul. "Blackening English: Polyphonic Poetics of George Elliott Clarke." *Poetics.ca #2* http://www.poetics.ca/pocticso2/02fiorentinoprint.htm (accessed 2004–09–05. 1–10.

Foster, Clarisse and Sharanpal Ruprai. "Interview with George Elliott Clarke." *Contemporary Verse 2*. 24.2 (2001) 15–24.

Gates, Jr. Henry Louis. *The Signifying Monkey: A Theory of African-American Literary Criticism*. New York: Oxford U P, 1988.

Hill, Lawrence. *Any Known Blood.* Toronto: Harper Perennial, 1998.

Johnson, Lemuel A. *Shakespeare in Africa (And Other Venues).* New York: African World P. 1998.

Loomba, Ania. "'Local-manufacture made in India Othello fellows' Issues of race, hybridity and location in post-colonial Shakespeares." *Post-Colonial Shakespeares*. eds. Ania Loomba and Martin Orkin. London: Routledge, 1998.

Moynagh, Maureen. "Mapping Africadia's Imaginary Geography: An Interview with George Elliott Clarke." *Ariel* 27.4 (1996) 71–94.

—. "George Elliott Clarke's Redeptive Vision." *Testifying* ed. Djanet Sears. Toronto: Playwrights Canada, 2000, 217–19.

Sears, Djanet. *Harlem Duet.* Winnipeg: Scirocco Drama, 1997.

Shakespeare, William. *Othello*. ed. Celia Hilton. London: MacMillan, 1984.

Sharpe, Jenny. *Ghosts of Slavery: A Literary Archeology of Black Women's Lives*. Minneapolis: U. of Minnesota P. 2003.

Walcott, Rinaldo. *Black Like Who? Writing Black Canada.* Toronto: Insomniac, 1997.

—. *Rude: Contemporary Black Canadian Cultural Criticism.* Toronto: Insomniac, 2000.

Wells, Dorothy. "A Rose Grows in Whylah Falls: Transplanted Traditions in George Elliott Clarke's Africadia." *Canadian Literature* 155 (1997) 56–73.

Workman, Sharon. "A poet's philosophy of beauty." *Globe and Mail.* Fri. Jan 10, 1997. C9.

Yeats, W.B. "Sailing to Byzantium." *Selected Poems.* ed. A. Norman Jeffares. London: Macmillan, 1974. 104–5.

"*Oui*, let's scat": Listening to Multi-Vocality in George Elliott Clarke's Jazz Opera *Québécité*

KATHERINE MCLEOD

Listening, as a critical practice, fundamentally alters the interaction between audience and text from passive to participatory, but the question remains as to what enables this listening to be political. In George Elliott Clarke's jazz opera *Québécité*, listening happens on and off the page, among performers, musicians, librettist, composer, director, and audiences. Premiered at the Guelph Jazz Festival in 2003, *Québécité* performs a combination of texts: Clarke's libretto, published as *Québécité: A Jazz Fantasia in Three Cantos*, and the musical score, composed by D.D. Jackson, whose collaboration with Clarke continues with the scoring of Clarke's subsequent libretto, *Trudeau*. A second production of *Québécité* took place in Vancouver alongside the conference "Transcultural Improvisations: Performing Hybridity," organized by Sneja Gunew and held at the University of British Columbia in October 2003. Thus, from this performance history, a dialogue has already begun between the terminology of "transcultural improvisations" (Gunew 125) and *Québécité* itself, a dialogue that I continue in this paper by asking how sound offers a particular medium through which to theorize the cultural crossings of these improvisations. Set on the apple-blossomed streets of Quebec City, with the iconic Chateau Frontenac in the backdrop, Clarke's libretto *Québécité* sings the story of two multicultural couples—Laxmi Bharati and Ovide Rimbaud, and Malcolm States and Colette Chan—whose loves are thwarted and recovered as they negotiate familial, personal, and cultural prejudices. Colette, a University of Laval law student, must decide whether to abide by her Chinese parents' disapproval of her love for Malcolm, an Africadian saxophonist. Laxmi, a Hindu architecture student from Montreal, questions the fidelity of her lover, Haitian-Québécois architect Ovide, and refuses to allow him to cast her as what she calls "une lascivité proprement asiatique" (Clarke 80). Through Clarke's libretto and Jackson's score, these characters negotiate cultural identifications within visual and acoustic spaces that simultaneously reify and unfix differences. While difference need not necessarily connote dissonance, the reception of *Québécité* frames the cultural differences between characters in terms of whether or not they *sound* alike. The female characters—Laxmi Bharati as sung by Kiran Ahluwalia and Colette Chan as sung by Yoon Choi—sparked extensive debate among critics regarding issues of dissonance, and therefore I ask how these characters, in particular, embody political action through sound. Situating this question amid current debates on performing multiculturalism (Bannerji; Kamboureli; Gunew), I argue that *Québécité* exemplifies the ways in which sound offers a medium through which to redefine understandings of multicultural and multivocal improvisations.

The work of jazz and literary critic Ajay Heble (artistic director of the Guelph Jazz Festival who commissioned the production of *Québécité* for the festival's tenth anniversary) outlines the theoretical background to the approach to listening that I apply to *Québécité* in this paper. Although his writing on jazz provides the most relevant connection, I argue that this writing needs to be contextualized by his essay "New Contexts for Canadian Criticism: Democracy, Counterpoint, Responsibility." Here, Heble makes the compelling claim that Glenn Gould's radio documentary *The Idea of North* necessitates a responsible, contrapuntal listening. Since Gould's editing techniques allow for all voices to speak simultaneously, Heble contends that this simultaneity not only democratizes the voice but also implicates audiences in the production of meaning out of this dissonance—requiring a participation that *Québécité's* characters are themselves conscious of, for example when Laxmi sings to Ovide in the opening scene, "You've invited me to savour jazz" (19). Furthermore, Gould's technique of polyphonic counterpoint highlights the interstitial space of what Heble calls "cultural listening" (86), which permits cross-cultural listening to take place along the lines of Edward Said's notion of "a simultaneous awareness both of the metropolitan history that is narrated and that of those other histories against which (and together with which) the dominating discourse acts" (qtd. in Heble 87). In this argument, Heble suggests that if we learn to practise new modes of cultural listening, then there exists the potential to unsettle processes of identity formation: "If identity, as Gould's contrapuntal method invites us to see, is multiple, dialogic, and ever-evolving, then what is at issue is, in large part, an attack on forms and structures of authority, on constructions and representations which authoritatively claim to be able to have access to some pure, definitive, or whole truth about, say, the identity of Canada" (90). While Clarke's libretto is not written in contrapuntal verse, both the visual and acoustic signifiers of *Québécité* produce a multi-vocal effect that enables a version of this ongoing, reciprocal cultural listening.

D.D. Jackson's score for *Québécité* is composed of lush, scintillating jazz. In this hybrid performance of jazz opera, as heard in the Guelph and Vancouver performances of Jackson's score, the music balances melodic love scenes with dissonant wails of characters' voices fighting against the politics and prejudices that prevent them from musically fulfilling their desires. For instance, Colette and Malcolm fall in love amid the soft sound of their duet, in which their words sing for exquisite accompaniment:

> Lushly, a dewed light falls,
> blushing branches.
> It clears what doubts had pressed down leaves
> and lets kissed lips—
> lilacs, lilies, tulips—
> flourish,
> lushly flourish. (28)

As if the libretto can already imagine how the piano keys press down softly like this image of pressed leaves, the characters utter the words, "it's your music that resembles / beautiful, fragrant, apple blossoms" (29). Yet the music of this couple changes dramatically at the end of Act II, when Colette tells Malcolm of her parents' disapproval. The music rages with his anger, culminating in his leaving of the jazz café, La Revolution Tranquille, with the statement, "We'll put our silver instruments / And our sable music away. Away! / This ain't no time for innocence" (71).

Thus, while the music is often harmonious jazz, there are moments of dissonance that respond to cultural dissonances among characters themselves.[1] It is in this sense that I hear *Québécité* through Heble's book *Landing on the Wrong Note*, in which he aims "to postulate a theory of musical dissonance as social practice" (170). While Heble's study includes musicological elements, its focus is on the discursive community that constructs our perception of sound as *wrong*, or rather on "sounds (and, more generally, cultural practices) that are 'out of tune' with orthodox habits of coherence and judgment" (9). He explains how this playing "out of tune" allows for a re-imagining of the self, which results in his questioning of what role "dissonant jazz played for subordinated social groups struggling to achieve control over the ways in which their identities have been constructed, framed, and interpreted" (9). It is this discursive element of dissonance that I apply to *Québécité*, because it provides a model for understanding how identities—such as Laxmi's and Colette's—are politicized as improvisatory and continually in flux. Heble's "Postlude" to the libretto supports this reading of Laxmi's and Colette's identities because he hears the spaces for these improvised identities as opening up from within the hybrid form of jazz opera: "Offering an alternative to the doggedly Eurological operatic tradition, *Québécité* marks an unprecedented opportunity on the Canadian operatic stage to generate bold new stagings of identity" (100). Given Heble's commissioning of *Québécité*, the performance itself offers what could be called an enacted version of his theoretical writing, or rather an example through which to test the applicability of "musical dissonance as social practice" (170) that underlines the theoretical arguments in *Landing on the Wrong Note*.

Immersed in a mimicking of the operatic tradition, the amorous language of the lovers, which strives to be sincere (as Laxmi articulates, jazz itself fears "cadences of decadence" [19]), reveals the extent to which *eros* needs to be taken into account in any definition of dissonance. What I mean is that *Québécité* shows that dissonance need not be heard as jarring collisions; it can be heard instead as disparate arcs of longing. The stage directions to Canto III, scene v, speak to how the voices meet—"Their songs interlock" (80)—as if depicting these arcs of sound waves overlapping in their mutual expressions of the characters' desires. Yet, if we consider that these voices are depicted as multicultural voices, then we realize that the performance calls for a critique of the listening audience and of whether these interlocking voices are heard as distinct or assimilated. Such a critique is necessary in order to avoid what Canadian critic Smaro Kamboureli calls "sedative politics," a re-organization of ethnic differences in order to control them (82). In *Scandalous Bodies: Diasporic Literature in Canada*, Kamboureli locates this debate in modes of legitimating ethnic diversity; namely, she points to a failure in confronting multicultural issues *through bodies*. It is here that *Québécité* provides a site for examining these issues through its use of both sight and sound to embody multiculturalism. Furthermore, given that the reviews of *Québécité* participate in this phenomenon of documenting multiculturalism through the media, I mention Kamboureli in order to set up the importance of media in constructing bodies as multicultural. (Further readings of, and listenings to, *Québécité* through Bannerji's deconstructions of the discourses of diversity, as well as through a critique of hybridity along the lines of what informs Gunew's global approach to "transcultural improvisations" [125], would lead to equally productive insights. I am pursuing these approaches elsewhere, but, unfortunately, I can only gesture towards them in the scope of this paper.) Using Kamboureli's argument as a starting point through which to ask how we might think ourselves out of this problematic reification of difference, I propose a listening to *Québécité* that emphasizes how *sound* foregrounds the complexity of its attempt to embody multiculturalism, and I suggest that the sound itself is what enables a critical path outside discourses of control.

Where Kamboureli's work further resonates with this theoretical approach to *Québécité* is in her positing of "a mastery of discomfort that would involve shuttling between centre and margin while displacing both" (130), which I argue offers a version of dissonance grounded in a failure of recognition. This failure plays upon the Althusserian hailing of *the Other* into being, or rather into subjectivity. For Kamboureli, the power of the hail can be subverted through a misrecognition, which thereby enacts a version of what Judith Butler describes as "a community in which the recognition [...] of the Other is always also the failure to know that Other" (qtd. in Kamboureli 130). Such a misrecognition occurs in *Québécité* in Canto II, scene v, in which Clarke's stage directions describe Colette, who is Chinese, as wearing "a Nova Scotian tartan sari" (62) when meeting Laxmi, who is wearing "a blazing pink sarong—and a turquoise necklace—and white pumps" (62). With expectations of appearances already subverted through clothing, the conversation between these two characters further complicates any attempt to classify them based on appearance: for instance, in this same encounter, Laxmi says to Colette, "I see saris are in vogue, and you're in love" (62), observing the playful capacity of visual signifiers to determine how characters are *seen*.[2] Moreover, as Kamboureli comments in relation to Butler's notion of misrecognition, "failure to know the Other means failure to accommodate existing stereotypes and failure to produce new ones" (130). I argue that the music of *Québécité* works with and against the visual in order to resist and challenge what it means to hear identity as fixed or known.

Québécité, as libretto and as jazz opera, calls attention to itself as a performance, and thus also calls attention to the performance of cultural identities. Magda Wojtyra's visuals for the performance translate this attention to performance from words into images. The image for La Revolution Tranquille echoes Clarke's stage description of this jazz café as decorated with posters of iconic figures of both jazz and politics, as if reminding the reader that politics and music cannot be separated:

> On the walls appear early 1960s-era posters of (your choice among) Martin Luther King, Pierre Elliott Trudeau, Ho Chi Minh, Rene Levesque, Fidel Castro, Oscar Peterson, Lili St. Cyr, John Coltrane, Golda Meir, Miles Davis, James Brown, Indira Gandhi, Ella Fitzgerald, Jean Lesage, Buffy Saint-Marie, Portia White (photographed by Karsh), Josephine Baker, Adrienne Clarkson, Malcolm X, Gamal Abdel Nasser, Oliver Jones, Leonard Cohen, Bruce Lee, Ravi Shankar, Astrud Gilberto, Genevieve Bujold, Nancy Kwan, and Jawaharlal Nehru. The bar is Warhol retro, with chrome and brass fixtures, and marble frills, soft-lit. (23)

Although these images are imagined as posters, they simultaneously evoke the acoustic by providing a version of a listening-list for the reader to imagine what La Revolution Tranquille would *sound* like; thus, as shown in this example, the libretto overflows with visual images, and yet these images very much engage with the acoustic space of the text and its performance. Just as the language oscillates between subverting and reifying embodiments of culture, the sound too performs this oscillation, an action that is not necessarily problematic but most certainly becomes complicated when reviewers, particularly with reference to Laxmi's character, read cultural signification through sound. Thus, beginning with Laxmi, I listen to how the acoustic challenges what takes place visually in the text and on the stage in order to unsettle how this character fits into discourses of performing multiculturalism.

In *Québécité*, visual signifiers occur within the larger signifying realm of sound, a medium in which expectations can be subverted. The libretto portrays identities that border upon being essentialized, as we hear when Ovide sings, "Laxmi mirrors *belle époque* India, / Exquisite, sepia-toned, lavish, precise" (81). These words hint at a performative element through mirroring but also, more significantly, align Laxmi with a physical exoticized Indian-ness. Although the medium of jazz opera makes an overarching gesture towards the fact that identity is performative, the recognition of this performativity in sound has proven to be difficult for reviewers to employ in their reviews of Kiran Ahluwalia as Laxmi, whose performance of culture has been often misread as naturalized. Ahluwalia refers to this troublesome point during a conversation cited in Vish Khanna's online review of *Québécité*: "I am Indian, but I'm Canadian as well so, when I'm improvising, is that Indian music or Canadian music? Well, you know what? It's a bit of both; I'm doing Canadian music even if it sounds foreign to you." Improvisation provides Ahluwalia with a space for transcultural crossings, which allows her to produce a sound that subverts expectations. In the above quotation, her statement, "I'm doing Canadian music even if it sounds foreign to you," speaks back to critics who insist upon labelling her music as *other*. As Ahluwalia herself recognizes, blending jazz with Indian styles of music is a significant performative statement, and when the complexities of such a statement are dismissed with an insistence upon hearing her music as "Indian," it seems to say more about the listener than about her performance.

Khanna's review focuses on Ahluwalia's participation in creating a cross-cultural sound through mixing jazz and Indian music. In her conversation with Khanna, Ahluwalia explains, "Ajay had an idea where he said, 'Let me bring this actual composer who does this kind of western music and let me bring all of these singers together with him.' He actually had this idea of bringing it out, and I think it's definitely something that's never been done before. I think it's really quite a pioneering effort in defining Canadian music." Her comment draws attention to the ways in which the acoustics of *Québécité* exist in a larger context of redefining what composes a Canadian soundscape. In the specific space of the performance, the intersection of jazz and Indian music can be heard when she sings the words to Canto III, scene iv, "Laxmi sur le quai." She begins the song with a citational gesture of singing what *sounds like* a classical Indian ghazal before moving into the scored lyrics. Her citing of the ghazal performs a version of what Henry Louis Gates calls "signifyin'" (46). As Gates explains in *The Signifying Monkey*, "the bracketed or aurally erased *g*, like the discourse of black English and dialect poetry generally, stands as the trace of black difference in a remarkably sophisticated and fascinating (re)naming ritual graphically in evidence here" (46). For both Laxmi and Colette, the concept of signifyin' allows us to understand how they sing riffs upon cultural difference, such as when Laxmi invokes the opening style of the ghazal in the scene "Laxmi sur le quai" (a scene in which the language of the libretto performs its own invocation of difference in a powerful description of Laxmi as a Québécoise Hindu Goddess, "a diva devi—de souche" [79]), or when Colette's scat solo mimics the intonations of English and Chinese dialogue, as if she is arguing with her father (discussed in the next section of the paper). Signifyin' as a culturally infused citation of codes further highlights the degree to which Ahluwalia's singing of Laxmi is a performance, which is important to keep in mind when reading reviews such as Geoff Chapman's for the *Toronto Star*, in which he describes Ahluwalia's Laxmi as relying upon her Indianness: "Kiran Ahluwalia was the least effective, except when she could employ her classical Indian style." This comment disregards the crossing of borders that is at the centre of both Ahluwalia's musical projects and *Québécité* itself. On Ahluwalia's Juno Award-winning CD *Border Crossings*, the ghazals are written in Punjabi and Urdu by Toronto-based poets and set to music by Ahluwalia, thereby creating what the liner notes refer to as "Canadian ghazals." Ahluwalia's singing of Laxmi in *Québécité* performs another version of these Canadian ghazals. Just as the ghazals on her CD are poetry set to music, the poetry of Clarke's libretto becomes the text for the ghazals of *Québécité*, resulting in a linguistic shift that marks the crossing of borders. The poetry is no longer written in Punjabi or Urdu but rather in a heteroglossic English that remains aware of its historical context.

Hearing is not a passive act, and yet the politics of music can often be unheard, or rather, confused with notions of taste. This conflation has important implications for *Québécité*, which refuses to separate the aesthetic from the political. Throughout the jazz opera, politics and aesthetics are fused, for example in Canto I, scene ii, when Malcolm, the saxophone player, riffs upon the meaning of jazz through language: "Jazz is saxes stroked like violins, pianos beat like drums. [...] Jazz is multiculti-Aboriginal-Semitic-Afro-Asian-Caucasian" (36). Malcolm's metaphors exemplify ways in which language fluidly slips between the aesthetic and political. There is no clearer example of this slippage than in Clarke's dedication of the libretto to his mother and D.D. Jackson's mother, "Two Dreamers of Beauty" (5), which appears alongside the names of Adrienne Clarkson and Pierre Elliott Trudeau, "Two Visionaries of Liberty" (5). At once the jazz opera becomes intensely personal and overtly political, a slippery status that pervades the libretto until the end, where we find the statement: "Without Love, it is impossible to live" (90) juxtaposed with: "Love is a tyrannical democracy" (92). Which is it? Are we to hear *Québécité* as a dream of "Beauty" or as a vision of "Liberty"? The complicated answer is yes and yes, because through jazz theory we can understand jazz as always already implicated within politics and yet still functioning within the discourse of aesthetics, as gestured towards in Clarke's use of the capitalization of ideals such as "Beauty" throughout his libretto. Another way of phrasing this complexity would be to situate it within a pressing need to locate the ideal within the real, or within what M. Nourbese Philip recognizes as the failure of multiculturalism to operate within this space of the real: "The mechanism of multiculturalism is [...] based on a presumption of equality, a presumption which is not necessarily borne out in reality" (181).

The political and the aesthetic, the real and the ideal, continue to blur throughout the jazz opera right up to the last line: "*Vive notre québécité*" (92), which sings of a political unity and of marital unities among the lovers. But what has been overcome in order for this word *notre* to be sung freely, given that the characters were confronted with the racial prejudices that prevented them from claiming such a word for themselves? Earlier in the jazz opera, for instance, Malcolm argues against Colette's concerns about mixed-race parentage when angrily asking her: "Do you think our kids'd be striped like zebras? / Or look like Neapolitan ice-cream? Or amoebas?" (71); yet, in the final chorus, Malcolm and Colette happily sing in unison: "Our children will be / every colour eyes can know / and free" (92). The image of their children as "coloured" appears in both scenes, but by the end this colouring takes on a positive connotation, as if reflected in the multi-coloured Quebec flag that emerges on the screen. While the inclusivity of this image makes an integral contribution to the political message of the pieces, the hyper-celebratory style of both the music and the image draws attention to the performance as a performance, a mask that hides behind it hyperbolic form.[3] Evidence for such a reading exists within Clarke's "Prelude" to the libretto, in which he describes *Québécité* as "an Absinthe-Amarula-Brandy-Champagne-Chartreuse-Chicouti-Cognac-Grappa-Palm-Port-Pastis-Rum-Saki-Sangria-Scotch-Tequila-Vodka opera, one coloured spicily with notes of ebony-dark-cherry, India indigo ink, and bronze-beige the shade of papyrus or bamboo" (12). His superlatively hyphenated definition, when taken in the context of his political message, becomes a serious kind of playfulness. For jazz theorist John Corbett, improvisation functions through sessions of "playing," with an intended pun on both the playing of an instrument and a playing with the semiotics of sound, which he understands as the two components through which jazz signifies itself (233). Perhaps the word *play*, with its double meaning as a trickster flirtation and a musical performance, best describes the *poiesis*, or linguistic making, of this jazz opera. Including the word *polyhexamethyleneudiapide* (53) signals a playfulness on the part of the librettist, which Keith Garebian highlights when he asks, in his review of the libretto, "How is a performer to cope with such hypertrophic phrases as the following: 'Polyhexamethyleneudiapide, simmering' or 'Flaunt a florilegium of dazzling perfume'?" When Haydain Neale as Ovide sings the word *polyhexamethyleneudiapide* in performances of the jazz opera, his voice not only glides over a word that depicts his character's obsession with lavish love and language but also signals the seriousness of such a word, which is capable of surpassing the boundary of what is or is not considered to be speakable, or rather singable.

As if commenting upon Clarke's playfulness in exploding the boundaries of what is singable, the female characters express wariness towards the male characters' words. As Laxmi says to Ovide: "Ovide, I prefer Puccini with cappuccino [...] to vain talk that bleeds like a vein" (22), and as Colette says to Malcolm: "Words have an annoying tendency / to turn into lies" (40). Yet the sincerity of Clarke's project emerges from this linguistic play to the degree that, even though the final scene seems self-reflexive of its over-the-top-ness, there is a serious message in the image of the multi-coloured flag that needs to be spoken: namely, the message that Clarke articulates in his comments following the CBC Radio broadcast of the jazz opera regarding the possibility "of having people from different cultural, linguistic, religious and racial backgrounds being able to collectively identify, without any irony, themselves as Canadian. To seize that label for everybody and not just a select group." Heble's "Postlude" to *Québécité* elaborates on this inclusivity when he speaks of the necessity for "an inclusive vision of community-building and intellectual stock-taking for the new millennium" (101), a vision that informs the text and music of Clarke's and Jackson's jazz opera. It is the *sound* of this performance that both enables and challenges this vision of inclusivity.

The words "*Oui,* let's scat" not only end the first scene of *Québécité* but also offer the audience a method of participatory listening through which to hear Clarke's libretto and D.D. Jackson's music. For audiences listening to the first two performances of *Québécité,* one at the Guelph Jazz Festival in September 2003 and the other in Vancouver in October 2003, one of the most poignant moments was Yoon Choi's evocative scat solo, a solo that was expanded in the Vancouver production into an elaborate improvisatory session, or rather an acoustic battle within Choi's character, Colette Chan, between dismissing or embracing familial ties to Chinese tradition and history. Choi's solo enacts what might be called a "talking back" to colonialist discourse through scatting, a musical practice that is non-semantic yet enables her to speak that which is otherwise unspeakable. Yoon Choi's evocative scat solo in the Vancouver production of *Québécité* pushes the boundaries of speakable and unspeakable. In this version of talking back, her scat solo foregrounds the limits of language itself and the extent to which language can be performed.

In the Vancouver performance of Colette's solo entitled "Colette au bar" (76), Yoon Choi, accompanied by bassist Mark Dresser, extended her solo into what Kevin McNeilly calls a "duo" between Choi and Dresser: "Their five minute exchange—which occurred in a musical space on the verge of score or script—was one of the highpoints of an exceptional evening" (122). Even though Dresser's contribution to this duo could be heard as linguistically unintelligible, McNeilly's comment highlights the extent to which Dresser's instrumental medium provided a dialogic form of call-and-response through which Choi could interrogate the very borders of semiotic intelligibility. Within this unwritten musical space, Choi sings an emotionally rough, visceral interrogation of the *sound* of cultural identity. Fluctuating between deep moans, staccato phonemes, tearful murmurs, and high-pitched wails, Choi scats in sounds that foreground their relation to language, sounds that are outside of signification yet still gesture towards it by mimicking culturally signifying tones, and vocal patterns that imitate dialogue. Her scatting is always already involved in this semiotic process even while attempting to interrogate the boundary between the semiotic and symbolic. The self-reflexiveness of her scat singing's interrogatory process can be read as *thetic*, in the Kristevan sense that "it posits its own process as an undecidable process between sense and nonsense, between language and rhythm, [and] between the symbolic and the semiotic" (103). As if angrily testing how long her sound can hover between the limits of signification, Choi foregrounds the process of attaching meaning to sound, a process that she argues is a product of hegemony in the lyrics that follow her scatting: "Finally I'm *called* to the bar—the bar of prosecution, / the bar of ripped-up bars of Music" (Clarke 76–77, emph. Clarke's). These lyrics create their own rupture not with scatting but with language, beginning with a word, *Finally*, that functions as a speech act to signal the end to scat's hovering between the semiotic and symbolic.

The lyrics that follow the scat solo sung by Yoon Choi as Colette Chan invite the audience to consider the "nonsense" that they just heard in the context of speaking the unspeakable; although her lyrics impose a linguistic explanation of her scatting, they also continue to challenge authoritative discourses through her repetition of a phrase that becomes a memorable refrain amid her solo: "Finally I'm called to the bar of prosecution, bars of ripped up music, bars of persecution" (*Québécité*, Vancouver), which differs both in phrasing and in the number of times it repeats from the libretto's version of this scene. In addition to the linguistic play resulting from the fact that the scene takes place in a bar and Colette is a law student, the repetition of the word bar within the context of speaking the unspeakable strongly aligns itself with Judith Butler's concept of the "bar" as imposing foreclosure upon language. In *Excitable Speech*, Butler discusses political speech acts in relation to a "bar" that functions both as a bar that impedes access and as a judicial bar. In reading censorship as a form of foreclosure, Butler argues that censorship "produces discursive regimes through the production of the unspeakable" (139). Since foreclosure takes place not because of a single action but because of "the reiterated effect of a structure" (138), Butler states that one cannot speak *against* the bar; instead, one must use the "force," consisting of both speech and body, of the performative in restructuring social utterance (141). In the case of Colette, the anger in her singing, such as in the words, "the bar of prosecution, bars of ripped up music" (*Québécité*, Vancouver), conveys a bodily force already undermining the "bar" that she stands before; moreover, in addition to the deconstruction of the various "bars"' in her song, the fervent repetition of the previously quoted line throughout her solo enacts what Butler proposes as "a repetition in language that forces change" (163).

The *change* necessary in Colette's solo is connected to a history of what lies "unspeakable" in jazz music itself. In discussing early recording practices, Jed Rasula offers the valuable differentiation between what is unrecordable and what is unspeakable. For Rasula, the "unspoken" in jazz is not the "live" immediacy of the performance but rather "the things that will never be known, people that will forever go unheard, words that will remain unsaid" (152). Both Butler's and Rasula's theories underline Edwards' reading of how scat has been constructed as "nonsense" (622); furthermore, Edwards draws on the theories of Nathaniel Mackey in order to suggest that scat testifies to an "unspeakable history" (Edwards 624). Although Mackey speaks of a link between scat and "a common predilection in black musical expression for the edges of the voice" (qtd. in Edwards 625) that does not apply directly to the Asian cultural context of the scat solo in *Québécité*, Mackey's focus on alterity allows us to hear the scatting voice tracing around the edges of the "bar" that Butler refers to, and this tracing draws our attention to it as a structure, therefore possibly leading to its dismantling, as in Colette's phrase, "the bar of ripped-up bars of Music" (Clarke 77).

Once Colette bursts out of the semiotic and into the symbolic, she critiques authoritative discourses, especially when she sings as a jazz singer about how "Mao declared jazz seditious contraband" (Clarke 77). But can scatting itself "talk back"? One way in which Colette does perform a subversive talking back is through a playful yet poignant exploration of culturally inflected sound, producing a version of Henry Louis Gates' notion of signifyin', with the absent g, as representing what Gates calls "a figure for the Signifyin[g] black difference" (46). Similar to Laxmi's citation of cultural codes through music, Colette's scat signifies by shifting between vocal improvisations that verge upon sounding like English and those that verge upon sounding like Chinese dialogue (*Québécité*, Vancouver). Furthermore, I apply the term *signifyin'* to Colette in the same way that jazz theorist Robert Walser applies it to Miles Davis, in order to explore signification through "performance and dialogic engagement" (168). Korean-born and Toronto-raised singer Yoon Choi succeeds in revealing the complexity of the character of Colette through this notion of "performance and dialogic engagement," which signifies cultural tension outside of the semantic realm. Colette mimes conversational "norms" to the extent that we can almost hear the offstage argument with her parents over her choice to love an Africadian man of African-Mi'kmaq-Nova Scotian heritage rather than a Chinese man who could enable what Colette calls her parents' "dream of golden, Chinese grandchildren" (77). In Walser's reading of signifyin' in jazz music, he hears this technique as striving to produce a contested, unfixed meaning—meaning that, as in the case of Colette, defies boundaries of semantic knowledge and remains unstable, kinetic, and alive.

Refrains in which the characters voice their desires to speak *meaningfully* echo throughout *Québécité*, as if aspiring towards a semiotics of "signifyin" that recognizes itself as performative and dialogic. As Ovide insinuates in his opening duet with Laxmi, to be meaningful already lies in the realm of eros: "Will you fulfill my meaning /

Am I meaningful?" (19). When Laxmi responds: "You invited me to savour jazz [...] Why taint it with saccharine hints, / Such sick cadence of decadence?" (19), she reveals her attitudes towards Ovide's seemingly *meaningless* words while foreshadowing a possible reaction to the meaning of the performance itself. As if in reaction to Laxmi's skepticism, the language of *Québécité* expresses a preoccupation with being *meaningful.* When Colette protests to Malcolm: "We can still love. Don't be so mean!" (69), he responds by reiterating the importance of meaning: "I want to love meaningfully / not meanly" (69). Although performing in a medium that often resists meaning, or at least "meaning" in a Western hermeneutic sense of the word, the characters reiterate the desire to be meaningful, which brings to mind Corbett's description of jazz improvisation as fluctuating among "*meaning nothing, meaning something,* and *being interpreted as meaning something*" (221). Both in scripted language and in improvised scat, *Québécité* foregrounds the suspiciousness of *meaning* as an abstract concept, yet still asserts the importance of meaning, with the characters' desire to be meaningful intertwined with their desire to love—"If you were to die right now, you'd regret / Not having loved, not having been fit," says Ovide to Laxmi, who responds: "Why would I regret not being lied to?" (68). If we read the plot of the love story as motivated by the characters' attempts to sing and to hear meaning as both performative and unfixed in its acoustic space, then the reuniting of the couples suggests that, at least momentarily, they understand what informs Malcolm's wish "to love meaningfully" (69).

Wandering in the fog, searching for each other and for meaning, the four characters' voices merge in the line: "I miss you as a kite misses the wind" (81). Here, in Canto III, scene v, entitled "Dans le brouillard," their voices remain distant and distinct, yet their distinct voices also form a collective sentiment of desire that applies to language itself. Desiring to be meaningful, even when challenging the boundaries of signification, the language of *Québécité* performs its own longing for performance, missing the breath "as a kite misses the wind."

I propose that this scene exemplifies the multi-vocality of the jazz opera. It is a multi-vocality that the jazz opera enacts while, simultaneously, aspiring towards; and yet, is this longing on behalf of the jazz opera itself discordant or harmonious? It is, perhaps, in the dialectic tension between these two states that the jazz opera most fervently longs to linger. A dismissal of this dialectic overlooks the fact that sound performs the tension between and among cultural systems of sound, therein producing a cultural hybridity, in the sense that cultural theorist Ien Ang speaks of when she suggests that "rather than seeing hybridity as a synonym for an easy multicultural harmony, or as an instrument for the achievement thereof, I want to suggest that the concept of hybridity should be mobilized to address and analyze the fundamental *uneasiness* inherent in our global condition of togetherness-in-difference" (200).

Critics who try to hear "an easy multicultural harmony" will not find it in *Québécité*; however, they will find an articulation of the "uneasiness" that Ang refers to, and this is what, I think, complicates any reading of the jazz opera as resolved form. The hybrid form of jazz opera, or what Clarke calls a "gumbo concoction" (11), presents itself not as a way to speak about this uneasiness, but as a solution to it. As Heble concludes in his "Postlude" to the jazz opera's libretto, pairing this state of "uneasiness" with one of hope, "In an era when demands for tighter controls on immigration and border-crossing threaten the dreams of the aggrieved, the structures of hope, possibility, and momentum embodied in Clarke's rainbow quartet of lovers seem particularly pertinent" (101).[4] I suggest that scene v, "Dans le brouillard," shows this rainbow quartet of lovers as characterized by the desire underlining their words, longing for what we might call togetherness. It is a scene in which all four characters are "lost in the fog, each oblivious to the others" (80). Yet, as they sing, Clarke's stage directions imagine how "their songs interlock" (80) and, in the performance of this interlocking, their songs produce polyphonic music.

Importantly, the scene of interlocking voices combines a desire for togetherness with a state of unease. As McNeilly observes in his review of the performance: "[*Québécité*] is not a work about easy resolutions, but an attempt to embody, and to extemporize upon, difference" (123). Just as the voices remain distinct in their cultural associations as the jazz opera comes to a close, those voices, though distinct, overlap in this scene to form a collective sentiment of desire, a desire for togetherness that coincides with Clarke's desire to claim the term *québécité* for all, not just a select group. But does the voicing of this togetherness successfully navigate a path outside the "sedative politics" of control that Kamboureli warns of?

In answering this question, we must keep in mind that, both in Kamboureli's reading of the Multiculturalism Act and in the moment of this final scene, there is "a striving to an 'ideal' community" (Kamboureli 112). This does not mean that we should abandon multiculturalism discourses, but rather that we need to see the value in applying multiculturalism as a framework that allows for a thinking, not of centres and margins, but, as Kamboureli suggests, of "relational knowledge" (161). In this way, her argument draws upon Ella Shohat and Robert Stam's compelling assertion that "the word multiculturalism has no essence; it points to a debate" (qtd. in Kamboureli 161).

Thus, in our critical responses to *Québécité*, we must grapple with its call for an awareness of how the textual and embodied performances of this piece *point towards* a debate larger than what we see and hear. Moreover, *Québécité* points towards a space of dialogue that extends out and among performers and audience. Yet can this space of dialogue also involve productive listening? Exemplifying this concern is McNeilly's apt questioning of whether Laxmi represents "a critical scepticism about the ease with which ethnically distinct interlocutors can actually listen to one another" (123). Nevertheless, the relationality that McNeilly calls for in terms of the performers' own voices offers a model for the audience to follow as well. It is in this way that the piece calls for a critical *polyphony* on behalf of the listener, to hear it from within and *among* multiple voices: a polyphonic listening that listens across languages, musical genres, and cultures, and then listens back upon itself. These actions require a rethinking of what is asked of a critical audience. Thus, *if* the debate that multiculturalism points towards is one that can be, as Kamboureli notes, cacophonous and discordant while demanding "that both interlocutors change" (161), then a polyphonic listening provides a valid approach to enacting this change. As a performance that combines the textual libretto with embodied sound, *Québécité* moves us towards this change through its words—words waiting to be sung.

Endnotes

1. Julia C. Obert's "The Cultural Capital of Sound: *Québécité's* Acoustic Hybridity" (*Postcolonial Text* [online] 2.4 [2006]: 1–14) frames the transcultural sound of this jazz opera in terms of its acoustic space, which "exceeds the bilingual, and approximates the multicultural" (2). As Obert notes, "while Clarke often celebrates creolization and cross-cultural exchange, he also sounds the *difficulties* of such exchange" (10), which foregrounds the by-products of cultural exchange and speaks to the issue of what creates productive dissonance.
2. It is this embodiment of difference that cultural theorist Sarah Ahmed, in "Multiculturalism and the Proximity of Strangers" (in *Strange Encounters: Embodied Others in Post-Coloniality*. New York: Routledge, 2000. 95–113), hears in the discourse of Australian multiculturalism, which offers a comparative framework for the Canadian context. Ahmed critiques this formation of a national identity through the claiming of difference because this allows the nation "to imagine itself as heterogeneous (to claim their differences as 'our differences')" (96). Ahmed posits the "stranger stranger" as the re-doubled figure who cannot be "taken in" by the nation (97). However, I suggest that the acoustic challenges the very process of assimilation itself.
3. In *The Protestant Ethnic and the Spirit of Late Capitalism* (New York: Columbia UP, 2002), cultural theorist Rey Chow reads the Canadian Multiculturalism Act as exemplifying how what she calls the "difference revolution" has been deployed across both high theory and

national politics (128). Chow describes the Act as "an attempt to be inclusive and celebratory [that] serves, in the end, to mask and perpetuate the persistent problems of social inequality" (133). The words "inclusive and celebratory" are particularly relevant to *Québécité* because they encapsulate the *jouissance* expressed by the characters as they sing the final chorus, "*Vive notre québécité*" (92).

4. In the libretto, Clarke's stage directions describe how the jazz opera should conclude with a polyphony of multicultural sounds and a multi-coloured Québécois flag: "The lovers exit as couples—riding Vespa scooters. Then church bells, horns, sitar, Chinese violin (p'i-p'a), harmonium, harp, tabla, and thumb piano commix. The Quebec flag descends from the rafters, but its four panels are, here, beige, pink, gold, and indigo, and its fleurs-de-lys are, correspondingly, violet, orange, black, and crimson, and its cruciform segmentation is green" (92). Wojtyra's visual image for this final scene includes elements of this description, yet it depicts the rainbow as rays of light shining through the flag, rather than re-colouring the flag itself. While it could be argued that this adaptation of the stage directions does not convey the full effect of re-defining a Québécois icon, the rainbow of light still evokes the multicultural message of the opera's politics and gestures towards a hopeful future for these characters, which, for myself as a reader of the libretto, brings to mind the words that Clarke uses to conclude his introductory Prelude: "And—look!—light gilds the sky" (12).

Works Cited

Ang, Ien. *On Not Speaking Chinese: Living Between Asia and the West.* New York: Routledge. 2001.

Bannerji, Himani. *Dark Side of the Nation: Essays on Multiculturalism, Nationalism, Gender.* Toronto: Canadian Scholar's P, 2000.

Butler, Judith. *Excitable Speech.* New York: Routledge, 1997.

Chapman, Geoff. "A Bumpy Operatic Ride to Quebec City." *The Toronto Star.* 8 Sept. 2003. 20 July 2004 <http://www.yoonsunchoi.com/reviews/TheStar.com>.

Clarke, George Elliott. *Québécité: A Jazz Fantasia in Three Cantos.* Kentville, NS: Gaspereau P, 2003.

Corbett, John. "Ephemera Underscored: Writing Around Free Improvisation." *Jazz Among the Discourses.* Ed. Krin Gabbard. Durham, NC: Duke UP, 1995. 217–40.

Edwards, Brent Hayes. "Louis Armstrong and the Syntax of Scat." *Critical Inquiry* 28 (2002): 618–50.

Garebian, Keith. "A Review of *Québécité: A Jazz Fantasia in Three Cantos.*" *Books in Canada.* Dec. 2003. 20 July 2004 <http://booksincanada.com>.

Gates, Henry Louis. *The Signifying Monkey: A Theory of Afro-American Literary Criticism.* New York: Oxford UP, 1988.

Gunew, Sneja. *Haunted Nations: The Colonial Dimensions of Multiculturalisms.* London: Routledge, 2004.

Heble, Ajay. *Landing on the Wrong Note: Jazz, Dissonance, and Critical Practice.* New York: Routledge, 2000.

—. "New Contexts for Canadian Criticism: Democracy, Counterpoint, Responsibility." *New Contexts of Canadian Criticism.* Ed. Ajay Heble and Donna

Palmateer Pennee. Peterborough, ON: Broadview, 1997. 78–97.

—. "'You know you break no laws by dreaming': George Elliott Clarke's *Québécité*. A Postlude." *Québécité*. Kentville, NS: Gaspereau P, 2003. 97–101.

Hutcheon, Linda, and Michael Hutcheon. *Bodily Charm: Living Opera*. Lincoln: U of Nebraska P, 2000.

Kamboureli, Smaro. *Scandalous Bodies: Diasporic Literature in English Canada*. Don Mills, ON: Oxford UP, 2000.

Khanna, Vish. "La Belle *Québécité*: Multiculturalism Examined in Festival's Jazz Opera." Excerpted from *Echo* Magazine: Sept. 2003. 20 Sept. 2004 <http://www.echoweekly.com/viewstory.php?storyid=114-page=1>.

Kristeva, Julia. "Desire in Language: From One Identity to the Other." *The Portable Kristeva*. Ed. Kelly Oliver. New York: Columbia UP, 2002. 93–115.

McNeilly, Kevin. "This Ain't No Time for Innocence: *Québécité*, a Jazz Opera by George Elliott Clarke and D.D. Jackson." *Canadian Theatre Review* 118 (2004): 121–123.

Philip, M. Nourbese. "Why Multiculturalism Can't End Racism." *Frontiers: Selected Essays and Writings on Racism and Culture*. Stratford, ON: Mercury, 1992. 181–86.

Québécité. In Performance. CBC Radio 2. 10 Oct 2003.

Québécité. By George Elliott Clarke and D.D. Jackson. Dir. Colin Taylor. River Run Centre, Guelph. 5 Sept 2003.

Québécité. By George Elliott Clarke and D.D. Jackson. Dir. Colin Taylor. Vancouver East Cultural Centre, Vancouver. 18 Oct. 2003.

Rasula, Jed. "The Media of Memory: The Seductive Menace of Records in Jazz History." *Jazz Among the Discourses.* Ed. Krin Gabbard. Durham, NC: Duke UP, 1995. 134–62.

Walser, Robert. "'Out of Notes': Signification, Interpretation, and the Problem of Miles Davis." *Jazz Among the Discourses.* Ed. Krin Gabbard. Durham, NC: Duke UP, 1995. 16–88.

Creating a Canadian Odyssey: George Elliott Clarke's Global Perspective in *Trudeau: Long March / Shining Path*

LYDIA WILKINSON

The cast of *Trudeau: Long March/Shining Path* saw their workshop production at the Harbourfront Centre's Enwave Theatre open to a packed house. The sizable audience was transported on a trip around the world, as D.D. Jackson's score and George Elliott Clarke's libretto accompanied Trudeau's travels, moving from the soulful strings of Chinese folk, to the dance beats of the Cuban rumba, to the jazz piano of a Montreal bar. The transcultural score was called for by Clarke's narrative, which follows Trudeau through his tours of 1949 and 1960, and Trudeaumania of 1968, before revisiting the Prime Minister in Montreal for his death in 2000. Focused on his world travels and meetings with international leaders, Clarke and Jackson sketch a picture of Pierre Elliott Trudeau as global traveller, adventurer, cosmopolitan and worldly sage, or to borrow Clarke's more lyrical description, a "romantic, chevalier, feisty, swashbuckling, Napoleonic, Caesarian, Ulyssean, Maoist character" (Clarke, 2007). Clarke's excess of descriptors here denotes a character that even in a single representation is complicated and multifaceted, offering up any number of interpretations for other biographies and biographical performances. Thus the Trudeau of *Long March/Shining Path* differs from Brooke Johnson's pensive intellect in *Trudeau Stories*, from the obscenely sexualized Trudeau of the Shameless Dames Burlesque Troupe, from the coldly rational of Griffiths' *Maggie & Pierre*, and from the parodic of the *VideoCab* cycles.

Characterizations of Trudeau reflect the individual concerns of their author, and in Clarke's case his interest lies in multiculturalism, as he provides an alternative view to a historical record that often recalls Trudeau's policies on culture and diversity as simplistic, exclusionary and ultimately unrealized. Trudeau's 1971 Multicultural Policy responded, as did his cultural policies more generally, to Canada's social and political scene as well as his personal politics. Trudeau's public career, spanning the 60s and 70s, coincided with a period of increased independence within Canada, a coming of age marked on one side by the country's 100th anniversary and on the other by the patriation of the constitution. Yet this same period was also a time of instability. Provinces were divided over regional interests, and often vied for greater freedom from federal intervention. Separatists in Quebec, especially, fought for an independent French nation; a struggle later legitimized with the ascent of the PQ and the 1980 referendum.

Whether declaiming regional individuality or federal commonalities this time was an important one for the founding of Canadian culture. The country's identity crisis seemingly had its solution in the nurturing of a shared national character; yet Trudeau was a leader who refused to subscribe to a project that insisted solely on cultural similarities. In *The Teeth of Time* Ramsay Cook cites two of Trudeau's major political influences as Lord Acton and

Elie Kedourie, both of whom argue that a nation should not be defined by a homogeneous culture, but rather be a unit constituted by multiple intersecting and sometimes overlapping identities. Trudeau attempted to navigate the potentially divergent interests of encouraging multiculturalism and building national character, laying out the importance of acknowledging cultural difference within the nation while maintaining its territorial boundaries.

Trudeau: Long March/Shining Path sees Trudeau's multiculturalism realized in its ideal form, as a culturally diverse Canada is literally embodied on the stage, through a staging that dispenses with traditional colour-conscious and colour-blind casting to enact the overlapping ethnic-cultural identities posited by Acton, Kedourie and later Trudeau. The Prime Minister's tenor "may be Aboriginal/ First Nations (or Metis) person," Margaret "should be Indian (out of Kashmir or Bihar) with a command of Indian vocal/musical traditions. Or she could be Italian. Let her identity be as indeterminate as Canadian actress Rae Dawn Chong in Jean Jacques Annaud's film *Quest for Fire*," while Mao Zedong's baritone, "may also play Fidel Castro and Jacques Fanon, and may be Chinese or Cuban or Quebecois" (Clarke 27–28). The potential of a single performer to embody multiculturalism mirrors Trudeau's ideal Canada, in which distinct cultures are acknowledged and included within one national space. By rejecting ethnic-cultural divides, and emphasizing the importance of global influences on Trudeau's political growth, Clarke and composer D.D. Jackson create a Trudeau that can testify to the advantages of multiculturalism while simultaneously personifying it in Trudeau's ideal form.

I met Clarke's PET on five different occasions last year. The first was in the early publication of the libretto in

Canadian Theatre Review. New to the subject of Trudeau biographies, I glossed over Clarke's introduction and notes, all but missing the complex characterizations and their symbolic meaning, and mistakenly imagining a Maggie whose pale skin and chestnut hair resembled that of the "real" Margaret, and a Trudeau whose voice resonated with his recognizable Quebec-Anglais lilt. The second was in the Hart House reading room, where Clarke rushed in between two commitments to embody a thoroughly engaging Trudeau, despite his frenetic pace. This Trudeau shared physical, visual and aural space with his author, beginning to enact the layered characterizations suggested by Clarke's directions, in which the human body becomes a palimpsest for multiple identities and experiences. The third was in Harbourfront's Enwave theatre, where the musical score accompanied the melding and mixing of physical identities upon the stage. The fourth was in a noisy diner where Clarke riffed for myself and my co-interviewer on subjects from adaptation, to a Canadian multicultural geography, to the Kennedy assassination, and finally to his Trudeau. The fifth was in the published version of the libretto, where Clarke's script is joined by an extensive paratext, what Robert Stam, citing Gérard Genette, describes as "titles, prefaces, postfaces, epigraphs, dedications, illustrations, and even book jackets and signed autographs, in short all the accessory messages and commentaries which come to surround the text and which at times become virtually indistinguishable from it" (Stam 28).

Clarke's presence grew with each of my meetings with Trudeau; by the time I reached the published text, Trudeau was equally sharing his space with Clarke as creator, who acknowledged his authorial intervention into the narrative of Trudeau, by redefining his subject as his own and writing a Trudeau that could embody the Prime Minister while also embodying a multicultural Canada. At the same time, Clarke's own commentary, provided through interviews, essays, prefaces and endnotes, highlights the inevitable limitations of the work as one individual's rendering of the Prime Minister. While I may have left the Enwave theatre praising the legacy of Trudeau, I left my interview with Clarke and completed my reading of the published text reminded of the subjectivity of any portrayal of any public figure. Rather than simply asking how Clarke constructed his Trudeau as a citizen of the world then, I would like to complicate things a little, to consider how he concomitantly undermines the "truth" of this telling, and his political purpose for using this strategy.

While re-imagining Trudeau, Clarke complicated his subject's ethno-cultural identity. In our interview Clarke recalled: "I did want to produce a 'black' version of Trudeau (no sense doing what others will do): so he's a wanderer, a fighter, and a skirt-chaser, who speaks in Hip Hop rhythms" (Clarke, 2007). Trudeau's importance as a representative public figure to Canadian minorities, despite his privileged, white, upper middle class French and Scottish origins is an important point for Clarke, and is taken up in greater detail in his preface to the published libretto entitled "Vrai: Un Essai". He writes:

> … As a 'visible minority' person (my official identity in white-majority Canada), I seize the right to 'write what I like' including this libretto about a wealthy, European male; one canonized—and demonized—by hordes of white Canuck lawyers and social scientists, but also by poets, artists, journalists, and historians.
>
> Trudeau was, is, though, a cult figure for many Canadians de couleur …

> Considerations of Trudeau by 'Third World' Canadians are absent, however, from media celebrations or interrogations of the man and his legacy. In line with the precept that Canada is a white country, 'multicultural' Canadians are expected to limit their political expression to raucous, ghettoized, candidate-nomination meetings. Yet, our vision of Trudeau would be enhanced were we to appreciate that he really was un citoyen du monde, the first Prime Minister who was comfortable with a Canada that looked more like Expo '67 and less like the grand Ole Opry. (Clarke 21–22)

While positioning Trudeau as inclusive and internationalist here, Clarke concurrently articulates his motivation, as a visible minority Canadian, for writing and righting Trudeau: he is inserting a "multicultural" voice into Trudeau's story and, by extension, offering an alternative to the demonizing and canonizing tales told by his "white" biographers. He is also appropriating the theatrical and political stage as a place for multiple voices and identities, allowing a politician who is representative of multicultural Canada to play out his ideal in a space where the objections of his detractors can be controlled and contained. Through this process Clarke performs a type of dramaturgical reification on the late Prime Minister, using his play to turn Trudeau into a symbol of multiculturalism that can exist outside of and even in contradiction to the established historical record.

The most extended discussion of Trudeau's shortcomings occurs quite late in the libretto. It is 1970 and Trudeau is met in the lobby of the House of Commons by Simone Cixous, a Quebecoise reporter, who voices the complaints of the people, arguing that the PM panders to big business, destroys First Nations culture, and has instituted a bilingualism policy that is alienating both the English and French electorate. The scene is framed by two asides by jazz musician Roscoe Robertson. His first reads:

> An empty mirror,
> A naked emp'ror,
> A hackneyed athlete,
> An acne'd aesthete,
> An old news story,
> He's rusted glory:
> A yesterday craze
> In a purple haze! (Clarke 88)

This scene recalls three earlier scenes. In 1960 Cixous and Robertson spy the young Trudeau in a Montreal jazz bar and proceed to sing his praises, noting his trip to China, his handling of the Asbestos strike and his scenester status in French Canada. Eight years later, they join him first for a leadership speech in Ottawa and second for the Jean-Baptiste parade in Quebec. Both venues provide a space to record and participate in Trudeaumania, as he whips up an English Canadian frenzy in Ottawa and shows his strength by stoically sitting through a whipping by beer bottles in Quebec. Cixous and Robertson, disenchanted by 1970, articulate Canada's changing response to Trudeau over the course of his leadership, but these exchanges take place within just twenty pages of Clarke's text and fifteen or so minutes of the performed opera. In fact, Canada's own response to the Prime Minister is only explored towards the end of Clarke's libretto, and seems to move at a more heightened pace than the proceeding fifty pages of travel. This structure serves a number of purposes. Firstly, it contains and diminishes the oppositional voices in a small controllable space, just twenty pages of text, recalling the containment of minority voices to "raucous, ghettoized, candidate-nomination meetings." Secondly, while quelling this opposition, it also calls attention to the potential for a rapid loss of support within political spheres, pointing to the fickleness of Canada's voting public. Thirdly, the manipulation of time and pace, as a convention, reminds us of Clarke's authorial intervention as subjective biographer.

Clarke's active intervention is first introduced in his disclaimer, which reads:

> This literary work offers an interpretation of the lives of several historical personages, all rendered fictitiously. The author has distorted known facts, altered dates, imagined dialogues, and invented situations. His characters should not be confused with actual individuals, either living or dead. This dramatic poem is purely a theatre of imagination (Clarke 15).

While Clarke can reasonably insist on the fiction of his characters' lines and behaviour they take on a more complicated meaning when read in conjunction with the playwright's preface, in which he clearly sketches out his "reading" of the Prime Minister, and supports his personal beliefs with hefty footnotes linking observations to real, factual events. For example, Clarke's claim in the essay that "study and travel transformed the erstwhile provincial fascist into a cosmo, anti-nationalist liberal" (Clarke 22), is supported by a page length footnote detailing the global political environment of the 60s and its effect on Trudeau as a young traveller. A correlation between the PM's experiences and ascent to Canadian power can be read onto Clarke's libretto, but it is only in the preface that the link is explicitly stated and supported with evidence.

Conversely, while Clarke's preface may reference Trudeau's travels as central to his political development, it is only through the play proper that we get a sense of their novelty and danger to a young intellectual. Read in tandem then the essay and libretto serve a dialogic function; the content of one exposes the gaps of the other, and these gaps make clear the limitations of both monolithic historic narratives and imagined, subjective histories to accurately represent the complexities of a lived subject.

Clarke similarly exposes the self-conscious construction of his particular Trudeau by dispensing with a "real" or accurate chronology to allow for a Trudeau whose growth in response to particular meetings and relationships with world leaders reflects and supports Clarke's own understanding of the public figure. Trudeau's first meeting with Chairman Mao is staged during the People's Liberation Army's capture of Nanjing in 1949, eleven years prior to their first meeting on historical record, and fourteen before they spoke at any length in an official capacity. During this fictionalized meeting, Trudeau recollects a favourite anecdote, recalling an encounter with three threatening locals on a trip to Ur. He recounts:

> In Palestine,
> Two bandits, to seize what was mine,
> Brandished daggers at my visage,
> But I astonished each savage
> By seizing one of their daggers,
> Then stabbed the air and staggered,
> Cried out poems, spewed mad madrigals,
> Alexandrines, octosyllables,
> So the bandits feared me insane—
> Or a saint—and so fled the terrain … (Clarke 38)

The possibility of Mao as a captive audience to this story is impossible given Trudeau's non-existent political position and, even more problematically, Mao's commitment to the war being raged around them at the time.

Having accused Trudeau of plagiarizing *Cyrano de Bergerac* in his tale, Mao returns with some political advice:

> Firing squads accomplish more than bureaucrats:
> I trust devils more than I trust diplomats
> The State must mandate counterweights
> And balance artists and elites. (Clarke 38–39)

Trudeau subscribed to Mao's counterweights throughout his political career, and thus Clarke has provided an exchange that on the one hand is entirely probable in a different context, but entirely untrue within the "real" history of Trudeau's life. While his around the world journey in 1949 certainly contributed to Trudeau's growing social consciousness, it was likely due to his voyeuristic participation in decolonization movements rather than any political mentoring by other world leaders. In our interview, Clarke suggested that Trudeau's interest in experiencing violent upheavals in China and the Middle East may have been motivated by a need to compensate for his non-action in the most focal Western conflict of his generation: World War II. While Trudeau's writings do not directly suggest that he regretted his lack of participation, they do tend to focus quite heavily on the role of these travels in forming his political position. It follows, then, that his witnessing of conflicts encouraged him to reflect upon strategies for political unification and cultural tolerance over divisive political action. By beginning his political dialogue in 1949, Clarke purposefully eliminates a time in which Trudeau was politically disengaged with global conflicts.

Clarke's interest in uncovering and learning from Trudeau's political interests is discussed further in a section entitled "Hansard," in which Clarke lists his various sources, including *Cyrano de Bergerac* and Mao Zedong's *Little Red Book*, as well as the Prime Minister's own writing in *Against the Current* and *Two Innocents in Red China*. Yet Clarke also catalogues many of his own influences; they include, but are not limited to, Thulani Davis's *The Life and Times of Malcolm X*, Ian Fleming's *You Only Live Twice*, and Mandela and Castro's *How Far We Slaves Have Come*. Clarke, then, seems to be acknowledging the plurality of voices and literary works that shape both his writing strategy and his understanding of his subject. As the structuring principle for Clarke's influences, the Hansard reminds us of the politicization of any and every source, while underscoring the varied influences inherent in any one work or any one cultural figure. Clarke has chosen to animate his own Trudeau, but this Trudeau is informed and interpreted by multiple authorial voices.

Similarly, the characters on the stage are animated by a single performer who enacts several identities. The script calls for actors who, like Trudeau, can represent varied characters. It is worth returning here to Roscoe Robertson's jazz aside. He claims that Trudeau offers up "an empty mirror;" for a country searching for its identity this empty mirror is a negative, but for a country made up of distinct, strong and varied identities the empty mirror offers a space to be filled by each individual, and often, this individual is not reducible to a single cultural identity. Clarke creates a portrait of the Prime Minister as a multicultural and global leader that is as self-consciously constructed as any other rendering of the public figure. In turn he provides Canadians with an imagined narrative that reifies Canada's evolving multiculturalism in the person of Trudeau. Clarke seems to be suggesting, then, that Trudeau provides Canadians with a slate that is limitless and rewritable, allowing every Clarke, Griffiths and Johnson to cover it with their image of a Canadian culture.

Works Cited

Clarke, George Elliott. "Personal Interview." April 2007.

Clarke, George Elliott. *Trudeau: Long March/Shining Path.* Kentville, NS: Gaspereau Publishers, 2007.

Stam, Robert. "Introduction: The Theory and Practice of Adaptation." *Literature and Film: a Guide to the Theory and Practice of Film Adaptation.* Oxford: Blackwell, 2005. 1–52.

“The Little State of Africadia is a Community of Believers”: Replacing the Regional and Remaking the Real in the Work of George Elliott Clarke

ALEXANDER MACLEOD

In keeping with the geographic vocabulary which seems almost unavoidable in any discussion of the relationship between literature and place, this paper opens by surveying the landscape of contemporary Atlantic-Canadian writing and mapping two distinct lines of critical inquiry. These two paths cover different territory and, in the beginning, they move along separate routes before eventually coming together in the end. The first path follows the career trajectory of George Elliott Clarke from his early work up to the present day and attempts to evaluate the unique contribution he has made to Canadian literature as an award-winning poet, dramatist, editor and essayist. The second re-examines some of the traditional challenges, as well as new developments, that have recently enlivened the debate surrounding contemporary regionalist literary theory and its relationship to current trends in the field of cultural geography. Where the two paths intersect, I return to Clarke's work and demonstrate how his efforts to establish an "Africadian" literary canon transgress the normal boundaries between real and imagined social space and, in the process, extend regionalist discourse into new areas of political and social action.[1]

The Departure of the Native

The story of George Elliott Clarke's career, thus far, has been a tale of rapid ascent through the hierarchy of academic and artistic celebrity in Canada. In less than twenty years, he has moved from the relatively peripheral standing of a young maritime poet and graduate student to become one of the country's most influential literary figures. Marginalized at the beginning of his writing life by his race, his regional affiliations, his age, his political beliefs and his aesthetic commitments, Clarke now occupies a position of central importance in Canada's largest literature department in Canada's largest university in Canada's largest city. He has won the nation's top literary prize for poetry, the Governor General's Award; he maintains a regular review column in Nova Scotia's largest circulating newspaper, *The Chronicle Herald*; and his work and public commentary are routinely featured in coast-to-coast radio and television broadcasts. In 2005, Clarke's first novel, *George & Rue,* a chilling but controversial re-telling of the events surrounding the 1949 murder of a Fredericton taxi driver and the subsequent executions of George and Rufus Hamilton, was published to widespread critical acclaim. When we consider all he has accomplished in such a relatively short amount of time (as I write this Clarke is still only 45 years old), it is easy to understand why some see Clarke not only as an essential poet and literary critic, but also as a more broadly defined cultural icon. Although he is perhaps at only the midpoint of his career, Clarke has already developed into one of those rare scholars that come along perhaps once in a generation: He is an academic who has at least partially escaped from the confines of the university's ivory tower stereotype to become a genuine public intellectual.

It is important to understand, however, that Clarke's precipitous rise to the status of a national figurehead and/or regional spokesperson has not come without its costs. Though he has always maintained close emotional and spiritual ties with his native Nova Scotia, for much of the last two decades, almost half his life, Clarke has lived outside the province. His academic training took him from Waterloo (BA) to Halifax (MA) to Kingston (PhD), and before he settled into his current position at the University of Toronto, Clarke's professional life was punctuated by longer stops in Ottawa, Durham, North Carolina and Montreal and countless other shorter journeys across the country and around the world. As anyone who has read his work will know, Clarke is a seventh-generation Canadian and his family can trace its genealogical lineage directly back to the arrival of the Black Loyalists and Black Refugees who migrated to the then-British colony of Nova Scotia in 1783 and 1815 respectively. Clarke's writing is unquestionably tied to the historical and contemporary experiences of this community, but this linkage between the poet and the place he represents to the wider world is not as one-dimensional or direct as many would assume. In a revealing interview with Maureen Moynagh, Clarke suggests there has always been a "terrific tension" in his work caused by the fact that for much of his career he has lived away from the community that defines both the centre and the limit of his poetry (78). In a particularly candid moment, Clarke admits that his relationship with Black Nova Scotia has not always been easy or positive: "I left here in 1979 to go off to the University of Waterloo, and in fact I left here quite deliberately because I was fed up with the place. I just had to get away. So I did, and immediately became tremendously homesick, and felt that I had made a drastic mistake in having left. And I started writing poems reflecting my Nova Scotianness, and my feelings about this place" (78).

In this statement Clarke interestingly identifies his physical departure from Nova Scotia as the key event which triggered and then intensified his creative engagement with the province. In this formulation (one we often see repeated with expatriate writers), the poet seems to gain the ability to imaginatively re-invent his or her home only after that place has been physically left behind. The vivid imaginary geography we encounter in Clarke's writing almost demands a separation from its referent, the "real world" social space that exists "out there" beyond his pages. This gap which opens up between Clarke's real and imagined geographies is hotly contested territory that critics can not take for granted. Though outside commentators may wish to treat Clarke's work as a direct and reliable ethnographic representation of Black Nova Scotia, advanced literary scholars must remember that there is absolutely nothing simple or one-dimensional about Clarke's connection to this community.

In his work absence and belonging are intimately intertwined and often Clarke is more interested in capturing the disorienting and dislocating experience of the exile or outsider than he is in accurately recording the rooted perspective we normally associate with the insider's point of view. As Michelle Banks' research ably demonstrates, rather than uncovering the "true" cultural geography of Black Nova Scotia, Clarke's work is motivated more by "the desire for a home place" (58). Despite the deep roots of his family tree, Clarke's writing originates from a profound sense of cultural deracination and it establishes what Banks calls a "thorough identification between the voice of the poems and the condition of homelessness" (67). In fact, when we look past Clarke's public persona, and engage carefully with only his work itself, we see that there may be no poet at work in Canadian literature today who is *less* comfortable with the blind embrace of community and *more* aware of the many demands and difficulties which lurk inside what, on the surface, might seem like a simple relationship between the poet and his or her home. In Clarke's writing, both creative and critical, the "exceptional" talent of the artist is caught in the struggle to speak both to and for the "average" experience of the community.

Clarke explores this troubling dynamic in more detail in another interview with Anne Compton. Here he tells an emotionally charged story about being almost completely rejected by precisely the people he is trying to serve:

> I had this horrifying experience which I think every writer should go through at one time or another. In the spring of 1986, I was invited to take part in a fund-raising event put on by the Black Cultural Centre of Nova Scotia. I was the only poet on the program. Every one else was a performer. I was there as the poet. I read in the way I had been taught to read in the university […] very plain, no emotion, just straightforward

> recitation. But this was in front of an audience of my peers, of my own community. So people started yelling at me: "Get off the stage." It was very direct: "You're boring. Go home." The people didn't want to hear some dry shit. (145)

Obviously, this kind of rejection is a traumatic experience for Clarke. It is very difficult to be told to "go home" when you believe you are already there. In response to his audience's initial negative reaction, Clarke changes strategies at this reading and later decides to "perform" some of his then-new material from *Whylah Falls*. As the rambunctious catcalls for his dismissal die down, the tide eventually turns and the people come back to their poet, cheering him on now with calls to "Preach it" and to "Testify" (146). Clarke's story about the reading (which begins so hopelessly) ultimately concludes with a happy ending. The *Whylah Falls* material succeeds where other, earlier poems failed.

For Clarke, this experience at the Black Cultural Centre serves as a kind of life lesson or perhaps as a very intense period of on-the-job training. After this initial rejection he decides that he "will never write again anything [he] cannot read before [his] own community" (146). When Compton pushes him to further explore his status as a "wanderer" and "a permanent exile," Clarke admits: "I haven't had an address in Nova Scotia since 1987. How can I write about this place any more when my connection to it is so tenuous? I really feel this dilemma between being away and wanting to get back" (157).

The anxiety Clarke feels about being torn between his literary presence within the province and his physical absence from Nova Scotia is understandable. From a national or international perspective, it may be easy to cast Clarke as the dominant and defining figure of contemporary Black writing within the region, but at home and on the ground, his status is more contentious. As is often the case, those individuals that the outside world recognizes as prophets are rarely seen in such an exalted light by the people who know them best. Like any other diverse collection of individuals, Black Nova Scotian society has its own internal divisions, and although Clarke has done more than any other individual to promote and publish local writers, his work offers us only one way of writing and reading his culture and not everyone in the community agrees with his portrayal. As an editor, reviewer and anthologist, Clarke has established himself as a fairly aggressive and exacting evaluator of poetic quality and achievement. Charged with the responsibility to call it like he sees it, and to judge harshly if he feels harsh judgements are required, Clarke's sometimes controversial commentary on his peers has often placed him at odds with the more nurturing support structure of the Nova Scotian writing community.

In his now infamous "unprejudiced" review of poetry collections by fellow Nova Scotians Maxine Tynes and David Woods, for example, Clarke serves up his compliments and criticism in equal measure. Though he believes Tynes and Woods are "irreplaceable contributors to the newly diversified canon of Canadian poetry," he also argues that their work lacks originality, is weakened by clichéd language, requires "ferocious editing," and should ultimately be considered "middling, but acceptable" (*Odysseys* 304). Obviously these are not the remarks of a critic who suspends his true opinion when addressing the work of his friends. As we might expect, the other side of this family feud holds different views on what constitutes literary merit. Tynes especially has made a clear effort to carve out her own place in Black Nova Scotian writing and to distance herself from Clarke's poetic and political agenda.

As Danielle Fuller and Marjorie Stone have both demonstrated, Tynes's writing and reading of the Black community are almost diametrically opposed to the models promoted by Clarke. According to Fuller, Tynes' staunchly feminist point of view, her more direct connection to the oral tradition of performance poetics, as well as her more accessible "emotive rhetoric" and "everyday imagery" provide a clear alternative to the masculine, textually privileged and more self-consciously "literary" aesthetic standards Clarke often endorses (106–107). In Stone's note on the Clarke vs. Tynes debate, she argues that, rather than ignoring or downplaying such differences of opinion within the Black Nova Scotian literary community, scholars should actually pay more attention to these divisions to ensure they do not portray "the current Black Nova Scotia cultural flowering as more homogenous that it in fact is" (243).

Denying such one-dimensional or artificially homogenous readings of Black Nova Scotian writing is essential if we are to fully appreciate Clarke's contribution to this literature. Clearly, Clarke is a writer who actively courts controversy and encourages dissent rather than politely shying away. From the very beginning of his career, he has positioned his work against any and all vaguely formulated critical readings which might encourage Black stereotyping or diminish the internal diversity of his community. The dominant recurring figure in his work has always been the intellectual exile, an individual who does not fit any standardized role within the society and cannot easily integrate him- or herself into pre-existing social structures.

Even as his poetry has helped re-inscribe the collective experience of Black Nova Scotia into the larger official historical narrative of the Canadian nation, Clarke, like so many of the characters we meet in his writing, has continually struggled with the burden of such a heavy responsibility. As far back as his first 1983 volume, *Saltwater Spirituals and Deeper Blues*, published when Clarke was only twenty-three years old, this focus on the exceptional outsider who longs to "escape" the embrace of the community was already present in masterpiece poems such as "Watercolour for Negro Expatriates in France," and "Crying the Beloved Country." In "Crying," the artistic figure is seen struggling with the decision to leave or to remain rooted:

> why can I not leave you
> like a refugee?
> . . . .
> why can I not depart from you
> like any proud, prodigal son,
> ignoring your eyes'
> black baptist churches?
> what keeps me from easy going?
> Mother, is it your death
> i fear
> or my life? (1–2, 7–14)

In these last lines, the poet wrestles with the personal and public consequences that accompany any decision to stay or go. The final question examines an interdependent relationship in which the survival or destruction of the community cannot be separated from the survival or destruction of the artist. In later volumes of Clarke's work, these same issues of displacement will be addressed again and the same kinds of refrains will repeat.

The very first poem in *Whylah Falls*, for example, is "Look Homeward Exile" and in the earliest stages of this poetic novel the reader is introduced to Xavier Zachary, another outcast/ intellectual figure. We learn that X has been away from home for five years, pursuing his studies in Montreal and that, while his body "drifted sad and tired, in the east," his mind remained focused on the lush landscape of Whylah Falls and on the equally ravishing beauty of his true love, Shelley Clemence ("The River Pilgrim: A Letter" 24). In *Beatrice Chancy*, Beatrice similarly returns home to the Annapolis Valley after three years of convent education and finds that she cannot easily bridge the gap between the woman she has become and the slavery-scarred community she has left behind. After bursting onto the stage with an introductory speech filled with pastoral language and a liberal sprinkling of high culture literary allusions, Beatrice is abruptly told by Lustra not to "be poetical" and reminded that there is no room for "Romanticism" in a world where "folk sweat day-long in fields" (32).

The theme of dislocation continues to dominate much of the 1994 compilation, *Lush Dreams, Blue Exile*. This book is subtitled "Fugitive Poems: 1978–1993" and its closing section focuses on the experience of the Black Loyalists who left Nova Scotia in 1792 and migrated to Sierra Leone in search of a better life. In his self-described "American" book, 2001's *Blue*, Clarke's tight focus on Nova Scotia expands again (9). Short poems, such as "Haligonian Market Cry" and "No Second N.S." are mixed into a now much broader catalogue that wrestles not only with local subjects but also with the wider experience of an African

Diaspora spread out across the country, the continent and the world.

By the time we reach *Execution Poems* in 2001 and 2003's *Québécité*, Clarke's creative work has temporarily left Nova Scotia behind and moved on to settings farther west in New Brunswick and Quebec. The same progression away from the immediately local and into the wider world can be seen in the author's critical work. After 1991's *Fire on the Water* project—a two-volume anthology specifically devoted to "Black Nova Scotian Writing"—Clarke's next two book-length projects—the anthology, *Eyeing the North Star,* and the essay collection *Odysseys Home*—were published with subtitles which revealingly replaced his former provincial focus with a new national concern for "African-Canadian Literature." With each step he takes, Clarke seems to expand his definition of the "home place" and to extend his geographical range over an ever-broadening cultural space.

Rethinking Regionalism

At this stage, I want to temporarily place Clarke's work to the side and turn back to our second line of inquiry. This path, I fear, may turn out to be far more challenging because it confronts the most basic theoretical assumptions on which any discussion of literary regionalism, Atlantic-Canadian or otherwise, must rest. I realize the concerns I raise here introduce more problems than solutions, but these issues deserve close attention, firstly because Clarke's work touches on so many of the central ideas related to regionalist literary thought, and secondly because I think scholars who have given so much energy to the study of Atlantic-Canadian literature often work at such a depth, and surrounded by so many like-minded colleagues, that it is often difficult to come back to the "surface" and articulate careful responses to what must be the first questions in this field.

Although generations of editors, anthologists and critics in Atlantic Canada have worked hard to establish, defend and extend a regionally defined canon, this same group of thinkers has never been able to articulate a clear critical statement that might once-and-for-all establish what the defining attributes of a regionalist aesthetic might be. Despite the best efforts of the leading regionalist scholars working in the field today—including Herb Wyile, David Jordan, Francesco Lorriggio, Michael Kowalewski, Alison Calder and Lisa Chalykoff—the theoretical arguments on which regionalist discourse rests are only beginning to be excavated and many of the essential questions remain unanswered.

For example: Where should we place regionalist discourse in a scholarly landscape that is already crowded with so many different (and usually positive) models of postcolonial theory? Or, on the other hand, where should we draw the line between traditional regionalist boosterism and all the other (usually negative) critiques of cultural nationalism that circulate in academia? Is regionalism, as Roberto Maria Dainotto forcefully argues, simply a devious way of reviving the old and discredited ideals of nationalism by "passing them off as 'new' regionalist ones" ("All the Regions" 488). Is regionalism nothing more than nationalism in disguise, working on a smaller and more politically correct scale, but still naively oversimplifying our complex contemporary realities and replacing them with what Dainotto calls pastoral portraits of "organic identity" ("All the Regions" 505)? What should we make of Frank Davey's aggressive charges against the "Maritime Powerlessness" which he believes dominates realist regional fiction in this part of the country (67)? More to the point, do regionalism and realism have to be considered inseparable discourses? Does such an unbreakable union between these two aesthetics inflict what Davey calls a "discursive determinism" on Atlantic-Canadian writers? (67) Does regionalism, as its harshest critics suggest, conceal its real ideology, its politics and its internal conflicts "beneath touristic images of landscape and inarticulately authentic individuals" (Davey "Towards" 5)?

The problems continue to pile up. Is a writer's regionalist status decided by biography or by subject matter? And if biography is our leading criteria, how much of a biography does one need? As we have seen in Clarke's particular case, this has become an important question, specifically in the Atlantic-Canadian context, because so many of the works under consideration were not actually written in the region and because so many of the writers that are studied do not (or did not) actually live in Atlantic Canada during their most productive years. Does it matter, for example, that so many of Lucy Maude Montgomery's novels were written in small-town Ontario, or that Hugh MacLennan spent most of his adult life in Montreal? Why do we argue so passionately about the fact that E. Annie Proulx has the wrong passport and why should we mourn for Elizabeth Bishop who spent only those few intense years of her childhood in the Great Village locale that shaped so much of her best work? Is a "real" presence in a particular geography required (or at least preferred) before scholars can seriously engage with an author's imaginary representations of that place? Clearly, the history of the regional canon seems to support such a claim. Like any other industry, Atlantic-Canadian literature prefers to keep its most talented employees at home. We find it troubling when writers have to go "down the road" to further their careers. When David Adams Richards finally moved from New Brunswick to Toronto in the late 1990's, for example, *Pottersfield Portfolio* marked that sad occasion with the publication of a special tribute issue devoted to the author's life and work. Normally such honours are reserved for writers who are recently deceased, but in Richards' case, luckily, he had only "passed away."

If it is not biography, but subject matter and setting which ultimately decide a work's regionalist status, then what subjects should be allowed and which settings prohibited? As Lynn Coady's introductory essay in *Victory Meat*, "Books that Say Arse," demonstrates with hilarious effectiveness, it is nearly impossible to police such a border, dividing what should be kept in from what should be kept out. No matter how valiantly some may wish to maintain what Coady calls a "fetishized" nineteenth-century pastoral reading of Atlantic Canada, the contemporary world keeps intruding on that vision, barging in with its mass-culture American influences, its technology and its references to contemporary politics (1).

What sort of relationship exists between the imaginary worlds we are presented with in literature and the real geographical facts we engage with in fully materialized concrete environments? Do contemporary scholars believe that nineteenth-century realist aesthetics should be applied to the writers we study today? Do we continue to see the external environment as a stable and reliable pre-existing referent that regionalist fiction unproblematically replicates? Is geography destiny? Do we think the place *makes* the artist, or has our long, if not unproblematic, exposure to cultural studies, postmodernism and the muddled world of "theory" mediated that former position somewhat, allowing us now to think more broadly about how, in even a partial reversal of that old thesis, we might be able to argue that artists actually create the places they inhabit rather than the other way around?

Like any question of origins, this is ultimately a useless kind of chicken and egg problem: What came first? The place or our representation of that place? At this stage of debate, however, even that gesture, the capacity to see a kind of balance between an over-materialized environmentally determinist doctrine and its doppelganger, an overly idealized, completely imaginary fictionalizing is a step in the right direction. As Wyile accurately and succinctly puts it, scholars working on regionalism today must "walk a fine line … between environmental deterministic conceptions of regionalism on the one hand and a deterritorializing postmodern textuality on the other" ("Regionalism, Postcolonialism" 158).

Rather than viewing these challenges as the inescapable weaknesses of regionalist writing and criticism, recent work by Clarke and many others proves that the complexity of regionalist aesthetics—that fine-line balancing act that regionalism and its study require—may actually be the greatest strength of this literature. Rescued from the state of discursive dormancy in which it has lingered for more than a century, contemporary regionalist writers and critics are beginning to shed their old reputations as simple, one-dimensional recorders of geographic reality and ethnographic culture. The old portrait of regionalism as an essentially conservative, inherently realistic, inescapably mimetic aesthetic is slowly giving way to a new model as today's writers effectively re-invent the genre for a new time and an entirely new way of thinking about place.

Led by the theoretical arguments initiated by the French philosopher Henri Lefebvre in his earth-shattering text, *The Production of Space*, and nurtured along by the excellent work of geographers such as Edward Soja, Derek Gregory and David Harvey, literary scholars are only now beginning to understand that regionalist writers are active participants in the cultural construction of the worlds they inhabit. Literary critics familiar with the teachings of current spatial theory are finally starting to examine the links that regionalist texts establish between what Soja calls "spatial ontology" (*Postmodern Geographies* 118) and "spatial epistemology" (*Thirdspace* 80). They are starting to see that "being placed" ontologically in any particular social environment is a never-ending intellectual process rather than a passive outcome, and that there is nothing fixed or predetermined about the strategies writers use to locate their work within the constantly shifting cultural spaces of what Soja calls a simultaneously "real-and-imagined" geography (*Thirdspace* 11).

Building a Past for The Future: The Imaginary Architecture of Africadia

The intersection between real-and-imagined spatiality is also the crossroads where the two lines of inquiry I have been tracing in this paper come together. As we have seen, Clarke's work straddles the line between traditional and contemporary interpretations of cultural geography. Read in a certain way, Clarke can be easily classified as a traditional regionalist. He is deeply committed to his role as an anthropological recorder and museum curator for Black Nova Scotian history. The omnipresent photographs in his books, the archival material, the recipes, the music, the newspaper clippings, the long lists of dedication and acknowledgement, the obvious indebtedness he feels to writers who preceded him in the eighteenth and nineteenth century waves of Black Nova Scotian literature—people such as David George, John Marrant and Boston King—all indicate that Clarke sees himself as a figure charged with a near religious, but definitely political, responsibility to collect, protect and nurture the cultural artefacts of his community. In the Moynagh interview, Clarke states very clearly:

> [T]he need to commemorate has fuelled my writing since my youth. I try to struggle against the general absence and repression of the existence of Black Nova Scotians or Africadians in every major discourse in this province … I feel I am constantly writing against our erasure and yet the erasure continues … we have a history here, a history full of trials, triumphs, struggles, etc., and there is just no legitimate way that we can be excluded from the history of this place. And so this explains my commemorative efforts and my general interest in involving history and photographs in my creative work, because it is a means of contesting that constant erasure, which has led ultimately I think to racism, to the idea that "you folks do not count; you're not even a fit subject for history." (73)

Obviously commemoration and cultural recording are essential to Clarke's work, but I think these elements play only a secondary role in what should be considered his primary project. Only when we take in the entire scope of Clarke's creative and critical contributions do we realize that, rather than being a writer who has been passively made by his home culture and is therefore predestined to defend that social space with his art, Clarke actively (and even aggressively) claims both the agency and the capacity to first re-imagine his home and then to actually re-construct it, physically, in the real world. The differences between these two types of literary ambition are difficult to overstate. Instead of being determined by his native land, Clarke is determined to change that place. His writing absolutely rejects the doctrine of a purely materialist environmental causality.

Unlike traditional regionalist writers, it cannot be said that George Elliott Clarke comes *from* Africadia. In fact, in his peculiar case, the writer's relationship with geography is directly opposed to that model. Ultimately, it should be argued that Clarke is *going* to Africadia. The imagined geography of this place is his destination rather than his point of origin and literature provides the means by which he travels between these two points, slowly tearing down the old, real world and gradually building up its replacement. Clarke's writing is devoted to a region that did not exist in the real world before he gave it a name and initiated the slow process of its creation. The religious overtones of such a project are obvious and Clarke has often drawn parallels between his own work and the "New Jerusalem, City-on-a-hill" thematic which runs through so much of America's early puritanical writing. "The little state of Africadia is a community of believers," he writes (*Fire on the Water* 15). It is an imaginary place, maintained by faith and by the desperate desire of a population who would wish to see the mythic materialized in the real world.

To support this somewhat outlandish claim, I want to suggest that the most important work Clarke has done thus far in his career is his introduction to the first volume of *Fire on the Water*. I am not sure if it is the intense youthful exuberance of the prose (Clarke had just turned 30 at the time of the book's release), the elevated evangelical rhetoric of the piece, or the overt political call to arms that Clarke launches at his peers in the closing sections of this short essay, but it should be clear to anyone familiar with Clarke's writing life that the intellectual concerns, the political issues, and the recurrent themes of exile, religious faith, and violence that come back so often in the rest of his oeuvre find their first full annunciation here.

This essay marks the formal launch of Clarke's Africadian nation-building project. In the opening paragraphs, Clarke sees himself standing at the precipice and he describes his position as one of both "luxury and anxiety" (9). He makes a special effort to emphasize that his work represents "not the last word, but the first" about the literary heritage of his community and he characterizes himself as an "explorer—stumbling, straying, yet striving to clear and map a path for future seekers to follow" (9). At the close of his "Declaration" section, Clarke humbly suggests that "the entire catalogue of classical Africadian literature appears at once" in this volume of his own creation, and that *Fire on the Water* should be read as "a monument to past and present writers and a beacon for those to come" (10). He concludes with a passionate plea to future generations of Africadians: "*Oh, you, who read these words in ages hence, may you add to this book further songs of the nation it honours. This work yearns, signals, calls, for you*" (10).

As Moynagh, Compton, Banks, Helmer and many other critics have noted, the "nation" Clarke honours in *Fire in the Water* is an idea rather than a reality. In conversation with Moynagh, Clarke readily admits that, because the Africadia he envisions is not *yet* "a real physical place," it must be considered as "a mythical notion, an intellectual construct, a soulful nation" (77). He goes on to explain:

> I've defined it as a place where the free self can live, a green space where the free self can live. It may not necessarily have to exist as a state with an anthem and a standing army, but it is important that we understand that we have this unique vantage point which does exist within ourselves, and which is manifested in different ways at different times, in different places with different groupings of people of African descent in this place that on paper we call Nova Scotia. But I don't think we have to accept these standard notions and that it's important to claim the place for ourselves, and to rename, reorder, rethink the whole thing. (77)

For scholars interested in regionalist theory and especially Atlantic-Canadian regionalist theory, these lines announce a dramatic changing of the guard. Clarke's call to "rename," "reorder" and "rethink" the imagined space of his nation is a direct assault on the doctrine of environmental determinism. In his always-pastoral green world of Africadia, the fixed facts of Nova Scotian geography become more flexible: Weymouth Falls can turn into Whylah Falls and Digby County can change its name to Jarvis County. Beatrice Chancy can come from Italy and be relocated to the Annapolis valley in 1801. Though he is aggressive with his changes, Clarke isn't naive about the charges that may be levelled at such a project. He is well-prepared to meet the criticisms of Dainotto and Davey. Rather than "concealing" its ideology, Clarke's fiery brand of regionalism blatantly flaunts its political commitments. Instead of promoting "touristic images" and "authentically inarticulate individuals," Clarke's writing takes its readers directly to the scenes that are left out of the tourist guides and it revels in the playful complexity of language.

In another important essay which has never received the critical attention it merits, "Treason of the Black Intellectuals?" Clarke returns to the potentially explosive topic of the relationship and responsibilities that connect the "average" needs of any community with the "exceptional" abilities of its intellectual class. Though he admits that Black thinkers "possess no immunity against the potentially toxic allure of nationalism" and that they must deny at every turn the "fallacious myths, misty romanticisms, and blood-rite fascisms" of the discourse (2), Clarke consistently argues that a "persuasive cultural nationalist scholarship is an absolute necessity" for his community and that "it is the precise task of African-Canadian intellectuals to determine the imperatives of African-Canadian culture (or cultures) and to build economic, political and cultural institutions that will allow us a measure of autonomy, pride and independence in our dealing with all other interest groups in the society" (18).

The socio-spatial index of Clarke's thought is unmistakable here. He believes that real and imagined geographies cannot be separated and that the intellectual work of the Black artist or intellectual should eventually take on a physical form and help build economic, political and cultural institutions in the real world. For Clarke, this material manifestation of the Africadian cause is an ultimate goal. He writes, "(e)ither African-Canadians are an assembly of miniature nations, or they are nowhere" (19).

Clarke's formulation of Africadian nationalism does not gloss over internal conflicts and division within the community. In a somewhat controversial claim in "The Death and Rebirth of Africadian Nationalism" (an essay that begins as a review of Shelagh Mackenzie's 1991 film, *Remember Africville)*, Clarke places at least some of the blame for Africville's destruction squarely on the shoulders of the then-leaders of the Black community. Characterizing this group as an elite aristocracy that was more interested in preserving its own position of influence within the community rather than defending the whole, Clarke argues that their "refusal to engage in more than token resistance to acts of discrimination, coupled with a failure to evolve a theology to counter the threat posed by modernity, left Africadia defenceless before the gospel of progress, which, by its very nature, could not accept the continued existence of Africville" (*Odysseys* 293). Clarke is absolutely convinced that:

> Africville was lost because we Africadians refused to sufficiently value our right to exist. Our leaders of the 1960's allowed themselves to be seduced into thinking of Africville as a slum rather than as a potentially strong Africadian community-neighbourhood in a prime location on peninsular Halifax. Had they been strong enough to resist the temptations of progress, Africville might have become the spiritual capital of Africadia, the conscious annunciation of our existence. (294)

Clarke's anger here could not be more clear, but alongside his mourning for the loss of the real Africville, his essay offers, again in overtly religious terms, the suggestion that the death of Africville—the "crucifixion," he calls it—may have been a necessary fall (295). In Clarke's version of events, the old Africville dies for the sins of "an apostate collective" so that the new Africville, the spiritual capital of Africadia, can be resurrected from the ashes. (295) Only after the bulldozers and the social workers have demolished the "real" physical structures of the neighbourhood can the imagined and remembered Africville begin to do its work. For Clarke, clearly taking his lead here from successful minority nationalist movements in Quebec and New Brunswick, the re-reading, re-writing and re-interpretation of Africville's cultural-geographic significance within the community is the single most important element of the Africadian nationalist renaissance. Exactly as a re-reading, re-writing and re-interpretation of the events of 1759 by Quebec intellectuals triggered a transformation that saw French Canadians begin to view themselves as *les Québécois* in the 1960's, and exactly as the Francophone community in New Brunswick used a re-reading, re-writing and re-interpretation of *Le Grand Dérangement* of 1755 to trigger an Acadian renaissance in the 1970's, Clarke's work demonstrates that a collective desire for the home place is infinitely more powerful than the passive defence of a real geographic site. Africville is more valuable to the Africadian cause as a lost place, a world that must be restored, a mistake that cannot be allowed to happen again.

If nothing else, Clarke is a scholar, perhaps even a rapid devotee, of nationalist theory and criticism. He has an encyclopaedic knowledge of Black nationalist movements in Canada and abroad and he is intimately familiar and clearly comfortable with the teachings of Benedict Anderson, Homi Bhabha, Julien Benda, Ernest Renan, Edward Said and Charles Taylor, among many others. His long-standing support for the model of conservative nationalism endorsed by George Grant in *Lament for a Nation* and his equally passionate distaste for the ideology of modern liberalism are well-known. Perhaps he is even aware of the Anglo-Irish argument of Seamus Deane which claims that "all nationalisms have a metaphysical dimension" that they are continually trying to "realize ... in some specific and tangible form" (8).

"Realizing" the metaphysical dimensions of Africadia has always been the tangible goal of Clarke's work. With each poem, essay, novel, opera or screenplay he writes, Clarke slowly wills an imaginary Africadia into existence. Obviously, this is not an easy process and it is impossible to avoid the inter and intra-community conflicts that necessarily accompany such an endeavour. To put it simply, it takes a fair bit of chutzpah, or guts, or perhaps just blind arrogance—traits for which Clarke may be criticized by those who are jealous of his courage—to, at the age of 31, name your own nationality and claim that simply by virtue of your creative and scholarly work, the collective identity of an entire population has been confirmed. My proof of this culture is enough to make the nation real, Clarke argues. He then outlines his case for the Africadian cause in clear and simple terms: If African Nova Scotian writers have produced a coherent canon, Clarke suggests, then let scholars recognize that canon as "Africadian" literature. And if there are recurrent issues and questions that come back again and again in this literature, then let those issues be recognized as the dominant themes of Africadian culture. And if this community possesses a recognizably distinct culture, and if that culture is strong, then let the people produce a state apparatus to nurture that culture and sustain its development. From here, the last step is obvious and Clarke makes it perfectly clear that "if Africadians constitute a state, let it be titled Africadia" (*Fire on the Water* 9).

It might be easy to interpret Clarke's project as yet another purely hypothetical, entirely intellectual pursuit that has absolutely no relationship or contact with the real world. Life in academia is often cluttered with such well-meaning, theoretical endeavours that never cross-over to produce concrete results in society at large. In this particular case, however, things are different and scholars do not have to look very far to see the startling transformations Clarke's work has already helped initiate in his community. In the aftermath of the 2003 provincial election in Nova Scotia, only two-hundred-and-twenty years after they first arrived in the colony, Black Nova Scotians were granted their first official representation in the government of the province. In July of that year, Barry Barnet, a white MLA for Hammonds Plains / Upper Sackville was named the first minister for "African Nova Scotian Affairs." In its official publications, the Government of Nova Scotia states that the "objects and purposes" of The Office of African Nova Scotian Affairs are as follows:

> [T]o create and promote an integrated approach to matters relating to the African Nova Scotian community; to represent Nova Scotia in intergovernmental and other initiatives and negotiations on matters integral to the African Nova Scotian community; to provide the minister responsible with research analysis and policy advice on African Nova Scotia issues; to develop cooperatively communication strategies and public education in order to improve general understanding and appreciation of African Nova Scotia culture, heritage and community identity; and to advocate for the interests and concerns of the African Nova Scotian community.

The bureaucratic language used here may not stir the soul, and at this stage, obviously, it would be too early to judge the overall effectiveness of this initiative, but no matter how we interpret it, this first official government recognition of the African Nova Scotian community is a momentous event. No other province in Canada offers its African community representation at such a high level. It is definitely not my intention to give Clarke exclusive credit for this political achievement. After all, he is only one of the many Black Nova Scotians who have helped the community reach this goal. However, he has undeniably made a key contribution and, since the very beginning of his career, Clarke's commitment to the cause has been passionate and unwavering.

We must remember that less than fifteen years ago "Africadia" was not even a word, let alone an official extension of the government of Nova Scotia with an office, a budget and a minister all paid for by provincial taxes. In this world, where power often flows directly from political office, this kind of state-sanctioned legitimacy is a clear indicator of "real" cultural significance. Back in 1991, when Clarke was just beginning his journey, Africadia may have been "only" an imaginary site, but thanks in part to his tireless work, the actual, material manifestation of this "community of believers" seems more and more like a real-world possibility.

Endnotes

1. In the "Confession" section of the introduction to volume one of *Fire on the Water: An Anthology of Black Nova Scotian Writing*, Clarke offers the following etymological explanation for his invention of the terms, "Africadian" and "Africadia": "I use the term

'Africadian,' a word I have minted from 'Africa' and 'Acadia' (the old name for Nova Scotia and New Brunswick), to denote the Black populations of the Maritimes and especially of Nova Scotia. Other appellations—'Afro-Nova Scotian,' 'Black Nova Scotian,' etc.—are unwieldy. Moreover, if Africadians constitute a state, let it be titled Africadia." (9)

Works Cited

Banks, Michelle. "Myth-making and Exile: the Desire for a Home Place in George Elliott Clarke's *Whylah Falls.*" *Canadian Poetry* 51 (2002): 58–85.

Clarke, George Elliott. *Beatrice Chancy.* Vancouver: Polestar, 1999.

—. *Blue.* Vancouver: Polestar, 2001.

—, ed. *Fire on the Water: An Anthology of Black Nova Scotian Writing.* Vol. 1. Lawrencetown Beach, N.S.: Pottersfield Press, 1991.

—. *Lush Dreams, Blue Exile.* Lawrencetown Beach, N.S.: Pottersfield Press, 1994.

—. *Odysseys Home: Mapping African-Canadian Literature.* Toronto: U of Toronto P, 2002.

—. *Saltwater Spirituals and Deeper Blues.* Lawrencetown Beach, N.S.: Pottersfield Press, 1983.

—. *Treason of the Black Intellectuals?* Montreal: McGill Institute for the Study of Canada, 1998.

—. *Whylah Falls.* 10th Anniversary ed. Vancouver: Polestar, 2000.

Compton, Anne. "Standing Your Ground: George Elliott Clarke in Conversation." *Studies in Canadian Literature* 23.2. (1998) 139–165.

Dainotto, Roberto Maria. "'All the Regions do Smilingly Revolt': The Literature of Place and Region." *Critical Inquiry* 22 (Spring 1996): 487–505.

—. *Place In Literature: Regions, Cultures, Communities.* Ithaca: Cornell UP, 2000.

Davey, Frank. "Maritime Powerlessness: *Nights Below Station Street.*" *Post-National Arguments: The Politics of the Anglophone-Canadian Novel since 1967.* Toronto: U of Toronto P, 1993. 67–80.

—. "Toward the Ends of Regionalism." *Textual Studies in Canada* 12 (1998): 1–17.

Deane, Seamus. "Introduction." *Nationalism, Colonialism and Literature.* Minneapolis: U of Minnesota P, 1990.

Fuller, Danielle. "'Raising the heart': The Politics of the Popular and the Poetics of Performance in the Work of Maxine Tynes." *Essays on Canadian Writing* (1999) 76–112.

Moynagh, Maureen. "Africville, an Imagined Community." *Canadian Literature* 157 (1998): 14–34.

—. "Mapping Africadia's Imaginary Geography: An Interview with George Elliott Clarke." *Ariel* 27.4 (1996): 71–94.

Office of African Nova Scotian Affairs. *The Government of Nova Scotia* 9 April 2005. <http://www.gov.ns.ca/nsarm/gaho/authority.asp?ID=136>

Soja, Edward. *Postmodern Geographies: The Reassertion of Space in Critical Social Theory.* New York: Verso, 1989.

—. *Thirdspace: Journeys to Los Angeles and Other Real and Imagined Places.* Oxford: Blackwell, 1996.

Stone, Marjorie. "The Poet as Whole-Body Camera: Maxine Tynes and the Pluralities of Otherness." *The Dalhousie Review* 77.2 (1997): 227–257.

Wells, Dorothy. "A Rose Grows in Whylah Falls: Transplanted Traditions in George Elliott Clarke's 'Africadia.'" *Canadian Literature* 155. (1997): 56–73.

Wyile, Herb. "Regionalism, Postcolonialism and (Canadian) Writing: A Comparative Approach for Postnational Times." *Essays on Canadian Writing* 68 (1998) 139–161.

"What We Desire is African": Intertextuality of Diaspora and Negritude in George Elliott Clarke's and Solano Trindade's Poetry.

MARISTELA CAMPOS

The African Diaspora is the common ground that performs a major role in shaping black poetry in the Americas. Enslavement, oppression, exclusion, racism, cultural resistance, and political unrest are shared histories suffered by African descendants in the New World. James Clifford states that diaspora does not simply signify movement and transnationality; the term conveys political conflicts and the endeavour to delimit frontiers in situations of displacement (252). These are the topics that I want to focus on in this comparative study of the poetics of George Elliott Clarke and Solano Trindade.[1] I attempt to establish a parallel between the authors' poems from the perspective of a common past of slavery and present of erasure or silencing of African-descendant culture. Nevertheless, the poets' differences in social and cultural backgrounds are not underestimated in my analysis. The poets' cultures, social conditions, geographical sites, and unique individual differences infuse their writings with diverse nuances which are instances of expression of black experience in Canada and in Brazil.

Clifford affirms that diaspora consciousness emerges from the positive identification with historical, cultural and political forces such as those depicted by Africa and China. The feelings of loss, exile, and marginality are counterbalanced by adapting strategies and constant "visions of renewal." Deprivation and hope define the tension in diaspora awareness (256–57). The discourse of the African diaspora in Brazil frequently depicts the sense of belonging to a mythical Africa which is not simply left behind but is the counterpoint to the contemporary hindrances of modernity and capitalism. The African continent is the signifier of a mother who comforts her divided and dispersed children in the Americas. Yet, this Afrocentric posture is an escapist and ahistorical attempt to reconnect Africa and the individuals of the diaspora.

The commonality of black experiences issues from enslavement, racialization, and exploitation. These structures are interwoven in the construct of modern hegemony. Black diaspora awareness does not have a linear temporality. The conceptions of "here" and "there" are disrupted by the Middle Passage. The present is constantly veiled by a past which also signifies a desired future and a renewed craving for rebuilding memory. In spite of being hostages of politically dominant and economically unequal regimes, diaspora peoples do not abandon the ability to maintain distinct communities which are politically and culturally resistant. The examples are Africville[2] in Canada and the rural community of Cafundó[3] in Brazil. Clifford's argument that "[...] the mix of destruction, adaptation, preservation, and creation varies with each historical case and moment" is particularly important to analyses of black diaspora consciousness in Brazil and Canada and its implications concerning black writing.

The concept of negritude is present in a variety of texts that convey the common experiences of black men and women in the diaspora. Alvaro Luiz Hattnher points out that the ideology of negritude is rooted in "self-acceptance of the black individual," "the construction and assertion of identity," the legitimacy of history, culture and "existential experience" of black individuals (54). Hattnher suggests that black identities can be revisited from a point of view that considers the forced dispersion of Africans as a movement which can provide new possibilities for depiction. Therefore, negritude is defined as an ongoing process that is woven with inter-discursive and inter-textual connections and has a broader meaning than the "special way to be black" proposed by Aimé Césaire[4] (1913–2008) and goes beyond the triangle formed by Césaire, Léopold Sédar Senghor (1906–2001) and Léon Damas (1912–78) in Paris in the late thirties and early forties (39).

Thus, I bring to bear a brief theoretical view about intertextuality to help establish the connection between the poets' works. Mikhail M. Bakhtin states that a text depends on the contact with another text (context) to survive. Therefore, the text cannot be read as a single detached unit. The contact between two texts, for instance, allows both to come alive and to provide one another with meaning. The juxtaposition between text and context is never static. The primary stage in understanding a text concerns the "mechanical contact of 'oppositions'." The stage is important to study structural definition; however it cannot be applied to apprehension of meaning. The approximation of personalities is "behind" the contact of text and context (*Speech Genre and Other Late Essays* 162). A work cannot be conceived outside the relationship with a certain context and the relationship the context may have with different systems.

Bakhtin asserts that an utterance is never isolated. Utterances carry impressions received from other utterances. An utterance is not self-validating; it is connected with others in verbal communication in an interdependent relationship. The utterance is a response that may either confirm or refute other utterances that have preceded it (*The Dialogic Imagination: Four Essays by M.M. Bakhtin* 316). According to Hattnher, the concept of intertextuality conveys not only the contact between text and context. Texts that individuals bring with themselves also permeate the interpretation of what is intertextual (17). Intertextuality prevents the final closure of a text. Intertextual events give the texts a dynamical characteristic and allow the continuity of meaning.

Intertextuality mediates the construction of texts through other texts. Social events and practices of discourse permeate the construction; therefore, texts depict social practices and discourse. Consequently, texts are not mere representatives of social practices, but are relevant components of discourse. Practices of discourse are dependent on each other in an institution as well as in society (20).

Still on this respect, Michel Foucault asserts that the margins of a book are not clearly defined. There are components that delimit and particularize the book: title, first lines, period, cover, etc. However, the book is inserted into a system of allusions to other writings. It is not possible to determine the "unity" of a book because it is "variable and relative." The unity cannot sustain itself because it emanates from a "complex field of discourses" (26). Foucault highlights the diffusion of events of discourse: its promptness and its possibility to be echoed, known, transformed, erased, or even veiled and hidden in books through time. For Foucault, it is not essential to pinpoint the origin of the discourse, but it is crucial to consider its occurrences (28).

It is possible to affirm that negritude is a formation of discourses which issue from common social and cultural practices originating within the African diaspora. The practices are interconnected and can be recreated, transformed, transmitted, and depicted so as to provide each other with meaning independently of time. In spite of the complexity of the experiences in blackness, negritude can be considered the formation of discourses that counterpoint racist postures and expose processes of assertion and construction of identity.

Diaspora is primarily a common framework which embodies the discourse of negritude in poems by the two authors. From this specific standpoint, textual evidence presents shared characteristics. In the current work I attempt to point out similarities and differences in Clarke's and Trindade's writings concerning the discourse of diaspora in poetry. The main characteristics to be discussed are the enunciating-self, the historical reconstitution, and the reverse of values. From colonial times up to the present, the literary canon has predominantly presented blacks as secondary and stereotyped characters in novels and poems whose heroes and heroines are constructed according to Eurocentric patterns. Zilá Bernd states that the enunciating-self in black literature "emerges from the process of becoming aware of what is to be black among whites" (48). The self embodies the "semantics of protest" where black identity takes on the standpoint and the speech in History and rejects being the "other" to be the "self" counteracting stereotypes, assimilation, and marginalization. The poems "I am black"[5] by Trindade and "Negation" by Clarke deal with these issues. Consider the poem "I am black" by Trindade:

I am black
my grandparents were burned
by the African sun
my soul was baptized by the drums
atabaques, gonguês and agogôs.[6]

I was told my grandparents
came from Loanda
as commodities at low price
they planted cane for the new sugar mill master
and founded the first Maracatu[7]

Later my grandfather fought bravely
in the lands of Zumbi
oh he was brave
[. . . . .]
Left in my soul
the samba
the batuque[8]
the bamboleio[9]
and the yearning for freedom. (1–14, 23–27)

Now, consider the poem "Negation" by Clarke:

Le négre negated, meager, *c'est moi:*
Denigrated, negative, a local
Caliban, unlikable and disliked
(slick black bastard—cannibal—sucking back
[. . . . .]

> Masticated scripture. Her Majesty's
> Nasty, Nofaskoshan Negro, I mean
> To go out shining instead of tarnished,
> To take apart Poetry like a heart.
> So my black face must preface your finish,
> Deface your *religion*—unerringly,
> Niggardly, like some *film noir* black guard's. (1–4, 8–14)

In Trindade's work the discourse of diaspora is presented in poetry through memories of slavery, denouncement of practices of racism and social exclusion, and the allusion to African heritage. The poetic voice constantly asserts and claims the legitimacy of African ancestry and reverses the route of the Middle Passage to rescue African origins. The line "I am black" (1) exposes the desire to make blackness visible and counterclaim negative delineations of negritude. The poem brings the timeless movement between "here" and "there" to reconstruct the present in which Africa signifies the source of fragmented pieces of memory which are necessary to rebuild diasporic identity: "I was told my grandparents/ came from Loanda" (6–7). The poet highlights the ancestors' virtues and the achievements in spite of the harsh conditions of inequality under colonial oppression.

In Clarke's poem, the enunciating-self calls for black awareness. The line "*La nègre* negated, meager, *c'est moi:*" (1), and "So my black face must preface your finish," (12) depict the assertion of black identity inside the Canadian Anglophone and Francophone conflict. The poet does not weave a timeless return to Africa like Trindade does, but there is a reference to a Black Loyalist past: "Nasty, Nofaskoshan Negro, I mean" (9). The poem utilizes the reconstruction of memories to rebuild consciousness and identity. As a discourse of diaspora, the writing denounces exclusion in words that delineate negation (the title speaks for itself) of the presence of African descendants and practices of racism in Canada. It is possible to affirm that both poems counterclaim negation of African-descendant culture. The assertion of blackness emerges from the need to directly confront the process of invisibility.

Thus, the common starting point of the poems is the enunciating-self that affirms negritude. From the assertion, the two poets engage in a reformulation of what it means to be black. Trindade revisits the Middle Passage to retell events from a black perspective. While the voice in the poem narrates the saga of ancestors, resistance and fight for freedom are emphasized. Therefore, black identity receives another meaning: it abandons obscurity and becomes an agent of history; the slaves sold at low prices reject submission and begin to organize towards a better future: "and founded the first Maracatu" (9–10).

Clarke applies different strategies to rebuild black meanings. The poet revisits negative terms believed to depict black experience in hegemonic discourse: "Denigrated, negative, a local / Caliban unlikable and disliked" (2–3). The words taken from racial discourse are used to answer back to oppressive practices. The line "To go out shining instead of tarnished" (10) transforms the meaning of what is to be black into a positive dimension. The poetic voice recreates black trajectory and consolidates current cultural and political struggle.

Clarke and Trindade face compromise in bridging the various gaps in African-descendant history in Canada and in Brazil. The appropriation of the epic retells history from the African standpoint depicting oppressed blacks as the real heroes and heroines in acts subverting the dominant order. Bernd affirms that the traditional epic conveys events of war where the traditional hero owns superior physical and psychological strength (92). The black anti-epic reverses such concepts depicting oppressed peoples as true heroes. The slaves fight not for the power in civilization, but for the right to maintain their traditions and the cultural and geographical sites that embody resistance. The poems celebrate fugitive slaves and martyrs of the struggle for freedom. The poems "III—Poetry" by Clarke and "Song of Palmares" by Trindade evidence historical reconstitution from the standpoint of negritude:

> *Madame Zajj* was first Zeferina –
>   a Yoruban warrior
>   weighted down by *Slavery*'s shadows.
> [. . . . .]
> Bullets came at her but couldn't hit her.
> She was a zephyr; her steed breezed lyrical.
> Her squads of machetes mashed and swished;
> her Amazon phalanx forked pallid bellies.
> Still, the slavers' shots slowly bled them
> And veered them back –
> [. . . . .]
> Surrounded Zeferina coolly dismounted;
> stood disdainfully atop the pale, piled dead,
> making their reddened bodies her royal dais.
> Dazzled, Salvadorans had to shout, "Queen!"
>
> (Poetry is like *Beauty*: what remains after dying,
> After the falling away, when flesh becomes song.)
>   (1–4, 19–24, 27–32)

Consider the poem "Song of Palmares" [10] by Trindade:

> And now we hear the cry of war,
> in the distance we see
> lighted torches,
> it is the bloodthirsty civilization,
> which is approaching.
> But my poem
> was not killed.
> Stronger
> Than any forces
> Liberty... [...] (177–186)

In "III—Poetry" Clarke refers to a heroine of the struggle for freedom in Brazil. Though most of the poet's work concerns depiction of African Nova Scotia, the poems in *Illuminated Verses* revisit black females' contribution and participation in the political resistance in other countries that received African slaves. Trindade, on his turn, tells of events that marked the fight in Palmares, the most important site of African resistance during slavery in Brazil. It is possible to affirm that the authors believe in the power of poetry to reconstruct consciousness and hope and thus redeem the oppressed. Clarke's line "Poetry is like beauty: what remains after dying" (31) and Trindade's "My poem / was not killed" expose the poetic voice that evokes the continuity of struggle against racism in present days. The poems of both authors depict the oppressed, the outlaw, and the marginalized as agents of heroic feats. The site which is considered marginal and threatening by the colonizer becomes a place of grace in Trindade's lines: "even the palm trees / love freedom" (84–5).

Negritude is permeated by the desire to turn negative stereotypes into positive assertion of black cultural values. To reverse the prevailing discourse, the poets reinfuse terms such as black/negro with a positive significance. The reconstitution of history and identity originated from the assertion of blackness through the enunciating-self makes the reverse of values possible. The reverse is also an attempt to transform negative depictions of black physical characteristics into positive delineations of blackness. The colour of skin becomes the poetic image of pride. "Black" is no longer a synonym of savage, violent, ugly, evil and primitive. In the poem entitled "*IV. iii*," Clarke does not only reverse the negative meaning of the term, but inscribes the dimensions of black experience:

> Black is black and black and black
> Black is a nègre nigger, a negrita nigger, a *schwartz* nigger
> Black is mulatto, sambo, negro, quadroon, octoroon
> Black is Africa, darkest Africa, as photographed by Leni Riefenstahl
> Black is the best Scotch, the best chocolates, the best sex
> [...]
> Black is the highest standard, highest caliber, of white [...]
>
> (1–5, 21)

In the poem entitled "Love," Trindade uses the term "negro" as a positive signifier. The poem associates "negro" with the adjective "good" to characterize blackness:

> Negro love is good
> long lasting and cheap
> if you have not tasted it
> take the chance
> There is a lot
> But it may end.

Negro love
is a national product
with calcium and vitamin
with all the ABC
abandon your conventions
take a negro for yourself

Negro love is tasty
Negro love is good!... (1–14)

Trindade's line "Negro love is tasty" (13) is similar to Clarke's "Black is puritanical sex, which is good, and depraved sex, which is very good" (24). The lines compose a provocative allusion that cancels stereotypes of black sexuality.

The poets also reverse signifiers by celebrating black women's beauty, strength and participation in black cultural and political stands against exclusion. As spokespersons for the black community, Clarke and Trindade engage in recreating female roles (traditional or not), maintaining African tradition and resisting against racial violence. More than mere depictions of African physical beauty, black women in Trindade's and Clarke's poetry are queens, warriors, matriarchs, martyrs, homemakers, mothers, muses, and lovers. There is plenty of textual evidence. In the poem entitled "Black Aesthetic," Trindade depicts African descendant females as builders of their own freedom:

Black woman in dreams insulted
Black woman in dreams oppressed
Always love...

Black woman's love always aesthetic
Her first liberation
Was in the Songs of Solomon
The second one was the sculpture by Picasso
The third one she achieved on her own (1–8)

In the beginning of the poem, the lines 1–3 depict oppression that black women have suffered. However, the poem ends with an unexpected move towards black women's freedom and independence: "The third one she achieved on her own" (8).

Consider Clarke's "Love Letter to an African Woman":

> Black Madonna! I love your African essence, your faith in children, your insatiable desire for freedom, your swift intelligence, your sharp passion, your secret strengths, your language that tells no lies, your fashion that is colour, your music that is gospel-lullaby, your lips like crimson berries, your skin like soft, moist night, your eyes like dusk, your hair like dark cotton, your scent like rich butter, your taste like raisins and dates and sweet wine.
> Let us join. My love, let us join. (28–36)

Before reaching further conclusions, it is necessary to consider the long record of sexual abuse, violence and extreme subjugation that black women suffered during slavery. The black female essence is disrupted by the impossibility of maintaining dignity and to assert status as a subject. Black females (particularly as slaves) are denied the right to take possession of their own bodies, to raise their own children, and are labelled inferior to white women in the sense of beauty, morality and virtue. The poem returns to black women their deserved place in African-Canadian culture as agents of history more than simply inspiring muses.

The poets similarly refer to positive depictions of black beauty in the Bible. In "Love Letter to an African Woman," Clarke quotes Songs of Solomon 1:5: "Are you not Sheba, 'black but comely,' who enlightened Solomon; [...] (10). The poem "Songs of Solomon" also exposes Clarke's ability to appropriate Shakespearean tradition to depict Africadian experience:

> Yea, thou art black
> but comely –
> like the Sixhiboux River,
> like Mount Eulah's pines.
>
> I have compared thee,
> O my love,
> to soft, black night
> and raisins and sweet wine. [...] (1–8)

Trindade uses the same reference to celebrate black female participation in search for liberty: "Her first liberation / Was in the songs of Solomon" (5–6). Black women's experiences are revisited through depictions of heroism, beauty, and love.

Rescuing history and culture as well as reversing values requires the destruction of stereotyped depictions of blackness. The allusion to suffering and oppression during slavery is an effort to raise consciousness concerning the enslaved past. The horrors of the largest forced movement in the world are not denied. Revisiting such events aims to push black identity towards a better future. The new symbolic order is a determinant of resistance against assimilation. In Trindade's poetry, the poetic image of the slave ship receives a completely opposite delineation. According to Paul Gilroy, ships allude to the Middle Passage, to the

African continent as an idyllic return, and the transportation of cultural information and political concepts that form the discourse of diaspora (4). In the poem "There comes the slave ship," the craft becomes a signifier of circulation of cultural and political organization:

> There comes the slave ship
> There it comes on the sea
> There comes the slave ship
> Let us look, my folks
>
> There comes the slave ship
> Through Brazilian waters
> There comes the slave ship
> Bringing human load …
>
> There comes the slave ship
> Crowded with melancholy
> There comes the slave ship
> Crowded with poetry …
>
> There comes the slave ship
> Crowded with resistance
> There comes the slave ship
> Crowded with intelligence … (9–16)

Trindade refers to slave ships as the means which transport cultural and political resistance. The voice in the poem invites people to observe the ship and reformulate the signifier of suffering into a vehicle of transmission of African culture and knowledge. The line "Let us look, my people (4)" is an invitation to observe and understand the Middle Passage from a positive standpoint. There is more than horror and death on board. The lines "Crowded with resistance" and "Crowded with intelligence" (14, 16) depict Trindade's warning that slave ships bring peoples who are empowered to be the agents of their own histories in spite of the condition of slaves.

Clarke also refers to ships in his poetry. The poetic voice denounces the practice of denial and erasure of events of slavery in official history. In the poem entitled "Tobago" the author applies the oral tradition of African culture to reconstitute the Middle Passage and the suffering of slavery:

> A black man, lean, grey, clear,
> preaches,
> "Signs don't tell you
> man nothing,
> but slaves was shipped
> to that fort here, then whipped.
> [.........................]
> (But *History* has not
> recovered some –
> sum
> of our loss.) (9–14, 23–26)

Paul Zumthor, in the book *A Letra e a Voz: A "Literatura" Medieval* (Letter and Voice: Medieval "Literature"), explains that the history of the composition of a poetical text presents five operations: "production, communication, reception, conservation, and repetition." Performance emerges when communication and reception happen at the same time. When a poet reads, the voice grants him or her authority. Tradition provides the poet with prestige, but it is the action of voice that connects the poet with such tradition (19). In *Introdução à Poesia Oral* (Introduction to Oral Poetry), Zumthor writes that oral communication plays the role of granting the permanence of a social group allowing the discourse that a certain society pronounces about itself to be heard. Voices in a society stimulate individuals against fear of extinction. Oral poetry is permeated by two different oralities: one that is based on individual experience, and another which is embodied by a certain tradition. Knowledge that is transmitted orally and appropriated through ears consequently results in recognition. Such recognition develops into beliefs and mental habits which constitute the mythology of a group (34–5).

Leda Maria Martins distinguishes the terms "oraliture" and orature to define the characteristics of oral tradition in African descendant cultures. According to Martins, "oraliture" concerns body and vocal expression. The term is wider than the set of forms and cultural practices of oral tradition. "Oraliture" is connected with performance of voice or body movement which exposes "knowledge, values, concepts, standpoints and styles." Literary studies use the term orature concerning "classic and contemporary oral traditions" which specifically distinguish verbal textuality in African cultures. Orature is also used to point out practices of oral rhetoric in written literature of several African authors (83–4).

In Clarke's *Whylah Falls* and Trindade's *Cantares ao meu Povo*, the presence of "oraliture" is clearly observed. Indeed, Clarke began to deliberately write poetry that can be performed after he delivered an unsuccessful reading in front of his community in 1986. Now, the Africadian poet writes lines in non-standard English interwoven with spirituals, jazz, and blues. In the introduction to *Blues and Bliss,* Jon Paul Fiorentino highlights that Clarke writes "[...] poems that combine abstract, intellectual, and specific literary content with a home-place vernacular" (xii). The poem entitled "King Bee Blues" reveals Clarke's ingenious use of musicality and language:

I'm an ol' king bee, honey,
Buzzin' from flower to flower.
I'm an ol' king bee, sweets,
Hummin' from flower to flower.
Women got good pollen;
I get some every hour. [. . .] (1–6)

Also, the prose poem "The Symposium" is rich in evidence of Clarke's use of home-place vernacular: "So don't put no business on the streets that's conducted 'tween your sheets. But if some big-mouth humbugs you, tell the black bitch not to mess 'cos she's terrible lookin' anyway; a knife gash 'cross her face would just be improvement" (38).

Trindade writes popular poetry that emerges from black rhythms (samba, frevo, and maracatu), socio-political claims, and love. The author rescues the vocabulary of African languages and non-standard Portuguese to create verse which can be recognized by the uneducated working class. Trindade considers that poetry needs to be intertwined with performance. The poem "Olorum Ekê" [11] depicts the cadence of African rhythms:

Olorum Ekê
Olorum Ekê
I am the People's poet
Olorum Ekê

My flag
Has the color of blood
Olorum Ekê
Olorum Ekê
Has the color of revolution
Olorum Ekê [. . .] (1–10)

Besides African-Brazilian rhythms, Trindade alludes to African-American music as well as Cuban rumba in the poem entitled "America's Song." The kinds of music in the lines of the poem delineate the rhythmic expressions of protest and resistance:

> Blues! swings! sambas! frevos!
> macumbas! jongos!
> Rhythms of anxiety and protests,
> Are hurting my ears! …
> They are secular groans of the wounded
> humanity,
> Impregnated in aesthetic
> emotions,
> of the American soul …
>
> It's America that sings …
> This rumba is a manifesto,
> against racial prejudices
> This conga is a cry of revolt,
> against social injustices,
> This frevo is an example of proximity
> and equality… […] (1–16)

The works of the poets expose common concerns with a kind of poetry that may reveal black experience in its several dimensions inside African-Brazilian and African-Canadian cultural sites. The poets apply common strategies to approach their communities especially through polyphonic and performative lines. Clarke's and Trindade's poems use the African verbal textuality and performance of voice along with rhythm and musicality.

Clarke and Trindade refer to the canon to establish a dialog with the European tradition. Diana Brydon writes that "[f]or Clarke, it seems partly a matter of self-validation, partly homage and partly a way of writing his own place into the great tradition, but on his own terms" (190). However, Fiorentina Souza explains that Trindade's allusions to the canon are delineations of a hybrid discourse that transmits the claims of an underprivileged group. Trindade is aware of the literary tradition but his objective is to unveil African descendant heritage. The poet's main concern is to rescue almost forgotten African tradition in rhythm and storytelling as well as aspects of popular culture (291). The poem "Warning" depicts the discourse of a poet who searches for transmitting a clear and straightforward message to his community:

> There are poets who write love poems only
> There are hermeticist and futurist poets
> while hydrogen and atomic
> bombs are manufactured
> while armies
> are getting ready for war
> while famine annihilates peoples …
>
> Eventually
> they will write lines of horror and remorse
> and will not escape from punishment
> because war and famine
> will reach them too
> and poets will fall into oblivion … (1–13)

Here Trindade warns intellectuals to perform active roles in standing against injustice. He criticizes "hermeticist and futurist" poets as writers of the elite not connected to social struggles. It is possible to point out a similarity with Clarke's "Nu(is)ance":

> Jabbering double-crossing double
> Pale-assed poetasters void my "blues-caucused,
> Raucous lyrics"—too Negroid and rowdy,
> While sable, sassy poets preach I ink
> Too blankly, *comme les blancs*, my bleached-out verse
> Bleating too whitey-like—worse in they ears.
> *What can I say?*
> All this blather about
> "Black" and "white" is blackmail and white noise.
> Cripes! English—fallacious—be finished here!
> I'd rather stutter a bastard's language
> Only spoken in gutters, a broken,
> Vulgar, Creole screech, loud with bawling, slurring,
> Balderdash, cussing and caterwauling,
> A corrupt palaver that bankrupts all meeching speech
> Because it be literal, guttural *Poetry*,
> I.e. *Hubbub*. (1–17)

In the two poems, the poetic voices assert commitment to social change. Trindade's universal concerns in the poem are poverty, famine, and war. In Clarke's poem, the poetic voice criticizes the intellectual elite disconnected from political engagement: "While sable, sassy poets preach I ink" […] (4). Furthermore, the poem counterclaims linguistic assimilation: "I'd rather stutter a bastard's language" […] (11).

By rejecting 'imperial' language standards, the poetic voice legitimates African culture. Clarke's mastery of language permits appropriation, translation, and revision of the canon to accommodate African-Canadian experience. On the other hand, Trindade's concern is to maintain the resonances of African languages to preserve African-Brazilian tradition and to use non-standard language to reach a working-class audience. The short poem "Lady Grammar" is another evidence of the poet's rejection of linguistic standards: "Lady grammar / forgive my grammatical trespasses. / if you won't forgive me / lady / I shall sin more. (1–5)

In Clarke's "Language," the poetic voice maintains the posture of anti-assimilation:

> 1
> I hate this language that *Hate* dictates to me.
> It gusts the tang and bray of a savage civilization –
> Violent words violently arrived at.
> [.................................]
>
> 2
> This homely poem's a queer nigger rig,
> A botch of art in slovenly English,
> Bad grammar, bad everything;
> It cannot perform ethically.
> It even fucks up Black English badly:
> The metre harries, but the words refuse to fit.
> [.................................]
>
> 5
> [.................................]
> My black, "Bluenose" brogue smacks lips and ears
> When I bite the bitter grapes of Creole verse –
> Or gripe and blab like a Protestant pope
> So rum-pungent Africa mutes perfumed Europe.
> (1–3, 10–15, 35–38)

The poetic voice confronts the colonizer's language and the violence of linguistic prejudice: "Violent words violently arrived at" (3). Language again is the cultural site for negotiation of legitimacy: "So rum-pungent Africa mutes perfumed Europe" (38).

In the anti-epic poem "Song of Palmares" Trindade quotes canonical poets acknowledging European tradition. Trindade rejects the canon to reverse historical standpoints. There is no rage against Western culture in Trindade's lines, but he celebrates the struggle of the race for freedom. In the second line, the poet affirms not to envy Virgil and Homer, which can be understood as an act of ignoring Western tradition.

> I sing to Palmares
> I do not envy Virgil Homer
> and Camões
> For my singing
> is the cry of a race
> in the fight for freedom! [...] (1–6)

Clarke and Trindade denounce violence through poetry. The poets clearly delineate events when blacks are unfairly judged by the colour of skin. Clarke's *Execution Poems* tells the story of his cousins, George and Rufus Hamilton, who are hanged for the murder of a taxi driver in Fredericton, New Brunswick. The two black men are sentenced by an all-white jury. The poetry exposes racism and poverty and their tragic consequences. For instance, "Ballad of a Hanged Man" provides textual evidence of despair caused by poverty:

> [...] I sidled in, easy, the taxi with a hammer,
> harsh, in my pocket. See as a wed man,
> I don't care if I wear uglified overalls.
> But I ain't gonna hear my child starve.

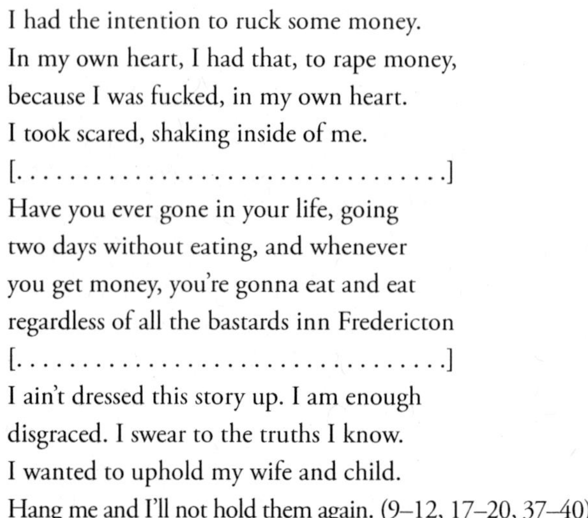

I had the intention to ruck some money.
In my own heart, I had that, to rape money,
because I was fucked, in my own heart.
I took scared, shaking inside of me.
[. . . . .]
Have you ever gone in your life, going
two days without eating, and whenever
you get money, you're gonna eat and eat
regardless of all the bastards inn Fredericton
[. . . . .]
I ain't dressed this story up. I am enough
disgraced. I swear to the truths I know.
I wanted to uphold my wife and child.
Hang me and I'll not hold them again. (9–12, 17–20, 37–40)

Trindade also alludes to crimes committed by individuals in extreme need. Moreover, he writes about oppressed people who lead ordinary lives and suffer in silence. The poet is the spokesperson for the excluded (not only blacks) who cannot stand up for their rights. However, the poem entitled "White civilization" clearly denounces racial violence:

A man was lynched
Among skyscrapers
(Read it in the paper)
I searched for the man's crime
The crime was not in the man
It was in the color of his epidermis (1–6)

Trindade writes about miserable conditions of the lower classes in Brazil. The lines of the poem "There are people dying, Ana" register the extreme inequality and famine in the Northeast, a region that is considered to be the poorest in the country:

There are people dying
In the dry Northeast
There are people dying
Of hunger and thirst
There are people dying
Ana
There are people dying [...] (1–9)

The poems presented reflect an attempt to point out intertextual evidences of negritude in Clarke's and Trindade's poetry. The most important of these elements of negritude is the presence of the enunciating-self which permits the authors to affirm blackness and establish a discourse which counterclaims hegemony. Black experience becomes the theme of poetry. This characteristic permits a major change concerning the reverse of values. Black is no longer a synonym of savagery; black is a signifier of beauty and virtue. From the assertion of blackness, the poets initiate a rescue of African-descendant culture. The poems convey the desire to rebuild history and destroy stereotyped depictions of negritude. Clarke and Trindade seek to legitimize African tradition. Both poets rely on linguistic resources that derive from oral African tradition. Trindade, as the spokesperson of the community, makes use of a simple language which can be heard and understood by his audience. He writes about social issues concerning Marxist ideals. His poems expose the desire for universal brotherhood that transcends the frontiers of race and nation. Clarke appropriates canonical forms, translates and revisits Eurocentric tradition to depict African Canadian experience. Clarke's claims possess a nationalist concern of exposing what it means to be black in white-dominant Canada. The poems analyzed in the essay convey cries for justice and the urgent need for change and the construction of less prejudiced societies.

Endnotes

1. Solano Trindade (1908–1974), "The People's Poet," is a Black Brazilian author, playwright, actor, and cultural researcher who participated in diverse black movements and cultural events from the early 1930s on. Along with other participants, he founded the Afro-Brazilian Cultural Center and the Black Brazilian Front in the state of Pernambuco. As a poet, his project does not involve only the specificity of race; however it is based on black experience.
2. Maureen Moynagh states that Africville, settled in the 1850s, is a cultural site whose belonging signifies act of resistance against "disavowal, exclusion, and displacement" (15).
3. Carlos Vogt, poet and linguist, and Peter Fry, anthropologist and professor at UFRJ (Federal University of Rio de Janeiro), write about the rural community of Cafundó which is situated 150 km from São Paulo. In spite of being close to the metropolis, the community maintains the lexis of an African language called *cupópia*. The majority of the population is made up of blacks who are divided in two families: the Almeida Caetanos and the Pires Cardosos. According to Vogt and Fry, Ifigênia and Antônia (two slave sisters and ancestors of the present inhabitants) received the land as a donation from the former slave master some time before abolition. The permanence of the African language and tradition evidences political and cultural resistance (16).
4. According to Kabengele Munanga, Césaire, Senghor and Damas, who produced the greatest writings of black literature of French expression, can be considered the founders of negritude as a movement (43).

5. In this study I translate poems and citations of originals in Portuguese.
6. African musical percussion instruments.
7. Maracatu is a parade of African-Brazilian percussionists and dancers. The origins of maracatu date back to slavery when it was a way of paying homage to blacks who played leadership roles among slaves. The parade follows a woman who carries a doll depicting African deities.
8. A rhythm produced by percussion instruments.
9. The act of swinging in dancing.
10. Palmares was the widest known *quilombo* which was led by Zumbi, the greatest hero of Black resistance in the XVII century. *Quilombos* were settlements mainly formed by runaway and free-born slaves. Palmares lasted for almost a hundred years before being defeated by the Portuguese expedition commanded by Domingos Jorge Velho in 1694.
11. Olorum is the African Yoruba divinity believed to be the creator of heaven and earth.

Works Cited

Primary Sources

Clarke, George Elliott. *Black*. Vancouver: Raincoast Books, 2006.

—. *Blue*. Vancouver: Raincoast Books, Vancouver, 2001.

—. *Execution Poems: The Black Acadian Tragedy of "George and Rue"*. Wolfville: Gaspereau, 2001.

—. *Illuminated Verses*. Toronto: Canadian Scholars' Press Inc., 2005.

—. *Whylah Falls*. Vancouver: Raincoast Books, 2000.

—. Fiorentino, Jon Paul, ed. *Blues and Bliss: The Poetry of George Elliott Clarke [...]*. Waterloo: Wilfrid Laurier University Press, 2008.

Trindade, Solano. *Cantares ao Meu Povo*. São Paulo: Editora Brasiliense, 1981.

—. *Canto Negro*. Ed. Zenir Campos Reis. São Paulo: Nova Alexandria, 2006.

—. *Poemas Antológicos de Solano Trindade*. Ed. Zenir Campos Reis. São Paulo: Nova Alexandria, 2008.

—. *Solano Trindade: O Poeta do Povo.* São Paulo: Ediouro, 2008.

Secondary Sources

Bakhtin, Mikhail M. *The Dialogic Imagination: Four Essays by M.M. Bakhtin*. Trans. Caryl Emmerson and Michael Holquist. Ed. Michel Holquist. London: Routledge, 1990. 259–422.

—. *Estética da Criação Verbal.* Trans. Maria Ermantina Galvão G. Pereira. São Paulo: Martins Fontes, 2000.

—. *Marxismo e Filosofia da Linguagem*. Trans. Michel Lahud and Yara Frateschi Vieira. São Paulo: Editora Hucitec, 2006.

—. "Methodology for the Human Sciences." Trans. Vern W. McGee. *Speech Genre and Other Late Essays*. Ed. Caryl Emmerson and Michael Holquist. Austin: U of Texas P, 1986. 159–172.

Bernd, Zilá. *Introdução à Literatura Negra*. São Paulo: Brasiliense, 1988.

—. *Negritude e Literatura na América Latina*. Porto Alegre: Mercado Aberto, 1987.

—, ed. *Poesia Negra Brasileira: Antologia*. Porto Alegre: Age; Porto Alegre: Instituto Estadual do Livro; Cachoeirinha: Igel, 1992.

Brydon, Diana. "George Elliott Clarke's Othello." *Canadian Literature* 182 (2004): 188–194.

Clifford, James. "Diasporas." *Routes: Travel and Translation in the Late Twentieth Century*. Cambridge: Harvard University Press, 1997.

Damasceno, Benedita Gouveia. *Poesia Negra no Modernismo Brasileiro*. 2nd ed. Campinas: 2003.

Duarte, Eduardo de Assis. "Literatura Afro-Brasileira: Um Conceito em Construção." *The Afro-Brazilian Mind: Contemporary Afro-Brazilian Literary and Cultural Criticism*. Ed. Niyi Afolabi, Márcio Barbosa, Esmeralda Ribeiro. Eritrea: África World Press, 2007: 101–110.

Fiorentino, Jon Paul. "Blackening English: The Polyphonic Poetics of George Elliott Clarke." *Poetics.ca* 2 (2002). 10 pp. 28 Nov 2006 <http://www.poetics.ca/poetics02/02fiorentinoprint.html>.

Foucault, Michel. *A Arqueologia do Saber.* Trans. Luiz Felipe Baeta Neves. Rio de Janeiro: Forense Universitária, 2000.

Gilroy, Paul. *The Black Atlantic: Modernity and Double Consciousness*. Massachusetts: Harvard University Press, 1993.

Hattnher, Alvaro Luiz. "Uma Ponte Sobre o Atlântico: Poesia de Autores Negros Angolanos, Brasileiros e Norte-Americanos em uma Perspectiva Comparativa Triangular." Diss. Universidade de São Paulo, 1998.

Holquist, Michael. *Dialogism—Bakhtin and his world.* London: Routledge, 1990.

Martins, Leda Maria. "Corpo, Lugar da Memória." *Brasil Afro-Brasileiro*. Ed. Maria Nazareth Soares Fonseca. Belo Horizonte: Autêntica, 2000: 63–86.

—. "A Fina Lâmina da Palavra." *O Negro na Sociedade Brasileira: Resistência, Participação, Contribuição*. Ed. Kabengele Munanga. Brasília: Fundação Cultural Palmares; MinC; CNPq, 2004: 263–285.

Moynagh, Maureen, "Africville, an Imagined Community." *Canadian Literature* 157 (1998): 14–34.

Munanga, Kabengele. *Negritude: Usos e Sentidos*. São Paulo: Ática, 1986.

Souza, Fiorentina. "Solano Trindade e a Produção Literária Afro-Brasileira." *Afro-Ásia* 31 (2004). 277–293. 27 Nov. 2008 <http://redalyc.uaemex.mx>.

Vogt, Carlos, and Peter Fry. *Cafundó: A África no Brasil*. São Paulo: Companhia das Letras, 1996.

Zumthor, Paul. *A Letra e a Voz: A "Literatura" Medieval*. Trans. Amalio Pinheiro and Jerusa Pires Ferreira. São Paulo: Companhia das Letras, 1993.

—. *Introdução à Poesia Oral*. Trans. Jerusa Pires Ferreira. São Paulo: Editora Educitec, 1997.

Resistance from the Margins in George Elliott Clarke's *Beatrice Chancy*

KATHERINE R. LARSON

George Elliott Clarke characterizes his 1999 verse drama *Beatrice Chancy* as "a feast of intertexts" (Personal interview).[1] His Acknowledgements catalogue the dramatic, visual, musical, historical, and even architectural texts to which *Beatrice Chancy* responds.[2] The list is long, testifying to an interpretative love affair with Beatrices in general and, in particular, with Beatrice Cenci, the noblewoman executed in Rome in 1599 for parricide after being raped by her father (Clarke, *Beatrice Chancy* 152–3). Although the notorious Cenci tragedy arguably stands as the primary intertext for Clarke's work, *Beatrice Chancy* also draws on the plethora of retellings, through sculpture, opera, and drama, which that story prompted, notably Shelley's 1819 drama *The Cenci*. Moreover, Clarke's "martyr-liberator" (*Beatrice Chancy* 10) Beatrice amalgamates elements from a host of Beatrices: Dante Alighieri's divine paragon; Shakespeare's romantic wit; Thomas Middleton's manipulator; Dante Rossetti's devout saint. Clarke combines, adapts, and elaborates on these intertexts, positioning his version of the Cenci story, set in the context of the early nineteenth-century Nova Scotia slave trade, as a conflict between the Black Acadian slave Beatrice and her lustful father/master.

Even as this list of works signals the intertextual richness of *Beatrice Chancy*, Clarke's Acknowledgements also foreground the strategic function within the verse drama of what Gérard Genette calls the paratext: the elements located on the peripheries of a text that together provide a guiding framework for a reader. Genette's coinage of the term draws on J. Hillis Miller's examination of the prefix "para" as a marker of threshold, a space of blurred boundaries "signifying at once proximity and distance, similarity and difference, interiority and exteriority" (219). The paratext operates as a "vestibule" (Genette, *Seuils* 8), a permeable area that facilitates a reader's approach to a text.[3] This liminal zone exists largely within the text itself, in what Genette dubs the peritext, namely the title, author name, publication information, chapter headings, dedications, epigraphs, preface, introduction, illustrations, afterword, or notes. The paratext also includes elements beyond the physical boundaries of a work that nonetheless influence a reader: the "epitext," which includes reviews, interviews with the author, letters, and editorial remarks. These peripheral elements, both peritextual and epitextual, assume a force that Genette likens to the performative impact of speech acts. They can impart information, relay authorial intention and interpretation, or signal a text's engagement within or against a particular genre. Indeed, Genette characterizes the paratext as a "lieu privilégié d'une pragmatique et d'une stratégie, d'une action sur le public au service, bien ou mal compris et accompli, d'un meilleur accueil du texte et d'une lecture plus pertinente" (*Seuils* 8).[4]

Crucial to Genette's understanding of the paratext is his insistence on its strategic role, a feature epitomized by *Beatrice Chancy*. For example, Clarke entitles the section containing his Acknowledgments "Conviction" and begins it with an epigraph by Chilean writer Antonio Skàrmeta: "*Las Beatrices producen amores incommensurables.*"[5] The function of both the section title and its epigraph is complex. On one level, these paratextual elements hearken back to the events of the verse drama. The title serves as a reminder of Beatrice's conviction and hanging; the epigraph recalls the blossoming love between Lead and Beatrice as well as the incestuous passion that Beatrice unwittingly sparks in her father. At the same time, the epigraph points forward to the "*amores incommensurables*" that Beatrice Cenci and Beatrices more generally have prompted in literature and history, the tradition that shapes *Beatrice Chancy*.

The ambiguity of the word "Conviction" in this context is even more problematic. If the word is taken to mean "[d]emonstration, proof" (*Oxford English Dictionary*), then it announces Clarke's list of historical, artistic, and literary sources as validation for his project. If it is understood as "detection and exposure" (*OED*), then it could set up the catalogue of intertexts as a key to Clarke's poetic code. "Conviction" can also mean "bringing any one to recognize the truth of what he [sic] has not before accepted; convincing" (*OED*), in which case the Acknowledgements become a crucial source of evidence grounding Clarke's depiction of the horrific reality of slavery in Nova Scotia. Regardless of how the reader interprets this section's title and epigraph, it becomes impossible to read Clarke's Acknowledgements in isolation from the rest of the work. The section occupies a liminal place, both part and outside of the text, prompting the reader to question the role of the ensuing catalogue of intertexts in shaping *Beatrice Chancy*. In so doing, "Conviction" exemplifies the paratextual strategies that inform the work.

One of the most powerful functions of the paratext is its ability to advise or command a reader to approach a text in a particular way. Genette offers the example of the Preface to Victor Hugo's Contemplations: "Ce livre … doit être lu comme on lirait le livre d'un mort" (Seuils 16).[6] Genette characterizes the fringe space of the paratext as a transaction zone that conveys direct authorial commentary or information validated by the author to the reader, thereby guiding the reader closer to the author's interpretation of the text. Interestingly, the prefix "para" can also mean "to make ready, prepare" or "to ward or defend" (OED). The space of the paratext both prepares a reader to enter into and interpret a text and defends that text against readings that clash with authorial and editorial goals. This emphasis on authorial control and strategy becomes particularly important in Beatrice Chancy, as Clarke deliberately constructs paratextual elements as framing devices to guide readers' interpretations of his verse drama.

It could be argued that Genette's insistence that the primary role of the paratext is to signal authorial intention problematically resurrects the figure of the author. Graham Allen points out that this emphasis on authorial intention helps to "neutralize the radically destabilizing … nature of intertextuality" and to "keep transtextual relations within a determinate and determinable field" (107). By extension, Genette implies that the author controls the meaning and function of the paratext. In reality, however, the paratext is profoundly vulnerable to outside influence. As editions change, original prefaces might be replaced with updated versions, sometimes after an author's death. In addition, the media helps to shape the epitext, highlighting certain aspects of an author's background or of a text at the expense of other, usually less marketable, features. Editors influence the relative impact of a peritext by exerting control over the physical layout of a text. Finally, the influence of the paratext may elude the reader who skips paratextual material, deeming a preface, notes, or acknowledgements to be separate from or even irrelevant to the text. What Genette lauds as the map leading a reader to an author's intentions appears rather as a surprisingly unstable area, susceptible to alteration, excision, omission, and subjective interpretation.

Indeed, not all readers will interpret authorial signals in identical ways. Genette's insistence on the paratext's ability to direct a reader towards the author's intended interpretation does not mitigate the potentially infinite range of intertextual relationships that might be triggered by a particular epigraph, dedication, or illustration. Genette is right to point out that a reader who, for example, recognizes the epigraph from Skàrmeta that begins the Acknowledgements in *Beatrice Chancy* will glean a different meaning from the text than a reader who does not recognize the intertext. Genette remarks: "Je ne dis pas qu'il faut le savoir: je dis seulement que ceux qui le savent ne lisent pas comme ceux qui l'ignorent" (*Seuils* 13).[7] If a reader knows that the epigraph is taken from *Ardiente Paciencia*, Skàrmeta's 1985 novel centering on poet and political activist Pablo Neruda who endured a period of exile from Chile for his political views, or knows that Skàrmeta himself was temporarily exiled from Chile and used his writing as a form of political resistance, that information will shape his or her interpretation of *Beatrice Chancy*. A reader may bring further unexpected intertexts to bear on a particular paratext on the basis of personal experience; Skàrmeta's quotation, for example, might trigger allusions to Michael Radford's interpretation of poetry's revolutionary potential and the relationship that develops between Mario and the idealized Beatrice in the 1994 film adaptation of Skàrmeta's novel, *Il Postino*. The paratext's function is best understood as a primary intertext coexisting with many possible subjective readings; indeed, in his discussion of hypertextuality, Genette recognizes the multiple intertexts that might hover behind a text, whether contributed by author or reader.[8]

Although the paratext's impact on a reader's interpretation of a text does not necessarily stem from authorial intent, authorial strategy and control remain integral to the function of the paratext, particularly in the case of *Beatrice Chancy*. *Beatrice Chancy*'s paratext—and especially its peritext—becomes a key tool through which to explore the role of intertextuality in Clarke's verse drama. The unusual attention which Clarke devotes to peritextual material in *Beatrice Chancy*, and indeed throughout his works, is manifested not only in his abundant use of epigraphs, photographs, and stage directions but also in his discussions of his verse drama. As such, it is fitting that an article devoted to Clarke's fascination with peripheral elements should itself rely on an authorial epitext in the form of an interview. Reflecting on *Beatrice Chancy*, Clarke consistently maintains that his poetry is meant to be violent, to jolt readers into memory, awareness, and action. The surfeit of peritextual material in *Beatrice Chancy* is vital to this process; even if a reader does not catch the nuance of every epigraph, their prominence and blatancy forces awareness. Moreover, Clarke deliberately formulates his peritext on both structural and thematic levels to provide intertextual commentary on the events of *Beatrice Chancy*.

Beatrice Chancy is consistently and persuasively framed by and infused with peritext. A sixteenth-century Italian map bookends the work on its front and back inside covers. The introductory pages are peppered with epigraphs. Clarke prefaces his verse drama with a reflection: "On Slavery in Nova Scotia." Two more epigraphs, coupled under the heading "Charge," separate this reflection from the *dramatis personae*. Each of the five acts of the verse drama itself is marked with an epigraph, a title drawn from John Fraser's *Violence in the Arts* ("Ambivalences," "Violators," "Victims," "Revolt," and "Responsibility"), and a photograph of a solitary Black woman. A poeticized article from *The Halifax Gazette* follows the conclusion of Act 5, along with another epigraph and an extract of newspaper "Apologies." Then come Clarke's Acknowledgements. Clarke goes on to include the performance histories of both the verse drama and its opera version, again prefacing the section with an epigraph. The Colophon positions typesetting credits under a final epigraph, and the work concludes with a brief biography of George Elliott Clarke. Not including stage directions, over 60 elements within the verse drama could be construed as peripheral.

Clarke describes *Beatrice Chancy* as the "maximum of my maximalist aesthetic" (Personal interview). In one sense, the plethora of peritextual material, particularly the number of epigraphs, characterizes Clarke's maximalist poetic style. However, the peritext of *Beatrice Chancy* plays a strategic role on both structural and thematic levels, positioning the events of the verse drama within a context evoking the resistance of Acadians, slaves, Black women, Black artists, and poetry itself. After briefly considering the structure of the peritext as a whole, this article will examine the function of the peritext in *Beatrice Chancy* through close analysis of two of the work's most pervasive peritextual elements: the epigraph and the stage direction. Throughout *Beatrice Chancy*, these peritexts reveal a preoccupation with resistance even as they themselves resist generic and linguistic categorization and containment. As such, they consistently mirror and enter into dialogue with the themes and events explored in the drama itself.

Genette posits that the impact of a peritext on a given work stems partly from its position in the narrative. Clarke's peritext identifies his verse drama as a response to late nineteenth- and early twentieth-century Nova Scotia travelogues and holiday brochures detailing journeys to sites associated with Longfellow's poem *Evangeline*. Clarke notes that, as a Nova Scotian, he could not ignore *Evangeline*, which tells the story of two lovers separated when the British deported the French Acadians from Nova Scotia in 1755.[9] The land associated with *Evangeline* became a popular tourist destination, marketed by Dominion Atlantic Railway and Windsor & Annapolis Railway among others. *Beatrice Chancy* mimics the structure of Dominion Atlantic Railway's travel brochures, guides for genteel travellers as they journeyed by ship from Boston to Yarmouth and then took the train through the Annapolis Valley (Clarke, Personal interview). The frontispiece of such brochures typically included a map of the area around Grand Pré, the site of the Acadians' deportation. The brochures then presented a brief history of the Acadians, a biography of Longfellow, a description of the sights one might see along the journey, with a special focus on the Annapolis Valley, and scheduling and hotel information.[10]

The structure of Clarke's introductory peritext, with its map, epigraphs, and brief account of slavery in Nova Scotia, self-consciously recalls these brochures. At the same time, Clarke's sixteenth-century Italian map of Acadia fuses the intertext of the Cenci tragedy with the commercialization of the Acadian deportation prompted by *Evangeline*.[11] Moreover, even as Clarke's reflection on slavery in Nova Scotia continues to mirror the structure of these travel brochures, it foregrounds Clarke's shift in focus from the Acadians' expulsion to slavery; coupled with the dedication to Lydia Jackson and Marie-Josèphe Angélique, two African Canadian slaves noted for their acts of resistance, the structure prepares the reader for his or her own journey into the Annapolis Valley.[12] By figuring these early peritextual elements as a travelogue, complete with map, Clarke ironically literalizes Genette's characterization of the paratext as a guide leading the reader into a text.

Clarke's strategic framework operates in conjunction with the peritext's thematic insistence on acts of oppression and resistance. The epigraphs establish a rich intertextual dialogue between the events of *Beatrice Chancy* and the context out of which each epigraph emerges. The epigraph, according to Genette, can comment on, clarify, or undermine a section or title; it can also provide valuable information about the time period, genre, and biases of a particular work. Frequently, the allusion to a specific political or historical context prompted by the identification of the author of the epigraph plays a more important role than the text of the epigraph itself (*Seuils* 145–8). If one ignores, for the moment, the identities of the authors to whom Clarke refers, the epigraphs still provide important strategic commentary on the events of the verse drama. Indeed, as Genette remarks, in many ways the epigraph remains "un geste muet dont l'interprétation reste à la charge du lecteur" (*Seuils* 145).[13] If a reader does not recognize the name of the author referred to, for example, the impact of the epigraph's intertexts shifts. Regardless of author identity, the epigraphs, positioned throughout the text, function as a thematic map. Clarke juxtaposes his depiction of the development of Beatrice's agency, the slaves' desperation, Beatrice and Lead's decision to kill Chancy, and the "violence" ("Embracing" 19) of his poetry with the epigraphs' consistent emphasis on the role of women in countering acts of oppression, contemporary manifestations of slavery, the ethical quagmire that surrounds the decision to kill an oppressor, and art's role in resisting tyranny.

The epigraphs instruct and even order the reader to approach the text with these themes in mind. Clarke positions two of the epigraphs that precede Act 1 under the performative title "Charge," a word that, mirroring the ambiguity of the Acknowledgements' "Conviction," brings with it paradoxical connotations of command, duty, attack, and accusation. The two epigraphs included in the section, emphasizing women's duty to abolish slavery and women's right to defend themselves from a rostrum rather than from a scaffold, reinforce all of these connotations (*Beatrice Chancy* 9).[14] At the same time, Clarke structures these epigraphs as thematic directives to the reader. Positioned amongst and already in dialogue with four other introductory epigraphs that range from a testimony to the power of beauty to a meditation on modern slavery manifested in "bondage to … financial institutions" (11), this charge implicitly extends to the epigraphs throughout

Beatrice Chancy. The lyrics of the spiritual "Lonesome valley" (67) hover over both Beatrice's rape and Lustra's "invisible, silent ... chains" (74) in Act 3; Trudeau's famous "Faut-il assassiner le tyran?" (123) problematizes Beatrice's parricide in Act 5 as well as the slaves' debates throughout the verse drama concerning the proper means of resisting their master.

Along with a map, Clarke bookends the verse drama with important reminders of the prevalence of slavery in contemporary society: "And if the African belief is true, then somewhere here with us, in the very air we breathe, all that whipping and chaining and raping and starving and branding and maiming and castrating and lynching and murdering—all of it—is still going on" (158). This concluding epigraph appears under the heading "Colophon," assuming the function of a thematic authorial imprint. Perhaps the overriding charge to the reader, shared by all of the epigraphs and reinforced by the allusions to the manifold guises of slavery, is an injunction to remember history. Clarke himself posits that *Beatrice Chancy* was meant to "jet blood and saliva in amnesiacs' faces" ("Embracing" 16). The sheer excess of Clarke's peritext underscores the implicit violence of that injunction.

The identities of the epigraphs' authors intensify these intertextual resonances. Clarke includes the words of Maryse Condé, a Black Caribbean writer, storyteller, and activist whose works deal extensively with slavery and racism; George Bourne, an American abolitionist who warned against the moral danger of slavery; Ann Plato, a nineteenth-century American educator who was the second Black woman to have her writing published in the United States; Hardial Bains, the Indian-born former head of the Canadian Communist party; Carrie Best, activist, journalist, and writer who founded the first newspaper for Blacks in Nova Scotia; Angela Carter, a novelist and a feminist fascinated with intertextuality and intertextual theorists, particularly Genette; Filippo Tommaso Marinetti, whose manifesto evinces the futurist demand for a cultural uprising against tradition and custom. The authors of the epigraphs span centuries, languages, countries, and genres, opening up a dynamic interrelationship among *Beatrice Chancy* and the history of slavery, the history of Nova Scotia, the history of Black women writers and activists, and the struggle against constraining customs that continues to be waged on political and artistic levels.

The epigraphs retain a focus on the revolutionary and defiant potential of art and artists, consistently reinforcing the artist's role in resisting tyranny. Marinetti, for instance, insists that beauty manifests itself in struggle, while the words of African American spirituals conjure up the history of hope and resistance that coexists with that of slavery's oppression. Similarly, Clarke's inclusion of the words of contemporary novelists, writers, and storytellers testifies to the continued political role of the writer and poet. Most important, Clarke marks his own poetry as a form of resistance. In a recent article, he maintains that poetry and, indeed, beauty in any form, functions as a form of justice ("Embracing" 24). The potency and agency of poetry, Clarke argues, stem from anger, ugliness, and violence: "My poetry must come from anger / Or nothing from it comes" (21). While the poetry of "the howl [and] the lament" (17) that characterizes *Beatrice Chancy* exemplifies this aesthetic, Clarke also inscribes himself into two of his epigraphs, discreetly joining the ranks of the abolitionists, writers, politicians, and activists whose words he invokes.

The first epigraphs in *Beatrice Chancy*, hidden at the bottom of the publication and copyright information on the title page's verso, are Clarke's own. Clarke playfully structures his disclaimer as two poetic epigraphs:[15]

> *Blessèd reader*
> Every line is true, or it is a lie:
> Honey poured—honest—over lye.
> *Ogni riferimento a fatti e persone è del tutto casuale e le vicende,*
> *Personaggi ed i loro nomi sono immaginari.*[16] (4)

By figuring these disclaimers, one conventional and one unconventional, as epigraphs, Clarke implicitly links them with the copious epigraphs interspersed throughout the text that testify to histories of oppression and resistance. Moreover, like the "Charge," Clarke presents the epigraphs as a direct address to the reader, appropriating the nineteenth-century appeal "*Blessèd reader*." The epigraphs mark Clarke's own poetry as a form of resistance, and problematize the way in which a reader should respond to *Beatrice Chancy* and its peritext. Surrounded by publication information that the reader usually skips en route to the main text, these epigraphs are not likely to be noticed by most readers. Even if they are noticed, the disclaimers are themselves ambiguous. The second epigraph is in Italian, which the average reader will not be able to read, thereby masking the story's fictional roots. Similarly, the first epigraph remains unwilling to commit to truth or fiction: "Every line is true, or it is a lie." The epigraphs occupy a liminal position between history and truth that echoes their physical position in relation to the verse drama. Warning readers of the danger of ignoring even the most seemingly irrelevant peritextual material, the epigraphs anticipate the strategic import of extra-textual material throughout the work. At the same time, they introduce Clarke's poetry as wielding historical and political consequences that are unmitigated, perhaps even intensified, by its imaginary roots.

The epigraph attributed to Junius, inserted within the excerpt from the *Halifax Gazette* at the conclusion of the verse drama, works in a similar way. This time, instead of concealing the epigraph within copyright details, Clarke appropriates a fictitious name. The true identity of Junius, the pseudonym of an eighteenth-century English writer noted for his consistent refusal to submit to arbitrary measures of authority, remains unknown. This epigraph, which parodies the Toronto *Globe and Mail*'s daily quotation from Junius, is in fact Clarke's own poetry: "Noises of panting, running, muskets, creaking hounds, snarling wheels, sagging wind, moon screaming in the trees, the Gaspereau River groaning" (151). In linking his words with those of Junius, Clarke positions his own poetry as a public and lasting voice with the power to challenge oppressive authority. Moreover, by introducing the epigraph into a newspaper excerpt that is itself poeticized, Clarke validates poetry as a medium for transmitting and defining news and history. The decision further problematizes the tenuous relation between truth and fiction introduced by the initial epigraphs, while also underscoring the defiant potency of poetry as a genre.

This partly fictionalized selection from the *Halifax Gazette*, like the hidden epigraphs, explicitly merges Clarke's poetry, the text, with peritext, foregrounding the question of where text ends and peritext begins. Genette's definition of the paratext emphasizes the difficulties of determining where the boundaries between text and peritext lie: "on ne sait pas toujours si l'on doit ou non considérer qu'elles lui appartiennent, mais [elles] en tout cas l'entourent et le prolongent" (*Seuils* 7).[17] The problem of differentiating between text and peritext becomes especially difficult in *Beatrice Chancy*, complicated not only by Clarke's explicit injection of poetry into seemingly peritextual material but by the question of performance.[18] As a verse drama, the work lies on the border between poetry and drama. What becomes of the peritext in performance? If it simply disappears, how does that omission affect audience response? If peritextual elements such as the epigraphs and the map are included in a theatre program, does a spectator interact with and respond to them in the same way that a reader does? What peritextual elements need to be included in performance in order for an audience to appreciate some of the subtleties available to a reader? If included, do those elements then become part of the text? These questions are further complicated by the reality that any performance is itself an interpretation, drawing out through costume, set design, blocking, and casting certain intertexts at the expense of others.[19] Despite the directorial challenges it represents, *Beatrice Chancy*'s refusal to adhere to generic limits and the resultant shifting boundary between text and peritext function strategically as large-scale enactments of art's resistant potential.

The poetic stage directions in *Beatrice Chancy* stand as a prime example. Genette does not include stage directions as an example of a peritext in *Seuils*, perhaps because they arguably function as integral to a printed dramatic text. Because dramatic texts are performance-based, however, stage directions generally assume a peritextual function, providing crucial guidance and commentary on characterization and setting. At the same time, they remain vulnerable to the omission and alteration characteristic of the peritext. Most audiences do not have access to stage directions. Moreover, a director retains the right to alter characterization and staging depending on his or her interpretation. Stage directions therefore become unstable elements operating at the border of a text, exemplifying the features of the peritext.[20]

Because Clarke's stage directions cross the line between the dramatic and the poetic, the boundaries between dramatic peritext and primary text remain continually blurred. Clarke's stage directions sometimes work to convey onstage action. Immediately following Beatrice's rape, for example, the stage directions simply establish the scene's location and announce Beatrice's arrival onstage: "*Lustra's chambers. Beatrice enters, staggering, bedraggled. Lustra shadows her*" (90). In the majority of cases, however, Clarke's stage directions are crucial to his poetry and the verse drama's thematic content, providing subtle commentary on the atmosphere of a scene even as they continue to implicate the reader or audience in writing stories of oppression.[21] In Act 4, scene 1 for instance, Clarke intensifies the impact of Beatrice's rape through stage directions: "*A violin mopes. Invisible shovelfuls of dirt thud upon the scene—as if those present were being buried alive—like ourselves*" (91). The highly sensory peritext, which continually features details of sound, sight, and smell, paradoxically does so in directives impossible to stage: "*A damp, mushroom odour of shame, a whiff of disease, prowls among the flowers*" (33). The force of the scent of shame, or of Peacock "*stink*[ing] *secretly of spit*" (24) lies in the language, not in staging.[22]

Clarke never intended his stage directions to be taken literally. He describes them as "gestures toward a kind of feeling" meant to be "enjoyed in terms of [their] poeticality" (Personal interview). Significantly, his description explicitly recalls Genette's paratext. He wrote them to be "a hint" or "a guide" (Personal interview) for a reader or a director, an atmospheric map that would shape interpretation of the larger work. However, in performance, the director ultimately determines how those directions are used. If they are omitted or ignored, *Beatrice Chancy* loses some of its most potent poetry. If a staging excises the harsh onomatopoetic quality of the directions surrounding Beatrice's whipping, for instance, much of the sharpness of the scene disappears: "*Moonlight grates upon the graveyard. The wind is staggered by the sounds of the whip—and worse—then resumes. The thin, biting tone of E-flat clarinet insinuates bitter silences*" (70).[23] Excluding the stage directions also deprives the work of the intertextual impact of such stage directions as, "*Beatrice remembers Jeremiah 8:21*" (119) and the critiques directed to reader or spectator concealed within the stage directions: "*Too many of us destroy ourselves*" (15); "*Slavery is global industry and trade—the future*" (25); "*There's no freedom this side of the grave*" (95). Indeed, recalling the language of the epigraphs, the stage directions play a crucial role in negotiating the relation between fiction and truth, history and the present.

The 1997 staged reading of *Beatrice Chancy*, directed by Colin Taylor, opted for a compromise.[24] Taylor omitted the stage directions that seemed limited to the action of the drama and included a narrator in the cast who would read the directions that, in Clarke's words, "added to the texture" (Personal interview). That compromise still requires the director to determine which directions constitute action and which texture. However, it testifies to the extent to which Clarke's poetry resists confinement within peritextual or generic limits. Clarke muses that a successful staging of the play would require Shakespearean actors "who could … carry the language" (Personal interview). The poetry of the verse drama must remain a priority in performance, a feature that blurs conventional distinctions between text and peritext, poem and play.

This linguistic and generic resistance mirrors the force of the poetry wielded by Clarke's enslaved protagonists. Ironically, it is Chancy who likens the resistance of his slaves to the defiance promised by poets: "Our world's infected by slaves and poets!" (27). Indeed, the slaves on the Paradise plantation continually invoke poetry as a means to freedom. Dumas likens Beatrice's courageous actions to "Seven millennia of poetry" (146) while Beatrice herself, eyeing the gallows, maintains that: "I find it hard to breathe / Outside of poetry" (142). Moses points to poetry's ability to wound (121). Clarke identifies Dumas, the revolutionary seer, as a poet. Even George, the escaped slave who is the subject of the *Halifax Gazette*'s Reward column, "fancies himself a poet" (150). Their poetry is far from innocent, exemplifying Maureen Moynagh's contention that Clarke "makes poetry the means of rending the veil of decorum historically dropped over the most violent and gruesome acts of slavery" (114). In Act 4, scene 5, for example, Lustra recoils when Beatrice describes her father as her "raper": "These words aren't poetry, Beatrice; they canker" (109). Throughout *Beatrice Chancy*, poetry, and Clarke's poetry in particular, embeds a language of anger, struggle, and revolution.[25] It offers freedom and condemns rape. It overflows the limits of the text to merge with the peritextual words of abolitionists and politicians and newspapers. It refuses generic categorization and demands to be performed. At the beginning of Act 2, scene 2, Francis Chancy unwittingly points to the political potency of poetry that Clarke inscribes in both text and peritext:

"Plays spawn treason, / Poems assassination" (49). The words echo Clarke's insistence that his words, springing from anger, "promise only murders [and] executions" ("Embracing" 21). The tyrant, it seems, is right to fear the poet.

Clarke's peritext guides the reader into a narrative of struggle continually framed by and in dialogue with peritextual elements that together testify to oppression and the work of those who choose to fight it. Even as *Beatrice Chancy*'s peritext enjoins the reader not to forget these histories, it itself resists categorization. Clarke enacts poetry's resistant potential on a textual level while simultaneously depicting Beatrice's acts of resistance through and as poetry. Fittingly, the peritext, verbal and visual elements lying on the physical margins of a work, plays a pivotal role in the intertextual strategies of *Beatrice Chancy*, a verse drama that centres on the resistance of people at the margins.

Endnotes

1. I would like to thank Linda Hutcheon and the anonymous readers at *Canadian Literature* who offered valuable suggestions and comments as this essay developed. I am also grateful to George Elliott Clarke and James Rolfe for the opportunity to interview them; this article is indebted to insights that emerged during those discussions.
2. The list is by no means exhaustive. Clarke's work draws on intertexts ranging from Titian's *Venus d'Urbino* to the Bible to aphorisms. For a judicious account of the influences pervading *Beatrice Chancy*, see Clarke, "Embracing" 15–24.

3. *Seuils* provides a comprehensive overview of Genette's theory of paratextuality. See also Allen 97–115; Maclean 273–80; and Hallyn and Jacques 202–15.
4. A privileged space—both pragmatic and strategic—that acts on the public and that aims, regardless of its ultimate success, at a better response to and a more accurate reading of the text (my translation).
5. Beatrices trigger incommensurable loves (my translation).
6. This book must be read like one would read the book of a dead person (my translation).
7. I'm not saying that one must know it [the intertext]: I'm only saying that those who do know it will not read like those who don't (my translation).
8. Genette divides the ways in which texts can enter into relation with others (what he calls transtextuality) into five categories: intertextuality, paratextuality, metatextuality, hypertextuality, and architextuality. For helpful overviews of these terms and the specific intertextual relationships to which each alludes, see Genette, *Palimpsests* 1–10 and Allen 101–15.
9. For judicious accounts of the history of the French Acadians and of the Acadian deportation, see Arsenault, Cazaux, N.E.S. Griffiths, and Naomi Griffiths.
10. For examples of these brochures, see Douglas; *Holiday Tours Through Evangeline's Land*; *The Land of Evangeline*; *Old Acadia in Nova Scotia*; and *Through the Land of Evangeline*.
11. Interestingly, editions of Longfellow's poem also often included a map of "Evangeline country."
12. Lydia Jackson, having arrived in Nova Scotia along with the eighteenth-century influx of Black Loyalists, was indentured and eventually impregnated by her

master, Dr. Bulman. She finally fled to Sierra Leone with other Black Loyalists in 1792. Marie-Josèphe Angélique was the slave of a wealthy Montreal tradesman. On April 17, 1734, hearing she was going to be sold, Angélique escaped, setting fire to her owner's house to distract her pursuers. In June 1734 she was captured, tortured, and hanged.

13. A mute gesture whose interpretation is the responsibility of the reader (my translation).
14. The two epigraphs are: "*The abolition of slavery … is emphatically the duty and privilege of women*" (Bourne) and "*La femme a le droit de monter sur l'échafaud; elle doit avoir également celui de monter à la tribune*" (Gouges). (Women have the right to ascend the scaffold; they must equally have the right to ascend the [court] rostrum [my translation].)
15. Clarke draws on a range of languages in his epigraphs and throughout *Beatrice Chancy*. His extensive use of French, Spanish, Italian, and Latin functions partly to reinforce the particular context of slavery in nineteenth-century Nova Scotia that grounds *Beatrice Chancy*. The slaveowners of Nova Scotia were landed gentry, well-educated and well-read individuals who established universities and libraries in Nova Scotia. Library records from the 1890s reveal a preponderance of multilingual book collections. The multilingual poetry of *Beatrice Chancy* invokes this history (Clarke, Personal interview).
16. Every reference to facts and persons is totally casual, and the events, people, and their names are imaginary (my translation).
17. We do not always know whether or not we must consider the paratextual elements as belonging to the

text, but in any case they surround the text and extend it (my translation).

18. Interestingly, the page numbers of *Beatrice Chancy* do not demarcate peritext and text by, for example, enumerating title page and publication information with lower case Roman numerals and marking the beginning of the verse drama with Arabic numerals. Page numbers are listed using Arabic numerals beginning with the first title page. In a way, therefore, Clarke signals that every page constitutes part of the text.
19. See Carlson 111–17.
20. The *dramatis personae* and the description of the setting assume similar roles in *Beatrice Chancy*. However, both of these elements would normally be included in a program and would therefore be available to an audience.
21. Maureen Moynagh points out that Clarke's stage directions even scan as poetry and goes on to argue that such peritextual features suggest that *Beatrice Chancy* should be read as poetry rather than as theatre (101).
22. Clarke's epigraph attributed to Junius shares these sensory qualities, implicitly connecting the stage directions to the epigraphs.
23. A large number of Clarke's stage directions centre on sound, particularly musical, imagery. Such references as "*African-tuned bagpipes*" (134) and "*F-minor music—note of immorality*" (82) abound. Significantly, the verse drama of *Beatrice Chancy* developed as an offshoot of George Elliott Clarke's collaboration with composer James Rolfe on the opera version of *Beatrice Chancy*. While neither Rolfe nor Clarke considers the music of *Beatrice Chancy* as exercising detailed influence on the stage directions of the verse

drama or vice versa, both artists maintain that there was inevitable "cross-fertilization" between the two projects on both linguistic and musical levels (Clarke, Personal interview). Rolfe credits Clarke's poetic stage directions with providing the "atmosphere" for much of his music, going on to argue that music assumes the role of the verse drama's stage directions in the opera (Rolfe, Telephone interview). While the vast majority of the peritextual material that pervades the verse drama is excised from the opera score and libretto, a few elements remain. Rolfe retains three of Clarke's musically descriptive stage directions in the libretto: "*A bell shivers the dusk*"; "*A violet bell bleeds in the white wind*"; and "*Slaves, sunflowers, stars, sparks.*" Moreover, Rolfe prefaces his score with a "Charge" to the listener consisting of the same epigraph by Hardial Bains that introduces Act 1 of the verse drama. Finally, the section entitled "Conviction" appears in nearly identical form at the conclusion of both verse drama and libretto. The libretto also includes a variation on the verse drama's "Charge" as well as the performance history of the opera. Even in the highly edited medium of a libretto, *Beatrice Chancy* continues to be informed by peritextual elements. For a summary of the development of the two projects, see Clarke, "Embracing" 15–17.

24. The verse drama was staged as a reading with minimal blocking on July 10 and 11, 1997 at the Theatre Passe Muraille in Toronto. It played to an audience of approximately eighty people over the two nights and received "reasonable acclaim" (Clarke, Personal interview). Unfortunately, the verse drama has not been performed since. For a detailed performance history

of both verse drama and opera versions of *Beatrice Chancy*, see Clarke, *Beatrice Chancy* 155–7.

25. See also Clarke, "Embracing" 19–21.

Works Cited

Alighieri, Dante. *The New Life* [*Vita Nuova*]. Trans. Dante Gabriel Rossetti. New York: New York Review of Books, 2002.

Allen, Graham. *Intertextuality*. London and New York: Routledge, 2000.

Arsenault, Bona. *Histoire des Acadiens*. St. Laurent, Québec: Éditions Fides, 1994.

Cazaux, Yves. *L'Acadie: Histoire des Acadiens du XVIIe siècle à nos jours*. Paris: Albin Michel S.A., 1992.

Clarke, George Elliott. *Beatrice Chancy*. Victoria, B.C.: Polestar Book Publishers, 1999.

—. *Beatrice Chancy: A Libretto in Four Acts*. *Canadian Theatre Review* 96 (Fall 1998): 62–79.

—. "Embracing *Beatrice Chancy*, or In Defence of Poetry." *New Quarterly: New Directions in Canadian Writing* 20.3 (Fall/Winter 2000–2001): 15–24.

—. Personal interview. 12 April 2004.

"Conviction." *The Oxford English Dictionary*. Online Edition. 17 May 2005 <http://www.oed.com>.

Douglas, Sir Charles George. *The Land of Evangeline: The Gateways Thither*. Kentville, N.S.: Dominion Atlantic Railway, [1895?]. CIHM no. 12498.

Fraser, John. *Violence in the Arts*. Cambridge: Cambridge University Press, 1974.

Genette, Gérard. *Palimpsests: Literature in the Second Degree*. Trans. Channa Newman and Claude Doubinsky. Lincoln: University of Nebraska Press, 1982.

—. *Seuils*. Paris: Editions du Seuil, 1987.

Griffiths, N. E. S. *The Acadian Deportation: Deliberate Perfidy or Cruel Necessity?* Toronto: The Copp Clark Publishing Company, 1969.

Griffiths, Naomi. *The Acadians: Creation of a People*. Toronto: McGraw-Hill Ryerson Limited, 1973.

Hallyn, Fernand and Georges Jacques. "Aspects du paratexte." *Introduction aux études littéraires*. Ed. Maurice Delcroix and Fernand Hallyn. Paris-Gembloux: Duculot, 1987. 202–15.

Holiday Tours Through Evangeline's Land. Kentville, N.S.: Dominion Atlantic Railway, [1896?]. CIHM no. 90913.

Hugo, Victor. *Les Contemplations*. Ed. Jean Gaudon. Paris: Le Livre de Poche, 1972.

Il Postino. Dir. Michael Radford. Perf. Phillippe Noiret, Massimo Troisi, and Maria Grazia Cucinotta. Miramax, 1994.

The Land of Evangeline, Nova Scotia: Annotated Guide. Ed. Dominion Atlantic Railway. Kentville, N.S.: The Kentville Publishing Co. Ltd., 1935.

Longfellow, Henry W. *Evangeline: A Tale of Acadie*. Halifax: H.H. Marshall, Ltd., 1951.

Maclean, Marie. "Pretexts and Paratexts: The Art of the Peripheral." *New Literary History* 22.2 (Spring 1991): 273–80.

Middleton, Thomas. *The Changeling. Five Plays: Thomas Middleton*. Ed. Bryan Loughrey and Neil Taylor. London and New York: Penguin Books, 1988. 345–421.

Miller, J. Hillis. "The Critic as Host." *Deconstruction and Criticism*. Ed. Harold Bloom, Paul de Man, Jacques Derrida, Geoffrey H. Hartman, and J. Hillis Miller. New York: The Seabury Press, 1979. 217–53.

Moynagh, Maureen. "'This history's only good for anger': Gender and Cultural Memory in *Beatrice Chancy*." *Signs* 28.1 (2002): 97–126.

Old Acadia in Nova Scotia. N.p.: Dominion Atlantic Railway, n.d.

"para-." *The Oxford English Dictionary*. Online Edition. 17 May 2005 <http://www.oed.com>.

Rolfe, James. *Beatrice Chancy: An Opera in Four Acts*, 1997.

—. Telephone interview. 10 April 2004.

Rossetti, Dante Gabriel. *Beata Beatrice*. Tate Gallery, London.

Shakespeare, William. *Much Ado About Nothing. The Norton Shakespeare*. Ed. Stephen Greenblatt, Walter Cohen, Jean E. Howard, and Katharine Eisaman Maus. New York and London: W. W. Norton & Co., 1997. 1381–1444.

Shelley, Percy Bysshe. *The Cenci*. Ed. George Edward Woodberry. Boston and London: D. C. Heath & Co., 1909.

Skàrmeta, Antonio. *Burning Patience* [*Ardiente Paciencia*]. Trans. Katherine Silver. New York: Pantheon Books, 1987.

Through the Land of Evangeline. [Nova Scotia?]: Windsor & Annapolis Railway, [1893?]. CIHM no. 94388.

Walking the Walk: George Elliott Clarke's Creative Practice

JOSEPH PIVATO

George Elliott Clarke is an artist whose creative practice involves constantly exploring genres both in theory and in his compositions. An integral part of his practice as an artist is his engagement in the questions of post-colonial theory, especially the nature of the writing of the African diaspora and the place of African-Canadian literature in that global phenomenon.

In Europe there is a long tradition of poets who have also produced significant works of literary criticism and theory. One of the first who comes to mind is Italian poet Dante who wrote a seminal volume on literary language, *De vulgari eloquentia* (1312). The English Renaissance poet Sir Philip Sidney produced *A Defence of Poesie* (1583) explaining the value of literature in the historical context of western philosophy. The Romantic poet Samuel Taylor Coleridge published his *Biographia Literaria* (1817) which contains an analysis of the literary imagination. There are more examples of writer-critics in the twentieth century such as Virginia Woolf. Two poets who often appear in the work of George Elliott Clarke are T.S. Eliot and Ezra Pound.

Early in his career Clarke realized that it is necessary for a writer to work in several genres, especially if he is also trying to establish the recognition of African-Canadian literature. The writer-critics that I am familiar with are among Italian-Canadian authors who not only produce original literary works but also participate in the critical analysis of the publications of other writers. Two examples who come to mind are Pasquale Verdicchio on the west coast and Antonio D'Alfonso in Quebec. Australian-Canadian scholar Sneja Gunew has pointed out that ethnic minority writers form communities not only to produce the primary texts, but also to edit anthologies, compile bibliographies, find the appropriate theoretical structures, write criticism, speak at conferences, and organize book launchings and public readings. In addition to the activities of writing, publishing, editing and reviewing, these writers must redefine the public sphere and the academic perception of this new literature. (Gunew 7–29)

Canadian literature itself was established as an academic area in the 1960s and 1970s by the practice of authors who also wrote criticism. Two of the earliest are prairie poet Eli Mandel with *Criticism: Silent-Speaking Words* (1967) and Montreal's Louis Dudek with *The Making of Modern Poetry in Canada* (1967). The goal of these authors was to identify Canadian writing as a national literature distinct from both the traditions in the UK and the USA.

There is now an established tradition of creative writers who have also produced literary criticism and theory. George Elliott Clarke is the latest member of this ambidextrous group of authors. In Ontario we have poet Frank

Davey who has produced provocative books of criticism such as *Surviving the Paraphrase* (1977) and *Canadian Literary Power* (1994). In Montreal, Quebecer Hubert Aquin's French novels were matched by his criticism such as *Blocs érratiques* (1977) and poet Paul Chamberland published much of his criticism in *Parti Pris* (1963–8). In Sherbrooke, Quebec poet D.G. Jones published a book of essays, *Butterfly on Rock* (1970) and along with novelist Ronald Sutherland founded the Sherbrooke School of Comparative Canadian Literature. Sutherland's critical books are *Second Image* (1971) and *The New Hero* (1977). In Alberta we have poet E.D. Blodgett who produced *Configurations: Essays on the Canadian Literatures* (1982) and contributed to the spread of the Sherbrooke approach to comparative Canadian literature. There is now no question that Canada has a distinct national literature in English and in French.

Since the 1960s the comparative approach to the study of literature has become more important in universities as has the preoccupation with theory. In an academic world of more and more narrow specializations, it is often difficult to do interdisciplinary studies. Some of the essays in this collection cross the disciplinary boundaries by examining writing and music, writing and theatre performance and writing and adaptation.

In the global context of post-colonial writing and controversies on theory, the individual author finds that creative writing and literary criticism are more and more problematic. Clarke has set himself the tasks of producing his own work, and writing in several genres, of editing anthologies, of historical documentation, of literary criticism and the general promotion of African-Canadian writing. He must also distinguish Black writing in Canada from the dominant tradition in the United States. His promotion of Africadian history and culture goes some way towards achieving this distinct identity and tradition.

To me Clarke's creative practice is informed by several factors: One is his constant restless reach for the best form for his text, the poetic language, and the performance. Second is his use of the oral traditions and language of Black communities in Canada. A third is his engagement with post-colonial theory and criticism.

The Restless Genres

As a creative artist Clarke has often explored working in various genres. It has become part of his creative practice to recreate individual texts in different forms. In the shifting genres we may find a different speaker, an alternative point of view and a text addressing a new audience. We can see movement through genres in the striking parallels between *Execution Poems* and the novel, *George and Rue*. Clarke explained that the expansive form of the novel allowed him to explore the history and social reality of this tragic story in greater detail: "I needed something big, something that was going to be able to contain everything I wanted to say" (Wyile 140).

In her detailed study of Clarke's use of models shaping *George and Rue*, Spanish scholar Ana Maria Fraile explores the intertexuality of the many layers in the narrative and beyond the texts itself. Two models that Clarke engaged with were William Styron's *Confessions of Nat Turner* (1966) and Gayl Jones' *Corregidora* (1975). Clarke admits that, "I do in my own secret heart consider *George and Rue* my own particular answer to Bill Styron" (Wyile 142).

By responding to these African-American novels Clarke asserts a distinct African-Canadian literature:

> Besides following Gayl Jones' creation of a Black vernacular bluesy voice in *Corregidora*, *George and Rue* signifies upon both *Native Son* and *Confessions* by contesting the standard narrative voice in these novels with a Black vernacular English deeply rooted in Canadian soil, thus claiming African-Canadian subjectivity through language and style. (Fraile 9)

The other significant examples of changing genres are his operas. Clarke's *Beatrice Chancy* was published as a play with Polestar in 1999 and was printed as a libretto in four acts in *Canadian Theatre Review* in 1998 and performed as a chamber opera in Toronto in 1998 and 1999, in Halifax in 1999, and in Edmonton in 2001. "Beatrice Chancy: The Opera: A Libretto in Four Acts," appeared in *Marigraph* edited by Bruce Barton with Playwrights Canada Press in 2004. When this original Canadian opera is next performed it will be in a different adaptation, if only because this work has now changed our expectations of new operas. But it will also be because that is how Clarke works as an artist sensitive to the needs of his story.

Clarke's second opera, *Québécité: A Jazz Fantasia in Three Cantos*, was published by Gaspereau Press in 2003, appeared as "Québécité: A Jazz Libretto in Three Cantos," in *Testifyin* edited by Djanet Sears with Playwrights Canada Press in 2003 and in *Kola* in 2003. His third opera, *Trudeau: Long March, Shining Path*, appeared as a play with Gaspereau Press in 2007 and was performed as an opera in a workshop production in Toronto's Harbourfront Centre in 2007 and in Halifax in 2010. In future performances these operas too will find different adaptations.

Clarke has published several works in different genres, but has sometimes kept the same titles. Clarke's *Whylah Falls*, the poetry collection called a verse-novel, appeared in 1990 with Polestar Books which brought out a second edition in 2000. A third edition was published with Gaspereau Press in 2010. The play, *Whylah Falls*, was published by Playwrights Canada Press in 1999 and 2000. Clarke's poetry often approaches prose and both are used to tell a story. The play *Whylah Falls* was translated into Italian for a 2002 production in Venice as *Le cascate di Whylah* and included a chorus singing jazz, blues and spirituals. This Italian production of a Canadian work changes our perception of the original regional characters and voices into universal men and women of the African diaspora.

In his restless exploration of the most suitable genre for his text Clarke is obliged to work very hard to master the form, to find the best language and style for the work and to engage the new audience. The author risks making mistakes and so is constantly learning. Not only is he telling Canadian stories for the first time, but must find the appropriate vehicle to reach his audience. Clarke's creative practice is one of continually exploring genres against the questions of the African diaspora.

The Post-Colonial Criticism

In an impressive stream of essays Clarke has debated the place of African-Canadian writing in North America in comparison to Black writing in the US and the West Indies. Many of these essays are collected in his seminal volumes: *Odysseys Home: Mapping African-Canadian Literature* (2002) and *Directions Home: Approaches to*

African-Canadian Literature (2011). In *Odysseys Home* Clarke's introductory essay, "Discovering African-Canadian Literature," has a note which explains, in part, his mission in establishing recognition for African-Canadian literature:

> My view is that the marginalized always possess residual knowledge, interests, perspectives, ideas, theories, philosophies, theologies, and literatures unimagined by their external examiners. Furthermore, black populations which have been censored or marred by insufficiently attentive scholarship reserve the right, I think, to exercise their own redactions and establish their own visions. This expectation is just, for the formation and dissemination of ontological knowledge, that is to say, of identities and images, enunciates social relations of power, subjugation, and resistance. (*Odysseys* 19)

These critical essays are an integral part of Clarke's creative practice since they give us some insight into his ideas on African-Canadian literature and its place in Canadian writing and in the African diaspora. In order to identify an African-Canadian literature and culture Clarke has to immerse himself in all the distinctions, particularities and disputes of African communities in Canada who have different origins, histories and languages. This includes the anglophone Afro-Caribbeans, francophone Afro-Caribbeans, Africans from the UK, immigrants from various African countries and African-Americans. He pays particular attention to the powerful influences of African-American models in literature, post-colonial theory, language and music. From this cultural mosaic as diverse as any in the world Clarke must try to distinguish an African-Canadian literature and he has articulated some of the obstacles he encountered:

> Given its perpetual campaign against these forms of erasure, African-Canadian literature occupies the contested space between the Euro-Canadian reluctance to accept an African presence and the African-American insistence on reading Canadian blackness as a lighter—and less—shade of its own. The sumptuous dilemma of African-Canadian literature is that it is caught between two nationalist pincer movements of exclusion. (*Odysseys* 36)

Clarke's discourse on the African diaspora and African-American writing is the focus of the first argumentative essay in *Odysseys*, entitled, "Contesting a Model Blackness: A Meditation on African-Canadian African-Americanism, or the Structure of African-Canadianité." He observes how African-Canadians have historically followed the African-American models of discourse, aesthetics and language, and how that adoption was never without some distortion or deforming violence. American writers and speakers have regarded the Black communities in Canada as extensions of those in the US; products of the legendary underground railroad and the American Civil War. Clarke also traces the history of denying that Black people in Canada as having any roots or culture in British North America. Nevertheless he reviews a number of Black writers in Canada who explore their sense of belonging, their identity in a country with an unstable national identity. He also examines discussions of various Black communities in Canada in search of a unified African-Canadian identity. This is represented by the volumes, *Canada in*

Us Now: The First Anthology of Black Poetry and Prose in Canada (1976) in which the editor Harold Head writes about "the collective consciousness of people" and *Voices: Canadian Writers of African Descent* (1992) in which editor Ayanna Black refers to "a collective African consciousness." At the end of his review Clarke introduces the term "African-Canadianité, a condition that involves a constant self-questioning of the grounds of identity." (48) These views are reflected in Clarke's critical analysis of other African-Canadian authors such as Austin Clarke, Dionne Brand and M. Nourbese Philip. These ideas and debates on African diaspora identity are constantly reflected in Clarke's own compositions: poem-after-poem in *Blue* (2001), in poems like, "Address to Tomorrow's Negro Haligonians," in *Red* (2011), and in characterization of the narrator in *George and Rue* (2005) "whose English ain't broken but blackened," in describing:

> The brothers was once scrawny, beaten-up black boys. Now they was black men, with black angular caps and second-hand denim shirts. They was needing so much, beginning with love and respect and ending with beer and cash. They'd have to clip a jerk and swipe his budget. If they had the spunk. If they had such verve, Rue'd extract his new clothes now trapped in the cleaners and go to Halifax to rescue India, and Georgie'd retrieve his wife and newborn child immured in the hospital.(103)

The second argumentative essay in *Odysseys* asks the question which haunts Clarke and other Canadian artists: "Must All Blackness Be American?" He begins by reviewing how Canadians have historically tended to view Black in Canada as misplaced Americans. And how American intellectuals have tended to absorb African-Canadian artists and writers into their dominant cultural matrix and simply ignored any Canadian links. His analysis of Walter M. Borden's *Tightrope Time* (1986) demonstrates how this writer revises the African-American models he uses. Borden's use of repeating someone else's words to undermine the original meaning and change the power relations is an example of what Clarke calls African-Canadianité.

In the rest of the essay Clarke takes up the debate over Blackness in Canada by a detailed critique of Paul Gilroy's *The Black Atlantic: Modernity and the Double Consciousness* (1993) as an exemplary book that excludes African-Canadian literature and culture, rendering it invisible. Clarke's criticism of Gilroy's shortcomings can be summarized in these words:

> Gilroy attempts to dismantle the 'US first' conception of 'blackness' by constructing a 'transcultural, international formation called the black Atlantic,' which consists of African communities in the United States, the Caribbean, Britain, and Africa. While Gilroy omits Canada (this gap in his map replicates a suspiciously 'Americocentric' blindness), his 'Pan-Atlanticism' is intended as a panacea for the 'ever-present danger' of 'ethnic absolutism' ... especially 'the easy claims of African-American exceptionalism.' (81)

The other essays in *Odysseys Home* make it an important and seminal book for the establishment of African-Canadian literature. They cover the topics of Black English in Nova Scotia, Africadian literature, modernity and cultural nationalism, Black writing in Quebec, Zebra poetics and essays on many individual authors and books. One of the most important essays in *Odysseys* is "Treason of the Black Intellectuals?", a clear indication that Clarke is not afraid to take on controversial topics in African literature and among academics.

Debate on the Nature of African-Canadian Literature

Within Canada, Clarke has taken a position that argues for an African-Canadian writing that has regional and national links, rooted deeply in the Canadian soil and history. Rinaldo Walcott has taken a different position that argues for a transnational, diasporic space with global "networks and connections as opposed to an explicitly national address." (Walcott 15). While Clarke may have begun as a writer from the Atlantic region of Canada and particularly the Black community of Nova Scotia, he has always had a broader perspective. In *Eyeing the North Star* (1997) he states: "I testify: African-Canadian literature has always been international." (xv)

A recent example of Clarke's dual perspective is his poem collection *Red* which is part of his series of colouring books that include *Blue* (2001) and *Black* (2006). In *Red* personal poems set in Nova Scotia such as "Going to Halifax" (61) are juxtaposed with poems set in Italy, Mexico, France or the U.S. Recent studies of Clarke's work, such as "Creating a Canadian Odyssey: George Elliott Clarke's Global Perspective" (2008) by Lydia Wilkinson, and "Replacing the Regional and Remaking the Real in the Work of George Elliott Clarke" (2008) by Alexander MacLeod and other essays included in this collection, point to a Clarke who has established links with transnational diasporic communities. (See Marra 2012)

Final Note from the Editor

It has been my pleasure to put together this collection of essays on George Elliott Clarke. I have enjoyed working with a number of scholars who have helped me to create this collection and I would like to thank each of these contributors.

Works Cited

Clarke, George Elliott. *Odysseys Home: Mapping African-Canadian Literature*. Toronto: University of Toronto Press, 2002.

—. *George and Rue*. Toronto: HarperCollins, 2005.

Fraile, Ana Maria. "The Transcultural Intertexuality of George Elliott Clarke's African Canadianité: African-American Models Shaping *George and Rue*." *African American Review* 46.2 (2013).

Gunew, Sneja. "Foreword: Speaking to Joseph." In Joseph Pivato, *Echo: Essays in Other Literatures*. Toronto: Guernica, 1994.

Marra, Giulio, ed. *George Elliott Clarke: Poesie e drammi* (Italian translations), Venezia: Studio LT2, 2012.

Walcott, Rinaldo. *Black Like Who! Writing Black Canada*. Toronto: Insomniac Press, 2003.

Wyile, Herb. ed. *Speaking in the Past Tense: Canadian Novelists on Writing Historical Fiction*. Waterloo: Wilfrid Laurier University Press, 2007.

Bibliography for George Elliott Clarke

Poetry

Saltwater Spirituals and Deeper Blues. Porter's Lake, N.S.: Pottersfield Press, 1983.

Whylah Falls. Winlaw, B.C.: Polestar Press, 1990, 2nd ed. Vancouver, Polestar Books, 2000. Poetry and prose.

Lush Dreams, Blue Exile: Fugitive Poems, 1978–1993. Lawrencetown Beach, N.S.: Pottersfield Press, 1994.

Gold Indigoes. Durham, N.C.: Carolina Wren Press, 2000. Poetry.

Execution Poems. Wolfville, N.S.: Gaspereau Press, 2001. Governor General's Award

Blue. Vancouver: Raincoat Books, 2001. Poetry.

Illuminated Verses. Toronto: Canadian Scholar Press—Kellom, 2005. Photographs by Ricardo Scipio.

Black. Vancouver: Polestar Books, 2006.

Blues and Bliss: The Poetry of George Elliott Clarke, ed. Jon Paul Fiorentino. Waterloo: Wilfrid Laurier University Press, 2008.

I & I. Fredericton: Goose Lane, 2009

Red. Kentville, N.S.: Gaspereau Press, 2011.

Plays

Whylah Falls: The Play. Toronto: Playwrights Canada Press, 1999. Also in *Testifyin': Contemporary African-Canadian Drama.* Vol. 1. Ed. Djanet Sears. Toronto: Playwrights Canada Press, 2000. 215–276.

Beatrice Chancy. (verse play) Victoria: Polstar Books, 1999.
Québécité: A Jazz Fantasia in Three Cantos. Kentville, N.S.: Gaspereau Press, 2003.
Trudeau: Long March/ Shining Path. Kentville, N.S.: Gaspereau Press, 2007.

Novel

George and Rue. Toronto: HarperCollins, 2005. London: Random House, 2005. New York: Carroll & Graf, 2006.

Libretti

"Beatrice Chancy: A Libretto in Four Acts." *Canadian Theatre Review.* 96 (Fall 1998).
"Québécité: An Opera Libretto in Three Cantos." *Canadian Theatre Review.* 2002.
"Trudeau: Long March, Shining Path." *Canadian Theatre Review*, 2006.

Anthologies Edited

Ed. *Fire on the Water: An Anthology of Black Nova Scotian Writing.* 2 vols. Lawrencetown Beach, N.S.: Potterfield Press, 1991–1992.
A Lifetime of Making: Ralph and Ada Cromwell. Halifax: Mount Saint Vincent University Art Gallery, 1992. Essays.
Co-ed., *Border Lines: Contemporary Poetry in English.* Toronto: Copp-Clark, 1995. Eds. J.A. Wainwright, Clarke, Ruth Grogan, Victor Li, R. Ross, A. Wallace.

Ed. *Eyeing the North Star: Directions in African-Canadian Literature.* Toronto: McClelland and Stewart, 1997.

Guest ed., *The Dalhousie Review.* Africadian Special Issue. 77.2 (summer, 1997), 1999.

Eyeing the North Star: Perspectives of African-Canadian Literature. Washington, D.C.: Canadian Embassy, 1997. Monograph.

Academic Books

Treason of the Black Intellectuals? Seagram Lecture, 1998. Montreal: McGill Institute for the Study of Canada, 1999. Monograph.

Odysseys Home: Mapping African-Canadian Literature. Toronto: University of Toronto Press, 2002. Essays and reviews.

Directions Home: Approaches to African-Canadian Literature. Toronto: University of Toronto Press, 2011.

Translations

Poeme Incendiare. Trans. Flavia Cosma. Oradea, Romania: Editura Cogito, 2006.

[*Many Kinds of Love: Heavenly, Earthly, and Hellish.* Trans of *Whylah Falls*] Trans. Tong Renshan. Beijing: International Publishing, 2006. [poetry]

Screenplays

One Heart Broken Into Song. Feature Film. Prod: CBC-TV 1999.

Beatrice Chancy: The Opera. Feature Film. Prod: CBC-TV 2001.

Articles and Essays in Journals and Books *(a selected list)*

"What Was Canada?" *Is Canada Postcolonial?: Unsettling Canadian Literature*. Ed. Laura Moss. Waterloo, On.: Wilfrid Laurier University Press, 2003.

"Correspondences and Divergences Between Italian-Canadian and African-Canadian Writers." *Canadian Multicultural Dreams, Realities, Expectations.* Eds. Matthew Zachariah, Allan Sheppard, Leona Barratt. Edmonton: Canadian Multicultural Education Foundation, 2004.

"Raising Raced and Erased Executions in African-Canadian Literature: Or, Unearthing Angélique." *Essays on Canadian Writing.* 75 (2002).

"Canadian Biraciality and Its 'Zebra' Poetics." *Intertexts.* 6.3 (2002).

"Harris, Philip, Brand: Three Authors in Search of Literary Criticism." *Journal of Canadian Studies* 35.1 (Spring, 2000): 161–189.

"Racing Shelley, or Reading *The Cenci* as a Gothic Slave Narrative." *European Romantic Review.* 11.2 (Spring, 2000): 168–185.

"Reading Ward's 'Blind Man's Blues'." *Arc.* 44 (summer, 2000): 50–52.

"Liberalism and Its Discontents: Reading Black and White in Contemporary Québécois Texts." in *Literary Pluralities*, ed. Christl Verduyn. Toronto: Broadview Press, 1998.

"Cool Politics: Styles of Honour in Malcolm X and Miles Davis." *Jouvert: A Journal of Post-Colonial Studies.* 2.1 (1998): see Vol 2, 1 in http://social.chass.ncsu.edu/jouvert.

"Contesting a Model Blackness: A Meditation on African-Canadian African Americanism, or The Structure of African-Canadianité." *Essays on Canadian Writing.* 63 (Spring, 1998): 1–55.

"Towards a Conservative Modernity: Cultural Nationalism in Contemporary Acadian and Africadian Poetry." in *Cultural Identities in Canadian Literature/ Identités culturelles dans la littérature canadienne,* ed. Bénédicte Mauguière. New York: Peter Lang, 1998. 49–63.

"Must We Burn Haliburton?" in *The Haliburton Bi-centenary Chaplet: Papers Presented at the 1996 Thomas Randall Symposium.* ed. Richard Davis. Wolfville, N.S.: Gaspereau Press, 1997. 1–40.

"Africana Canadiana: A Primary Bibliography of Literature by African-Canadian Authors, 1785–1996, in English, French and Translation." *Canadian Ethnic Studies.* 28.3 (1996): 106–209. Guest editor, Joseph Pivato.

"Must All Blackness Be American?: Locating Canada in Borden's 'Tightrope Time', or Nationalizing Gilroy's *The Black Atlantic.*" *Canadian Ethnic Studies.* 28.3 (1996): 56–71.

"Clarke vs Clarke: Tory Elitism in Austin Clarke's Short Fiction." *West Coast Line: A Journal of Contemporary Writing and Criticism.* 22 (Spring/Summer, 1997): 110–128.

"Birth and Rebirth of Africadian Literature." *Down East: Critical Essays on Contemporary Maritime Canadian Literature.* Eds. Wolfgang Hochbruck & James Taylor. Stuttgart: Wissenschaftlicher Verlag Trier, 1997. 55–80.

"A Primer of African-Canadian Literature." *Books In Canada.* 25.2 (March, 1996): 5–7. Included in the *Study Guide* for English 451 and English 551, at Athabasca University.

Articles About and Interviews With George Elliott Clarke

Andrews, Jennifer. "Re-Visioning Fredericton: Reading George Elliott Clarke's *Execution Poems*." *Studies in Canadian Literature*. 33.2 (2008).

Brydon, Diana. "George Elliott Clarke's *Othello*." *Canadian Literature* 182 (2004).

Chariandy, David. "'Canada in Us Now:' Locating the Criticism of Black Canadian Writing." *Essays in Canadian Writing* 75 (Winter 2002).

Compton, Anne. "Standing Your Ground: George Elliott Clarke in Conversation." *Studies in Canadian Literature*. 23.2 (1998): 138–164.

Compton, Wayde. "'Even the stars are temporal': The Historical Motion of George Elliott Clarke's *Saltwater Spirituals and Deeper Blues*." *West Coast Line: A Journal of Contemporary Writing and Criticism*. 22 (Spring/Summer, 1997): 156–163.

Davidson, Arnold E. "*Whylah Falls*: The Africadian Poetry of George Elliott Clarke." *Down East: Critical Essays on Contemporary Maritime Canadian Literature*. Eds. Wolfgang Hochbuck & James Taylor. Stuttgart: Wissemschaftlicher Verlag Trier, 1997.

Fiorentino, Jon Paul. "Blakening English: The Polyphonic Poetics of George Elliott Clarke." *Poetics.ca* #2 (2003) http://www.poetics.ca/poetics02/02fiorentino.html.

Fraile, Ana Maria. "The Transcultural Intertextuality of George Elliott Clarke's 'African Canadianité': African-American Models Shaping *George and Rue*." *African American Review* 46.2 (2013).

Greenblatt, Jordana. "Something Sadistic, Something Complicit: Text and Violence in *Execution Poems* and *Thirsty*." *Canadian Literature* 197 (2008).

Gordon, Spencer. "Interview, George Elliott Clarke: Suggesting a Potential Canon." *The Danforth Review*, May 2009.

Hlongwane, Gugu D. "Whips, Hammers and Ropes: The Burden of Race and Desire in Clarke's *George and Rue*." *Studies in Canadian Literature*. 33.1 (2008): 291–306.

Heiland, D. "George Elliott Clarke's *Beatrice Chancy*: Sublimity, Pain, Possibility". *Postfeminist Gothic: Critical Interventions in Contemporary Culture*. Ed. Benjamin A. Brabon & Stephanie Genz. Palgrave Macmillan, 2007.

Hutcheon, Linda. "In Defence of Literary Adaptation as Cultural Production." *M/C Journal*. 10.2 (2007).

—. "Music, Race, & Ideology: George Elliott Clarke's Canadian Operas." Online(2006) www.leeds.ac.uk/canadian_studies/…/Hutcheon%20posters%201.pdf

Knutson, Susan. "'I am become Aaron': George Elliott Clarke's *Execution Poems* and William Shakespeare's *Tutus Andronicus*." *Canadian Cultural Exchange: Translation and Transculturation*. Eds. Norman Cheadle & Lucien Palletier. Wilfrid Laurier University Press, 2007.

—. "The Mask of Aaron: 'Tall Screams Reared out of Three Mile Plains'—Shakespeare's *Tutus Andronicus* and George Elliott Clarke's Black Acadian Tragedy, *Execution Poems*. *Readings of the Particular: The Postcolonial in the Postnational*. Eds Anne Holden Ronning & Lene Johannesen. Amsterdam: Rodopi, 2007.

Lane, M. Travis. "An Unimpoverished Style: The Poetry of George Elliott Clarke." *Canadian Poetry*. 16 (Spring/Summer, 1985): 47–54. http://www.uwo.ca/english/canadianpoetry/cpjrn/vol16/lane.htm.

Larson, Katherine. “Resistance from the Margins in George Elliott Clarke’s *Beatrice Chancy*.” *Canadian Literature* 189 (2006).

MacLeod, Alexander. “The Little State of Africadia Is a Community of Believers: Replacing the Regional and Remaking the Real in the Work of George Elliott Clarke.” *Studies in Canadian Literature.* 33.2 (2008).

McLeod. Katherine. “Oui, let’s scat”: Listening to Multi-Vocality in George Elliott Clarke’s jazz opera *Québécité*.” *Mosaic* 42.1 (2009).

McNeilly, K. “The Crime of Poetry: George Elliott Clarke in Conversation with Kevin McNeilly & Wayde Compton.” *Canadian Literature* 182 (Autumn 2004).

Moynagh, Maureen. “Mapping Africadia’s Imaginary Geography: An Interview with George Elliott Clarke.” *Ariel: A Review of International English Literature*. 27.4 (Oct. 1996): 71–94.

—. “Signature Pieces: Revisiting Race and Authorship.” *Essays in Canadian Writing* 81 (2004).

—. “‘This history’s only good for anger’: Gender and Cultural Memory in *Beatrice Chancy*.” *Sign: Journal of Women in Culture and Society* 28.1 (2002).

Muller, Markus M. “En route to ‘Africadia’: Black North American History and Culture in George Elliott Clarke’s Nova Scotia.” University of Trier, Germany.

Obert, Julia Catherine. “The Cultural Capital of Sound: *Québécité’s* Acoustic Hybridity.” *Postcolonial Text* 2.4 (2006).

Steven, Laurence. “Transculturation in George Elliott Clarke’s *Whylah Falls*: or When Is It Appropriate to Appropriate?” *Canadian Cultural Exhange*. Op.cit. see Knutson 2007.

Thomas, H. Nigel. "Some Aspects of Blues Use in George Elliott Clarke's *Whylah Falls.*" *CLA Journal.* 43.1 (September, 1999): 1–18.

Verduyn, Christl. "Opera In Canada: A Conversation," G.E. Clarke and Linda Hutcheon. *Journal of Canadian Studies.* 35.3 (Fall, 2000): 184–198.

Wells, Dorothy. "A Rose Grows in Whylah Falls: Transplanted Traditions in George Elliott Clarke's 'Africadia'." *Canadian Literature.* 155 (Winter, 1997): 56–73.

Wilkinson, Lydia. "Creating a Canadan Odyssey: George Elliott Clarke's Global Perspective in *Trudeau: Long March, Shining Path.*" *Alt.theatre: Cultural diversity and the stage.* 6.2 (2008).

Willis, Susan. "Anansi History: George Elliott Clarke's *Whylah Falls.*" *Journal of Commonwealth and Postcolonial Studies.* 9.1 (2002).

Wilson, Ann. "*Beatrice Chancy*: Slavery, Martyrdom and the Female Body." *Sitting the Other: Re-Visions of Marginality in Australian and English-Canadian Drama.* Eds. Marc Maufort & Franca Bellarsi. Brussels, 2001.

Wyile, Herb. ed. *Speaking in the Past Tense: Canadian Novelists on Writing Historical Fiction.* Waterloo: Wilfrid Laurier University Press, 2007.

Theses on the Works of George Elliott Clarke

Beneventi, Domenic A. "Spatial exclusion and the abject other in Canadian urban literature." Ph.D. Thesis, English. Université de Montréal. 2005.

Boyd, Moira Kirstin. "Straddling the 49th Parallel." M.A. Thesis. Vermont College of Norwich University. 2003.

Chariandy, David. "*Whylah Falls* and the Cultural Politics of George Elliott Clarke." M.A. Thesis. Carleton University. Ottawa, September 1995.

Chariandy, David John. "Land to Light on: Black Canadian literature and the language of belonging." Ph.D. Thesis. Toronto, York University, 2003.

Dagger, Lindsay. "Righting Back: Africadian History in the works of George Elliott Clarke." M.A. Thesis. University of Nottingham, U.K. 2005.

Gordon, Scott. "Through An/Other Lens: Photographs in the work of three African-Canadian writers. M.A. Thesis. University of New Brunswick, Fredericton, N.B. 1999.

Hartley, M.R. "A dialogue between beauty and pain: the community of George Elliott Clarke's *Whylah Falls.*" M.A. Thesis. McMaster University, Hamilton, 1996.

Jones, Agassou. "George Elliott Clarke: Nova Scotia's Mythopoeic Poet." B.A. Honours Thesis, Saint Francis Xavier University, Antigonish, N.S., 1990.

Montague, Amanda. "Collective Memory and Performance: An Analysis of Two Adaptations of the Legend of Beatrice Cenci." M.A. Thesis, McMaster University, 2012.

Pielechaty, Colleen. E. "Witnessing the Invisibility: The Africadian Muses of George Elliott Clarke." M.A. Thesis. Dalhousie University, Halifax, September, 1997.

Stacey, Robert David. "The transformed pastoral in recent English-Canadian Literature."

M.A. Thesis, McGill University, Montreal, 1995.

Zapf, Donna Doris Anne. "Singing history, performing race: an analysis of three Canadian operas, *Beatrice Chancy, Elsewhereless,* and *Louis Riel.*" Ph.D. Thesis, University of Victoria, School of Music, 2005.

List of Contributors

Jennifer Andrews is professor of English at the University of New Brunswick in Fredericton and co-editor of *Studies in Canadian Literature.*

Diana Brydon (Ph.D.) is Canadian Research Chair in Global and Cultural Studies at the University of Manitoba, Winnipeg. Among her many books, she has published *Decolonising Fictions* (1993) written with Helen Tiffin, *Shakespeare in Canada: 'A World Elsewhere?'* (2002) co-ed. Irena R. Makaryk, and *Renegotiating Community: Interdisciplinary Perspectives, Global Contexts* (2008) co-ed. William Coleman.

Maristela Campos has a Ph.D. from the Universidade de Florianopolis, and teaches English at the Universidade Federal de Santa Catarina, Brazil.

Wayde Compton is a Vancouver writer who teaches at Simon Fraser University, Burnaby, B.C. His books include: *49th Parallel Psalm, Performance Bond* and *Blueprint: Black British Columbian Literature and Orature.*

Susan Knutson is professor of English at the Université Sainte-Anne, Nova Scotia. She has published *Narrative in the Feminine: Daphne Marlatt and Nicole Brossard* (2001).

Katherine Larson is a professor of English at the University of Toronto at Scarborough. She has published articles on Shakespeare and Mary Worth, Puccini and *Moulin Rouge*, and Richard Strauss' last years.

Giulio Marra is professor of English at the Università Ca'Foscari di Venezia, and has published studies on British literature, Canadian theatre and post-colonial writing. He has published two novels in Italy: *Et in Arcadia Ego* (2005) and *Ca'del Lov* (2008).

Alexander MacLeod teaches English and Atlantic Canadian Studies at St. Mary's University in Halifax. His short story collection, *Light Lifting* was nominated for the Scotiabank Giller Prize (2010), the Frank O'Connor International Short Story Award in Ireland (2011) and the Commonwealth Prize.

Katherine McLeod has a Ph.D. in English from the University of Toronto. Conducts research at the TransCanada Institute and teaches in the School of English and Theatre Studies at the University of Guelph in Ontario.

Amanda Montague earned an Honours B.A. in English from St. Jerome's University at the University of Waterloo, and an M.A. in English from McMaster University. She is currently pursuing a Ph.D. in English. Her research interests include Canadian opera as it relates to concepts of citizenship and national identity as well as the articulation of Canadian nationalisms through contemporary performance genres.

Maureen Moynagh is a professor of English at St. Francis Xavier University, Antigonish, Nova Scotia. Her area of research and teaching interest is post-colonial literature and theory, African-Canadian literature and theatre. She has published *Political Tourism and Its Texts* (2005).

Joseph Pivato has a Ph.D. in Comparative Literature from the University of Alberta and teaches at Athabasca University in Edmonton. He has published *Echo: Essays on Other Literatures* (2003), edited *The Anthology of Italian-Canadian Writing* (1998) and five other books.

H. Nigel Thomas is professor of English (retired) at Laval University, Quebec City, and now lives in Montreal. He has published extensively on post-colonial literature. His novels include *Behind the Face of Winter* (2001) and *Return to Arcadia* (2007).

Lydia Wilkinson has a Ph.D. in English from the University of Toronto. Her areas of research and teaching interest are Canadian literature and performance.

Acknowledgements

We would like to thank the following copyright holders for giving us permission to reprint the following previously published essays:

"'Even the stars are temporal': The Historical Motion of George Elliott Clarke's *Saltwater Spirituals and Deeper Blues*," by Wayde Compton appeared in *North: New African Canadian Writing*. Ed. Peter Hudson, Special Issue of *West Coast Line* 31.1, No. 22 (Spring/Summer 1997): 156–63.

"Re-Visioning Fredericton: Reading George Elliott Clarke's *Execution Poems*," by Jennifer Andrews. Guest edited by Herb Wyile and Jeanette Lynes. *Studies in Canadian Literature* 33.2 (2008): 115–132.

"'The Little State of Africadia Is a Community of Believers': Replacing the Regional and Remaking the Real in the Works of George Elliott Clarke," by Alexander MacLeod was published in *Studies in Canadian Literature* 33.2 (2008).

"'Oui, let's scat': Listening to Multi-Vocality in George Elliott Clarke's jazz opera *Québécité*," by Katherine McLeod appeared in *Mosaic*. 42.1 (2009).

"Resistance from the Margins in George Elliott Clarke's *Beatrice Chancy*," by Katherine Larson appeared in *Canadian Literature* 189 (Summer 2006): 103–118.

"George Elliott Clarke's *Othello*," by Diana Brydon was published in *Canadian Literature,* 182 (Autumn 2004): 188–194.

"'This history's only good for anger': Gender and Cultural Memory in *Beatrice Chancy*," by Maureen Moynagh appeared in *Sign: Journal of Women in Culture and Society*. 28.1 (2002).

"Creating a Canadian Odyssey: George Elliott Clarke's Global Perspective in *Trudeau: Long March/Shining Path,*" by Lydia Wilkinson appeared in *alt.theatre: cultural diversity and the stage*. 6.2 (Dec. 2008): 20–25.

"The Mask of Aaron: 'Tall Screams Reared out of Three Mile Plains'—Shakespeare's *Titus Andronicus* and George Elliott Clarke's Black Acadian Tragedy *Execution Poems*," by Susan Knutson appeared in *Readings of the Particular: The Postcolonial in the Postnational.* eds. Anne Holden Ronning and Lene Johannesen. Amsterdam: Rodopi, 2007.

"Some Aspects of Blues Use in George Elliott Clarke's *Whylah Falls*," by H. Nigel Thomas appeared in *CLA Journal* 43.1 (September 1999): 1–18. Copyright 1999 by the College Language Association.

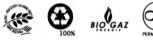

Printed on Rolland Enviro 100, containing 100 % post-consumer recycled fibers, Eco-Logo certified, Processed without chlorinate, FSC® Recycled and manufactured using biogas energy.